The Road to Castle Hill

To Midge, who opened my eyes and taught me
precision, persistence and patience.
A truly remarkable heading dog.

A catalogue record for this book is available from the
National Library of New Zealand

A RANDOM HOUSE BOOK
published by
Random House New Zealand
18 Poland Road, Glenfield, Auckland, New Zealand
www.randomhouse.co.nz

Random House International
Random House
20 Vauxhall Bridge Road
London, SW1V 2SA
United Kingdom

Random House Australia (Pty) Ltd
20 Alfred Street, Milsons Point, Sydney,
New South Wales 2061, Australia

Random House South Africa Pty Ltd
Isle of Houghton
Corner Boundary Road and Carse O'Gowrie
Houghton 2198, South Africa

Random House Publishers India Private Ltd
301 World Trade Tower, Hotel Intercontinental
Grand Complex,
Barakhamba Lane, New Delhi 110 001, India

First published 2007

© 2007 Christine Fernyhough (text) © John Bougen (all
photographs except where otherwise specified)

The moral rights of the author have been asserted

ISBN 978 1 86941 896 0

The publishers would like to thank the James K. Baxter
Trust for permission to reproduce 'High Country
Weather'.

Map by Holly Roach
Cover design: Katy Yiakmis
Text design: Sharon Grace and Katy Yiakmis
Cover photograph: Brendon O'Hagan
Cover inset: John Bougen
Printed in China

The Road to Castle Hill

A High Country love story

Christine Fernyhough

with Louise Callan

Photography by John Bougen

RANDOM HOUSE
NEW ZEALAND

Original wallpaper from the first Castle Hill Homestead, built for John and Charles Enys in 1865.

Contents

High Country Weather

Alone we are born
    And die alone;
Yet see the red-gold cirrus
    Over snow-mountain shine.

Upon the upland road
    Ride easy, stranger:
Surrender to the sky
    Your heart of anger.

JAMES K. BAXTER

Acknowledgements

To my wonderful family, especially my mother and late father, and my children, David, Kate and Joseph, who said, 'Go for it, Mum' and who continue to look out for me, to hold me close.

To my late husband, John, who encouraged me to be brave and enterprising. Buying Castle Hill was a quantum leap even for me.

To my friends, who support me as they eat and wear Merino, and particularly to Bets, who introduced me to half of Canterbury, and to Lindsay, Kathy, Anna, Pam and Julie, Craig, Riki, Dick and Jude Frizzell, and my South Island champions: Annie and John Chapman, Jess and Stewart Gunn, Gillie and Tim Deans and Pru and Tim Wallis.

To Snow, who in farming parlance has been on Castle Hill for a mere blink of the eye and who through his hard work, finely honed stock skills and wonderful sense of humour has changed for the best the fortunes of Castle Hill.

To Keith, who truly did look after his 'bonnie lass'.

To Emily and Anders Crofoot of Castlepoint Station and to my friends in and around the Waimakariri, the Rakaia and the Ashburton gorges, places where courtesies, consideration and the milk of human kindness reign supreme.

To Nicola Legat, a delight to work alongside and who said there was a story when I doubted her, and the rest of the team at Random House. It was the light in the eyes of a guy who had fallen in love with Mona Anderson's stories and who I met over a pint of Speight's that convinced me that my story of struggle and joy, laughter, hardship, mistakes and love in the high country was worth telling.

To Louise, thoughtful, erudite, incisive, patient, truly patient. Thank you for giving me time to come to terms with what it was to really talk, to do away with my lateral arabesques, to stop mustering at every opportunity and to make sense of my life, my thoughts, my emotions.

To John, for whom it must be a relief to stop saying 'What part of "look at me" don't you understand?' With your eye you have captured the essence of my Paradise. Your photographs traverse the many moods and seasons, light and subtlety of this special landscape. The people pictured whether in repose or in action, they too, exude a comfort, a contentment, a familiarity, a closeness to this wondrous land.

To the innovation and productivity of farmers, everywhere in New Zealand.

In the stones horizons sing.

Christine Fernyhough
Castle Hill Station
July 2007

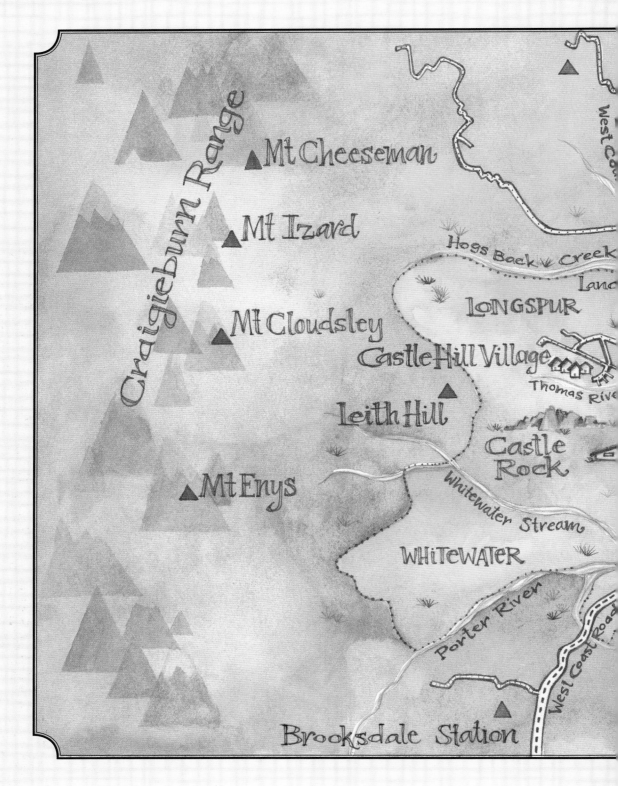

Craigieburn Range

▲ Mt Cheeseman

▲ Mt Izard

▲ Mt Cloudsley

▲ Mt Enys

West Co...

Hogs Back Creek

Lan...

LONGSPUR

Castle Hill Village

Thomas Rive...

▲ Leith Hill

Castle Rock

Whitewater Stream

WHITEWATER

Porter River

West Coast Road

▲ Brooksdale Station

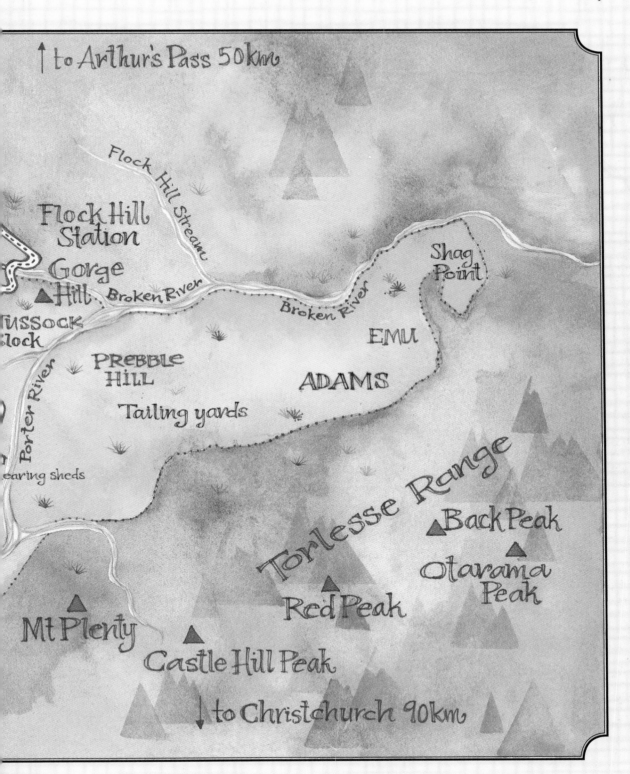

↑ to Arthur's Pass 50km

Flock Hill Stream

Flock Hill Station

Gorge Hill

Broken River

Shag Point

Tussock Block

Porter River

PREBBLE HILL

Tailing yards

Broken River

EMU

ADAMS

Shearing sheds

Torlesse Range

Back Peak

Otarama Peak

Red Peak

Mt Plenty

Castle Hill Peak

↓ to Christchurch 90km

CHAPTER 1

Castle
in the sky

S State Highway 73 runs from Christchurch across to Greymouth on the West Coast. It begins with a series of long straights through table-flat farm land, fields straddled by fine insect-like lines of irrigators, and small country towns — Yaldhurst, West Melton, Kirwee, Darfield, Waddington, Sheffield, Annat, Springfield — before climbing the distant ranges to cross over Arthur's Pass. At first the ranks of hills lie below the horizon; then rise and approach in a series of jump cuts until suddenly, beyond Springfield, you are amongst them on the climb up and over Porters Pass. The road winds between steep tussock, kanuka and matagouri-covered scree. On the lower slopes are hebes, tight mounds of vegetation which in flower look from a distance like sheep. Gorse and broom fill the stony river beds, colour the roadside verges and are colonising the boundary slopes above and below the highway. In late spring the first of the wild lupins flower in clumps on the long acre.

Opposite: The last of the original Castle Hill wethers found up the Porter River, having been alone and unshorn for five years.

I couldn't see the run-down state of the station. Neither was I aware of its fearsome reputation as a hard place to farm because of its altitude and climate . . . I was totally captured by the scale and grandeur of the place and the thought that I might become a part of it.

This is not a conventionally pretty landscape. Rather, it has a harsh beauty and an unforgiving terrain that at certain times — early morning or a summer twilight — can with a trick of the light deceive, making the erosion-exposed bones of the hillsides appear velvety soft, as if coated in the finest of grey powder.

On a morning in May 2004, I turned onto State Highway 73 out of Christchurch with my son David and son-in-law, Rob. We were on our way to Castle Hill, one of the oldest and best known of the South Island high country sheep stations. The week before I had learnt it was for sale. There were just days before the tender closed and amongst the family, David and Rob were the only ones who could take time to accompany me. At Lake Lyndon, Gerry McSweeney was to join us. Gerry is co-owner of Cora Lynn, a neighbouring station, and manager of its eco-tourism Wilderness Lodge. That day, however, he would be there in yet another of his roles, as a representative of the Nature Heritage Fund (NHF), the government's conservation land agent funded by the Department of Conservation. Nature Heritage was looking for a partner in a purchase that would give the heritage group two-thirds of Castle Hill's land. They wanted 'key recreation and conservation areas of national interest', basically the tops of the surrounding ranges above a certain level. This would leave the rest, the lower hills and flats, to be farmed. Also joining us was Allan McKenzie, manager of land purchases at the Department of Conservation in Wellington. Nature Heritage and DOC would be central players in any sale negotiations.

It was a fine day but cold, a freezing wind blowing across the lake; we were dressed for a mild Auckland autumn. Gerry, used to city guests' lack of appropriate wardrobe, handed out jackets before driving us a short way along the road and onto terraces that run below Mt Plenty, between Dry Stream and the Porter River. Even as he was telling me I would not want this particular piece of the station's patchwork of terraces, flats and hills, covered as it was with hieracium, I was assuring him it would be fine by me, already in thrall to my surroundings.

Castle Hill is the first station in the Waimakariri Valley between Porters Pass and Arthur's Pass. It sits in a basin cupped by the Craigieburn and Torlesse ranges, bisected by the main highway. That day there was a fierce clarity to the air. The sky was so vast, the landscape so grand with its great jumble of limestone rocks and castellated outcrops that so define the area. However, it is a vista that is not to everyone's taste. The first European explorer to look down across the country north of Porters Pass and the Torlesse Range thought it 'a romantic and chaotic mass of mountains'. On closer inspection Charles Torlesse was less enthusiastic: 'The scene did not strike me as promising a smiling or cheerful home. It chilled me to look at it.' Nine years later, in 1858, traversing the land around Castle Hill for the first time, he claimed that 'the wretched Broken River country . . . gave me positive pain to look at from its barren and misshapen appearance'. I could understand his disquiet. On previous trips south I would look with dismay at the emptiness, the tawny coloured expanses — few trees, few birds, vast and empty. I could only think of what was familiar: the lush green pastures of the north where you could see sheep grazing, unlike the high country's one sheep per acre.

I had first come to the South Island in the 1960s with my husband, Allan Tattersfield, to nail our gold mining rights on the claims assigned us in Central Otago and on the West Coast. Later, in the 1970s, we spent the mid-year school holidays in rental accommodation in Arrowtown, walking each day with the kids to our alluvial gold plant on a bend on the wild and unstoppable Arrow River. The steep gorge only allowed a slice of sun, leaving us in a noisy, cold, greyness so different from the usual holidays of white sand and snapper. Each day would bring a palpable anticipation of what might gleam in the silt. Most often it was simply the finest of dust. On a good day it might fill a thimble. Occasionally there was something of size that, when shown during Housie at the pub, would constitute a nugget. Then in the 1980s and 1990s I walked the usual tracks — Milford, Hollyford, Greenstone, Heaphy — where the need to keep your pack light forced wine and beer to give way to a flask of whisky and started me on the drink of choice in the high country.

At Castle Hill the land agent was waiting for us in the rough driveway to the station yard. There was already another group with him, suggesting I had competition. We had landed at Christchurch from Auckland at 11am and had to be back there by three o'clock for our return flight. Gerry gave us the view from the road, no more than a drive-by, and then took us for a closer look at the paddocks across the highway from the station yard. We drove down terraces to the pebbled bed of the Porter to ford its double channels; over to the deer paddock, one enormous block where spotting the deer was like looking for game on the Serengeti; through a stand of black beeches to the old wooden tailing yards and on, the rough track bouncing us past an enormous piece of limestone like a giant altar, and finally to the crest of another steep undulation that faced Flock Hill. Gerry handed out sandwiches provided by Wilderness Lodge — beautiful buns stacked with lettuce and thick cuts of smoked salmon. We gazed about us. It felt as if I had stepped into a land of natural plenty. We had seen trout in the stream and a pair of ducks on a swamp pond. A hawk circled and swooped beneath the brow of the next hill. Occasionally, at the sound of the four wheel drive, a hare started up from the tussock and loped away. By the time we left to go back to the airport and Auckland, I had committed to put in a combined tender with Nature Heritage, as long as we could make it work for both of us.

In the two or so hours in which we had skimmed across the tiniest portion of Castle Hill's more than 11,000 hectares (28,000 acres), I had not looked at fences or gates or pasture growth. The sales brochure promised a rural dream in 'one of New Zealand's Iconic High Country Stations with Opportunities for Productive Development and Expansion into Tourism or Related Ventures limited only by one's Imagination'. I couldn't see the run-down state of the station. Neither was I aware of its fearsome reputation as a hard place to farm because of its altitude and climate. I didn't care about (or for) the big new house that the current owners had built further up the hill. I loved the little limestone cottage that had been home to the station's owners in the 1860s. I was totally captured by the scale and grandeur of the place and the thought that I might become a part of it.

What some might see as frivolous or foolhardy in my approach to such a huge investment is second nature to me. I have tended to act spontaneously most of my life. I conceive ideas and act on them almost immediately. It is a modus operandi that has served me very well. I was fresh from two major ventures, one based on no more than a phone call to someone I had never met. Books in Homes and the Gifted Kids Programme had both been successful and exciting to create and develop. I like challenges and love learning new things and this new change of direction was not totally arbitrary. Country life had been part of my childhood, and I had investigated buying a farm in the past.

I spent the first five years of my life living with my mother, Aunt Phyllis and my older brother Malcolm on a working orchard at Kumeu in West Auckland. It was the war years, World War II, and my father was a navigator

Early paintings and photographs of Castle Hill. Clockwise from top left: Limestone homestead, circa 1900; Castle Hill's limestone rocks; the interior of Trelissick, the first home of an early owner, Charles Enys, who bought the run with his brother from the Porters in 1864. Charles Enys made numerous paintings of Canterbury runs and the Canterbury region, including the Trelissick exterior at far right. The circa 1900 photograph is of horse-drawn coaches on the West Coast Road (now State Highway 73) which continues on past the station gate to Arthur's Pass and the West Coast.

Alexander Turnbull Library

Alexander Turnbull Library

History in the hills

Even as he was telling me I would not want the station's patchwork of terraces, flats and hills, covered as it was with hieracium, I was assuring him it would be fine by me, in thrall to my surroundings.

Alexander Turnbull Library

National Library of Australia

Top: My mother, Gladys Don, my brother Malcolm, and me.

Below: Ready for school in hat and gloves with Malcolm and our younger sister Philippa.

in the RNZAF, fighting in the Pacific. Later, when I was at primary school, my little sister Philippa and I stayed with Aunty Phyl and Uncle George at what we always called 'the farm', when our parents went on an overseas trip for a year. The orchard was also where we spent school holidays. There are layers of memories. You reached the farmhouse down a long straight drive with flowered borders. The house was a simple bungalow with a long drop out the back until they did a little modernising. There were half a dozen cows. We would separate the milk from the cream and then Aunty Phyl would make butter, without salt, which tasted foul. She liked her garden and I remember picking pansies to put on trays or float in bowls around art deco naked ladies made of Depression glass.

The orchards were beyond the packing shed, over one, two hills and across and up from a stream with eels. Varieties of apples were grouped in sections — Docherty, Wine Sap, Granny Smith, Gentian, Giant Gentian and Red Delicious — then a new bay of pears, and grapefruit and plums. There were peaches, too, but they were very difficult to grow in Auckland. The rain would come and then they would turn brown and blacken and rot.

I can see my uncle spraying with a pack on his back, probably filled with DDT or something similar, and wearing a souwester, thinking it would somehow protect his head. No such thing as a mask then, or trying to spray when the wind wasn't blowing. The apple trees were huge and you needed long ladders to reach them for picking. There were canvas aprons that you pulled on over your head, flipped up the lower edge so you could pick into them and then flipped down to roll the apples into a trailer that went up to the packing shed.

But my strongest memory is the morning teas and lunches and afternoon teas outside. Phyl would spread the Onehunga blankets under the apple trees and put out the first cups Crown Lynn made, industrial cream and rimmed and looking like heater insulators, which was what Crown Lynn made to begin with. There was always home cooking, no bought biscuits, and lots of sugar and stirring. They were quiet times. We read and played ludo and snakes and ladders on the sun porch and listened to the country report on the Amalgamated Radio that looked like a gothic cathedral. There were big thick mattresses made of indeterminate things and really nice towels that smelled of camphor. At night you could hear the ocean at Muriwai. Somehow the roll and crash of the waves rose up over the dunes, through the pines, between the apple trees, across the hills and stream and in under my skin. Aunty Phyl's farm buried itself deep in my subconscious.

In the days following our return to Auckland from Castle Hill, we opened discussions with Nature Heritage on how the partnership might work. Allan McKenzie came up from Wellington, and a complicated three-way dance began between DOC, Nature Heritage and me and my lawyer, David Nicol. Some time before this, the station's owners, Mike and Lois Bradley, had begun the tenure review process and then decided to withdraw, but not before Nature Heritage discovered they had missed acquiring a limestone formation called Wuthering Heights. They were determined that none of the land they wanted would escape them this time. Then there was the question of price. Nature Heritage had just bought the whole of Birchwood Station for $11 million and considered Castle Hill second only to Birchwood in 'iconic' status. They might feel financially constrained after such a large purchase. One afternoon, sitting round the table, we each wrote on a piece of paper what we thought the station would sell for. The Thursday after our flying visit, we sent down a conditional tender and then negotiations opened.

The Bradleys came back wanting more money. I had a limit of $2.5 million and would not, could not, go beyond that. We then got an indication they would settle for $6 million. Nature Heritage raised their share of the price and finally we had an agreement to sell. I had a high country farm in Canterbury, and my share had cost me $2.4 million. In great excitement, I went out to dinner to celebrate with David Nicol and my kids. Used to me plunging into big projects, and having lived their lives alongside my ever-present can-do attitude, Kate, David and Joe were unfazed by this latest venture. We saw a new world opening up. For the family it was an incredible playground, totally different from the beaches they were used to and within a short drive of some of the South Island's best ski fields. It was also a chance for the next generation to gain an appreciation of the agricultural industry that continues to be the backbone of New Zealand. My philosophy has always been that life is for learning, learning is life-long, and with Castle Hill I would begin a whole new learning.

Now the hard work started as Nature Heritage, DOC and I began

View from the homestead, looking down Chrissie's Paddock across State Highway 73 to Old Quarters and the sheep yards, with, from left to right, Gorge Hill, Prebble Hill and Mt Torlesse.

negotiating how to divide the farm. I needed someone with expertise in my corner. Gerry McSweeney recommended his farm advisor who my brother, Malcolm, on the board of Richmond Meats, also knew. Malcolm thought him a good choice. First we revisited the station, this time traversing it carefully with the Bradleys' son-in-law, who had also been their farm manager. He recommended what land not to give up. Trading between us and Allan McKenzie for DOC on what we would keep and what we would relinquish went back and forth. Our greatest loss was the whole of the Cheeseman area — tussock flats and hills going up to the Mt Cheeseman ski field. It was not until I had started farming that I truly appreciated what I had lost — great country for stock to graze in summer and winter. Finally, at a meeting in Rotorua, my farm advisor rose saying, 'This is not going to work. I don't think I can recommend to Chrissie that she buy.' I drove back to Auckland in shock and called him. If it was as bad as he said, then what was I doing buying it?

It was, he assured me, just hard ball negotiating.

As we were buying the farm with NHF, the land purchasing arm of DOC we tried to preempt the tenure review process and have the pastoral lease converted to freehold as part of the joint venture purchase. However, NHF did not have such authority; tenure review is run exclusively by Land Information New Zealand (LINZ). Instead NHF promised to support us when we went for review. However, when two years later I formally signed up for tenure review, DOC came back wanting more land and more access than we had originally agreed with them. Negotiations continue to drag on and on.

Hand-over date was 30 July but the Bradleys asked for a couple of weeks' extension. I would take possession in mid August. I threw a wish-me-luck party. Presents included a sheep crook, books, violently coloured woolly slippers and hot-water bottles.

Friends tell me now that they thought I'd gone mad. In most eyes, buying a high country sheep station, when I had no farming experience vaulted over all my previous big and wild ideas to top the list. There was one other factor: for the first time in my life I was operating alone. I had family: a great brother and sister, my two sons and daughter and their spouses and children, and my mother, still the family matriarch. But a little over a year earlier, in just twelve hours, I lost the two most significant men in my life, the ones who gave me unconditional love and support — my father and my much loved husband of twenty years, John Fernyhough. My father's death was sudden and unexpected. He was old and his body was beginning to wear out, but he had not been sick. John's death, however, closed a long illness. Their loss precipitated a re-evaluation of what I was doing and what I was going to do. There was no shortage of friends and strangers with advice, but I kept returning to what I had observed as John's life changed and his cancer developed.

Looking back, I think I can see the first signs of that change, and maybe the first signs that something was wrong physically, when he decided to step away from the state-owned enterprises he had been involved in. John was the chairman and face of ECNZ during the time of the one-hundred-year drought in the late 1990s. He had done about ten years of community service in SOEs. They were very exacting responsibilities and, unlike the CEOs, chairmen were not well paid. He expended a lot of high powered thought on ECNZ and Forestry Corp in order to do the best for New Zealand. On the back of the drought he had an added stress. The government required a greater dividend and in order to pay it the price of electricity would have to go up. The government accepted the need for a modest price increase but when John, as chairman, made the announcement, he was left high and dry. The price rise was very unpopular. The CEO disappeared and the government, now in an MMP environment, ran for cover. Politicians and politics are like shifting sands.

In the end he became sick of political interference, fed up with politicians' sudden changes of direction, and the way they left the businessmen they had invited to manage the new state businesses unsupported when politics intervened. He was in his mid fifties, still a young man, and he went from someone with almost too much to do, to one with comparatively little demand on his time. Perhaps this is something all men go through on retirement. There was no office to go to; there was no imposed routine or timetable; there

*My late husband
John Fernyhough
and me in a French
field of poppies
on one of our
great adventures
overseas.*

were no colleagues around to talk to. He had a number of directorships, and
was mentoring some young businesses he had invested in. There was also his
Classic Car Museum which he was establishing. But none of that involved the
day-to-day running of a business. So with retirement came a kind of
loneliness. That was when he started to feel tired.

John was diagnosed with prostate cancer when he was fifty six. For a
number of reasons, and because we were told it had good results, he chose to
have radiotherapy treatment rather than surgery. Over the next few years we
juggled the cocktail of drugs prescribed and pressed on with life. The monthly
PSA tests were an emotional knock-about. Each time you hoped the levels
had dropped; and each time the news was bad, the body's balance never quite
under control. We explored alternative treatments in Australia and at the
Memorial Sloan-Kettering Cancer Centre in New York. On our first visit to
the clinic we were so jetlagged we slipped in and out of sleep. Next time we
came prepared with a list of all the questions we wanted to ask. The doctors
recommended a drug not yet available in New Zealand, Casodex, and once
the right dosage had been established, it seemed to work well.

We continued to travel. John had board meetings in New Zealand and
abroad to attend, there were family holidays and I was determined that his
illness would not mean an end to the kinds of adventures we both loved. One
of the last was a rally between Panama City and Anchorage, Alaska, in 1997.
About twenty three cars started in the touring division; five completed the
race. My son Joe and his wife Symmone set out with us in the Jeep Cherokee

Our harvest.

but only went as far as Las Vegas before deciding it was too scary and not much of a holiday. Race rules were rigidly adhered to: we were penalised on one leg for stopping to help another competitor whose car had developed serious mechanical problems because, the adjudicators said, no life was in imminent danger. Another of the drivers, an elderly man, dropped dead at the end of the first day, probably of excitement. It turned out his young navigator was not his wife and his wife did not know he was on the rally. We completed the race, coming second in the touring division, but it stretched us both. I began as navigator working with a tulip map for the first time and ended as driver on 'special sections', the most dangerous sectors, white-knuckling the wheel. John had begun to have dizzy spells, feeling so sick he would faint and then vomit.

Some months later, back in Auckland at dinner, John asked if the entrées were written in Chinese. He could not decipher the letters. He had had a comprehensive stroke. Suddenly he didn't know where familiar roads were, or at home where to find the kettle. He was bemused and lost until he started to reorient himself. Then the cancer spread. One kidney was completely gone and a cancerous growth had almost strangled the other before it was discovered and a stent inserted. Another small reprieve, another chance to get on with life; but each hopeful scenario would soon be dashed by another deterioration.

The disease became more and more pervasive and by Christmas 2002 the local district nurse was calling to see John at the bach at Mangawhai, giving him injections for pain relief. We returned to our house in Remuera, and once there, he went upstairs and never came down again. We moved his bed so that it was right next to the window. It is salutary to watch the very sick. Everyone wants to live another day and when you don't know whether you will wake tomorrow you come to value not just looking but really seeing in a way few of us take the time to. John would know which way the wind was blowing, what yachts were on the harbour, the habits of the local birds, small seasonal changes, the way trees moved. There would be no more reprieves. The hospice brought a morphine pump to help control his pain and showed me how to work it. The doctor warned he could go at any time.

That was when I got the phone call to say my father had fallen at home. When we had called an ambulance and settled him in hospital I went back and told John. They say hearing is the last of the senses to go. He used to listen to music and I would read to him and he would know it was me and would always be able to purse his lips, give me a kiss. But by then I was not sure how much he understood. On a Sunday night, two days after the fall, I saw my father for the last time. He was expected home soon. I remember it was lunchtime when my brother and sister came to tell me he had died. I went in to John and just cried and cried. I think he thought I was crying for him and somehow releasing him — it was as if I had given him permission to go.

Later that afternoon, I could no longer get a response. That night I was lying in bed holding him when I woke to hear him breathing differently. And then, very quietly, he died in my arms. It is strange at such moments how detail consumes you. I had a piece of paper explaining how to stretch out the body, something I thought I had to do, and I couldn't decide how to fold his hands. Movies had given me the idea that dying people make a special sound with their last breath. I was lying beside him when I heard a 'pssst-psst'. Was this it? Then I realised the pain pump was still going. I removed it, packed it back in its box and, after I had spent some time by myself, I began the phone calls, the first to John's brother who was staying next door. Two funerals: my father's on Saturday and John's the following Monday. It was terrible, hideous, incomprehensible. For such a long time I had been able to say that no one really close to me had died. Now suddenly two of the most important people were gone.

With John's death, my life lost a central focus. He had been sick for eight years. After his stroke I did almost all of the driving, nursed him and, until he became really sick, also kept up my work on Books in Homes and then the Gifted Kids Programme. It had taken much more out of me than I realised. I had been a person who had difficulty watching needles and blood on television. I began by giving John moral support and the belief we could get over it; but as his illness developed, what was needed became so much more. I went to every medical appointment with him. I became expert at having all his notes and tests with us when he had to go to hospital, and banging them down on the counter when we struck trouble at Admissions. And I got to handle more needles and catheters and deal with more blood and pain than I could ever have imagined I would be able to. My medicine, I used to joke with him, was cab-sav three times a day.

Right at the top of the list of life's most stressful experiences are the death of a spouse, loss of a parent and shifting house. I had all three. We had been preparing to move to a smaller place. John wanted me to feel secure after his death. It also seemed obscene to me to have tennis courts and swimming pools and three-quarters of an acre of land when I was the only one there. I wanted rid of the clutter and fewer outgoings than such a property requires. We bought two adjacent houses overlooking Judges Bay and John suggested to my daughter Kate and her husband, Rob, that they move in there with their two boys and the new twins. That way they would have more space and I would not be so alone. The renovations on my house were not finished so I lived in the downstairs bedroom at Kate and Rob's until I could cross the drive to my own place.

I was at a loss as to how to use my time. John had left me very well provided for but I had no interest in becoming a lady who lunches and plays a good round of golf, though I do both at times. It did not feel right to go back full time to Gifted Kids. The two women who had been so important in starting and growing the programme with me, and whom I had been closest to, were leaving. I would have to do something. I thought a week at the Australian health spa, Golden Door, on a regime of exercise and eating

Me with John's huntaway, Ed, and my heading dog, Midge.

When I sat on the tussock that day in
May, what part was about grieving, what
part about having a go at farming, what
part about farming in the South Island
high country — for many New Zealanders
their most treasured landscape?

politely might be a start. I liked the food but when I came home I hopped into the chardonnay again. It would have to be a real project. The decision to buy Castle Hill Station fulfilled all the criteria.

I have sometimes wondered since what really formed my decision. When I sat on the tussock that day in May, what part was about grieving, what part about having a go at farming, what part about farming in the South Island high country — for many New Zealanders their most treasured landscape? As we grow more and more urbanised, more and more dislocated from the countryside and rural matters, its vast land and sky scapes have become romantic emblems of an almost lost New Zealand.

On a drearily grey August afternoon, 2004, I set out again up State Highway 73, the same small settlements now lit against the descending night. For a time I kept pace with a freight train pulling a long line of empty wagons back to the West Coast and its coal mines, to load and return across the alps and plains, as coal trains have been doing for over a hundred years. In Porters Pass, scraps of snow reflected in the headlights' high beam. I was coming at last to take possession of my farm. This time my travelling companions were Judy and Dick Frizzell. I had told them they had a responsibility to help me move in since they had been there at the very beginning of this adventure. It had been the experience of visiting them in Hawke's Bay amidst the luxurious fertility of its orchards and farmland, olive groves and vineyards, the warmth and friendliness of its rural communities, that awakened the idea of a farming life. Admittedly, I had been thinking of something smaller than a high country station. It was a friend, ex-colleague and financial advisor who heard about Castle Hill while staying in Gerry McSweeney's Wilderness Lodge. We were having an ongoing discussion about investments. Back from another visit to Hawke's Bay I had called and asked, 'What about a farm?'

Colin Giffney, fresh from his Canterbury weekend, responded: what about a real farm?

It was late when we reached the station. The furniture and all the other contents would not arrive until early next morning so we had booked a night further up the road in Castle Hill Village. Excited and unable to wait, we drove up to the homestead. The power was not on, none of us knew where the mains switch was, and the dark country night made it impossible to see. We went on up to the B&B, hoping the weather would be kind to us for the big move, and woke on Monday to that particular muffling of sound that comes with snow. It had fallen heavily overnight, casting a deep coat across the landscape and icing the tops of the limestone rocks. We marvelled at its beauty; but with it came my first lesson in the realities of living in the South Island's high country.

The snow slowed the freight truck over Porters Pass and then defeated it completely on the driveway to the house. In the end, the farm manager dragged it up with the tractor. In the giant trailer was everything I thought I needed to start my new life. Some of it was specially bought and other pieces were part of the past, like furniture I put in storage when I moved into the smaller house in Auckland after John died. I had only seen the station

Baling winter feed on the flats from the paddock we call Chrissie's.

While things were going smoothly in and around the main house, the same could not be said of initial farm matters.

The homestead, with Midge heading a small mob and an out-of-season lamb. The snow-covered peaks at the back are part of the Craigieburn Range.

homestead once but I knew the pieces would fit and the big couches with their new tussock-coloured covers were just right for the comfortable informality I thought would suit rural living.

The unpacking began. I had less than a week before my son David and his family arrived to visit and then the Frizzells would move on. Dick's first job was to assemble all the furniture that came in pieces, like the beds, and to install the home entertainment unit. I found the tool kit I had bought and we began the task in high spirits. Before they left, the old owners had kindly measured the windows for me and so I started putting up blinds and curtains. One of Judy's early tasks was taking the sticky labels off all the glassware and washing it. There would be plenty of celebratory glasses of pinot and whisky to mark our progress through the week. With the eager help of the farm manager's wife, the kitchen unpacking went at such a rate that at one stage saucepan lids had to be retrieved from cartons thrown too soon into the horse float to be taken and burnt.

Dinner the first night was down at the farm manager's house. We would need to fill the homestead larder and fridge next. Back in Christchurch we stocked up on basics and treats and explored the second-hand and antique shops. Evening meals were fitted in round the ongoing organisation —

a chicken put into the oven in the late afternoon, ready to be eaten at the end of the day, washed down with a good glass or two of wine. I had never owned a freezer in any of my previous houses, much preferring to buy all my food fresh, and had not included one in my list of goods for the station. It would only take a short time before I came to realise what any farming family knows: a freezer is basic equipment and more than one is not an extravagance.

One evening during the news, Dick overheard a story about the start of the whitebait season. We had been working hard and agreed we deserved a break and something really delicious. What better than a meal of new season's whitebait fresh from its source. The next day we drove over Arthur's Pass and down to the coast. However, in a fuzz of tiredness, Dick had missed a salient part of the story: Greymouth was only preparing for whitebaiting. The season started the following week. Unable to let go of our original idea, we sat in a booth in a 1960s style bar and had truly awful fritters made from last season's frozen whitebait mixed with far too much flour and cooked in too much lard.

While things were going smoothly in and around the homestead, the same could not be said of initial farm matters. The first issue concerned the plant and machinery which were on the farm. The official take-over date was 30 July but when that was delayed I asked the farm advisor to draw up a schedule of items and prices and to fax it through to me before he signed it off. The decision not to come down earlier was one I came to rue. He failed to clear the schedule with me before he signed it and I found myself the reluctant owner of a whole range of things I didn't want or need. Worst was $28,000 worth of hardwood power poles which had been left on the station and would have cost the previous owner nothing. If I had known more, I would have had a clearing sale, the farm equivalent of a garage sale, as soon as I settled in.

The second issue was staff. Although there was a manager on the farm when it was sold, all the advice I received was to let him go and start afresh. Together with the farm advisor, we drew up a list of what I needed from whoever took the position. I wanted someone who would teach me, who I could go out with and learn from; someone I would find it easy to communicate with. Response to the advertisements was poor. Castle Hill's reputation as a hard station to farm may have been one of the reasons; and for a manager with a young family there was the issue of schooling — there is no school bus beyond Springfield and Porters Pass is often marginal in winter. There was, however, one applicant the advisor recommended. He said he was a hard worker and could manage the newly configured station alone. He would be modest in his demands and careful in budgeting. The prospective applicant was married and his wife was prepared to do some housekeeping while I was out starting to work on the farm. I was assured he would be an ideal fit. We called him in for an interview.

The end of that first week came in a rush. With some reluctance I drove the Frizzells back to Christchurch. Judy and Dick had been great fun and an enormous help, the best of companions, and I was sorry they had to go. With the house reasonably under control, I began to explore the farm with David and the family, but only as far as I felt comfortable. It is country that needs a powerful four-wheel drive, and even that will only take you so far. I was a novice at off-road driving and my nervousness made me cautious. We took picnics down to the stony edge of the Porter and climbed around the limestone rocks. Then it was time to take them in to Christchurch to return to Auckland.

It was different this time driving back across the plains and up over Porters Pass. The road was no longer strange, but it was the first time I had travelled it alone. It was dark and there was a snow storm. As I came up from the Porter River bridge and on to the long straight to the station gates, I could feel unwelcome tears pricking at the back of my eyes. My idea, my choice, my project, I reminded myself.

That evening I drove down to the main gates and closed them. It was to become a ritual at the end of each day. Up at the homestead I drew the curtains and pulled down the blinds, locked all the doors and built up the fire. I poached a couple of eggs and then wandered through my new home, a glass of whisky in hand while Bob

Marley's 'Redemption Song' blasted out. The snow lay thick on the ground and the cold breathed in hard and sharp.

One of the last things Dick had done after all the furniture had been placed was to hang my art. He came as painter-artist to the job, with strong opinions about some of the work. 'I'm not putting him up; he's no painter!' 'No, no! You can't hang those two together.' However, there was one canvas I wanted where people had time to sit and study it. That is how the original of the Duffy Pictorial History of New Zealand Aotearoa, the millennium poster for Books in Homes devised together with one of my best friends' daughters, came to hang on the wall of the lavatory between the back door and the kitchen. That night I stood in the doorway and drank a toast to it.

Duffy Books and Homes, the Gifted Kids Programme, the familiar sounds and securities of the city and the loving warmth of my family suddenly seemed far far away. I could feel the prick of unwanted tears again. I curled up in bed. Tomorrow, I promised, I would be ready to start the great adventure, learning everything about my high country farm.

CHAPTER 2

Books
for all seasons

One of my early images of Castle Hill was of books of poetry lying among copies of *Straight Furrow* and *Farmer's Weekly* on the window seats in the station owner's house. Beyond the large windows were the home paddock — soon to be called Chrissie's — a distinctively shaped limestone boulder I named The Rabbit and, stepping away, State Highway 73, the old shearing quarters and sheep yards, Prebble Hill and the peaks of the Torlesse Range. It conjured a delicious mix of time spent curled up indoors reading as well as the more obvious world of physical work awaiting me outside.

I've always been a reader, like my mother. I had books around me from when I was little, and my own kids and granny-kids are surrounded by books. Reading is everything people say it is: one of life's great pleasures, a way of learning about things, going to places you haven't been, confronting ideas that challenge and provoke your own beliefs. It's a key to unlock the potential and promise of life.

'And it occurred to Beth that her own house — no, not just her house but every house she'd ever been in — was bookless. The thought struck her like one of Jake's punches, dunno why. So much so she had to get up and walk around; paced up and down the downstairs passage, smoking, unable to ease her agitation. Bookless. Bookless. We're a bookless society. It kept hammering and hammering home. Soon it was like a sense of loss, almost grief. And she thinking, Jesus, what's wrong with me? So what if this house has no books, what's the big deal about books? But it kept nagging away at her . . . And she began to think that it was because a bookless society didn't stand a show in this modern world, not a damn show.'

When I first read those lines from Alan Duff's ground-breaking novel, *Once Were Warriors*, I thought they had real power and resonance: they sprang from a truth. The jolt it gave me may have been less than Beth's but it was still profound. Some time later I heard an interview with Alan in which he talked about a book project. I thought it sounded interesting so I dialled 018. This was in the early 1990s, and I had never called someone I didn't know before because of something I'd heard or read about them. Alan's initial response was gruff. I suggested that next time he was in Auckland he come and have dinner with the family. Months passed and I called again. He told me more about what he was doing. A couple of years earlier he had begun collecting books for children in one of the poorest schools in Hawke's Bay, where he lives. If he would come to Auckland and talk about it, I said, I would have a party and ask some friends. There were people who would be interested in helping. Later I thought about how crazy our beginning was, but then so many grand things are started by small spontaneous acts.

Alan came to dinner at our house in Auckland and talked about what he wanted to achieve and how his project had begun. On a visit to Camberley Primary during its writers' week he had asked the children how many of them had books at home. Hardly any of them had raised their hand. The man who had placed that thought about the power and role of books in the head of Beth was dismayed. The written word is the key to the modern world and a child who cannot read becomes an adult with real disadvantages. And New Zealand had many of them: a Ministry of Education survey on adult literacy had found one in five New Zealand adults had difficulty reading a bus timetable or understanding instructions on a medicine bottle. Maori and Pacific Island people's literacy was even worse. Our prisons were also filled with people who had almost no reading and writing skills. He wanted to make a difference, and so he had set out to collect over two thousand books, mainly second hand, for children at Camberley Primary. Alan talked about putting books in homes. It was a great idea but a struggle to keep going and even more difficult to expand beyond that one school.

I put a basket at the front door and asked my dinner guests to make a donation. Not all were fans of Alan but they liked his idea and they were generous. We collected about $15,000 that night. Then Alan and I talked. The principals in his local schools were supportive of the idea of getting books into their pupils' homes, but some felt that second-hand books lacked value in the kids' eyes. Too many of their children were surrounded by the second hand and second rate. (I had some sympathy as the less-than-thrilled recipient of the hand-me-downs from my cousins that augmented the clothes my mother made me as a child. I can still remember the first shop-bought dress I chose for myself from Sweet Sixteen to Sixty.) When Alan had been able to get new titles the children's reaction had been different. It seemed to me that if his idea was to be a real success, then not only must the books be new but the children must also be able to select what they took home to keep. Offer them a beautiful new book that they chose themselves and it becomes something special, something to be looked after and treasured.

The first thing we did was set up a charitable trust, the Alan Duff Charitable Foundation, with a board of trustees headed by the late Sir Peter Elworthy, whom Alan knew. The other trustees were ex-MP John Delamere, Andrew Morrison (then partner in the law firm Sainsbury Logan & Williams), John Marsh of the NZ Maori Arts & Crafts Institute, Rex Graham (a fruit grower from Hawke's Bay and friend of Alan's) and Terry Morrison, (a primary school principal from Rotorua). Our initial funds were those donations from the Auckland dinner. Then Alan announced that he had arranged for us to go to Wellington. We were off, he said, to ask the government for $5 million.

He was positive they would say yes: the idea was a world beater. Alan and I arrived at the Beehive with Peter Elworthy and our kaumatua, Ben Hona, full of fire and optimism. A photo in *The Dominion* shows us on the steps of Parliament buildings looking as if we were climbing out of the trenches of illiteracy, all ready and fired up for our assault. We were shown in to the office of John Luxton, then the Minister of Maori Affairs. Behind Luxton was a line of civil servants. Alan opened with little preamble and in his very direct way said something along the lines of, 'We are here for five million. We've got the

best idea out and you need to give it to us because we absolutely
guarantee we'll spend it wisely.' The civil servants began scribbling in
their large note books.

As the meeting progressed, it became more and more obvious there
wasn't going to be any $5 million for us. The questions kept coming:
What were we going to do? How were we going to do it? Where were
we going to do it? Looking back, it is hardly surprising. We had
nothing to show them. The Trust had only just formed and we had yet to
establish Books in Homes. Just as it was becoming awkward, Peter, who
had years of experience dealing with politicians as president of Federated
Farmers during the turbulent changes of the 1980s, found a way to
extricate us gracefully. We didn't get any government money that time, but
the following week a personal cheque for $500 arrived from John Luxton.

In retrospect, that experience with Luxton was the best thing that
could have happened. A project like the one we were proposing needs
government money; it would make the difference between struggling, and
possibly failing, and being able to keep going. We left Parliament realising
we had to organise something much more concrete. We would need to
have measurable results to back our claims for the programme. We would also
need support from the Ministry of Education. I suspected that to begin with it
was more likely to come from the grassroots level, from teachers.

There were three areas to organise: sponsors who would fund us, schools to
take part in Books in Homes and, most important of all, books — lots and lots
of them, and for the right price. Alan and I went to see Graham Beattie at
Ashton Scholastic, which published a wide range of titles including
educational books and texts for schools. Graham was to become an
enthusiastic and supportive believer in what we were trying to do. We
negotiated a contract that locked in the price per book at $4.20 for three
years. That way we were protected from unforeseen price increases, had a
base line for our costs and some rationale for a budget.

Next we needed to sign up schools. Books in Homes was aimed at primary
and intermediate schools graded decile one and two in the Ministry of
Education's rankings. Decile one and two schools take their pupils from the

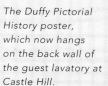

The Duffy Pictorial History poster, which now hangs on the back wall of the guest lavatory at Castle Hill.

Below: The fantastic Books in Homes team of the 90s. Clockwise from left: Jacqui Whyte, Jan Hellriegel, Tracey Gieck-Morris, Craig Anderson, Riki Conway, me, Ang Radford, Angel Elijas.

most financially disadvantaged suburbs and districts: there is a very high percentage of single parent families, many families reliant at least some of the time on government benefits, and over half the parents have no school qualifications. We began by concentrating on schools in Whangarei, Auckland and Hastings. I picked up the phone and cold-called, explained what we wanted to do and that we wanted to break the cycle of booklessness and illiteracy that so cramps opportunity. I followed up with a letter explaining the programme in detail. A large number of principals and teachers were interested in becoming a 'Duffy School'. As word got out, schools began calling us.

Alan and I had agreed at the outset it was vital the schools should be equal partners. They would sign up for three years and match us dollar for dollar. It was part of the self-help philosophy we both believed in. That way they were more likely to be committed to the programme and have an interest in making sure it was integrated into their school curriculum. Neither of us wanted it to be just another handout. It was not easy for many schools; it meant re-assessing budgets and resources that were already stretched.

Finally we needed sponsors. At the time I was redesigning and decorating an arts and crafts house belonging to a friend, Craig Heatley, who was turning the house into his office. Craig and Terry Jarvis had just started Sky, New Zealand's first pay television channel. Craig introduced me to Nate Smith, the new American CEO who was running the operation alongside John Fellett, and Alan and I went to see him. One of Nate's children had had reading difficulties. He and his wife Kate had been able to get help for their daughter, but they knew not everyone was in a position to do that. They understood the value of reading and the importance of the written word and how impossible life would be without the ability to read or write and without the dollars to employ someone to change that. Nate also comes from a country that has a history and culture of philanthropy. He was keen to help and be a part of the programme. At the end of that first meeting I only just managed to hold my shriek of delight until we had left the office.

Nate could also see the business advantages. Sky wanted to raise its profile, build subscription levels and increase its corporate base. He offered us the expertise of Peter Scutts and Sky's marketing department and together we developed Gold, Silver and Bronze sponsorship packages depending on the number of schools sponsored. Sky also offered several hours' free advertising and a number of additional hours at a subsidised rate to companies who became sponsors of Books in Homes. They gave us a couple of pages in their monthly magazine at no cost to promote the Duffy programme and our sponsors. In effect, Sky became a major conduit between Books in Homes and the corporates we wanted to back us. They became our founding sponsor along with the other originals, Carter Holt Harvey, *TV Guide*, Mitsubishi and Mainfreight. Fred Soar and his team at Soar Printing became generous supporters of our printing needs and Ernst & Young agreed to be our honorary auditors to make sure we kept the money side straight.

Sky TV also came with a secret weapon — Zinzan Brooke. They had employed the big rugby hero, one of the best to wear the No 8 jersey, when it looked like he would leave New Zealand for Japan; Zinzan would be available to visit and talk to our sponsors and schools. Bruce Plested of Mainfreight still has vivid memories of a tour of schools around the Far North with Alan and Zinzan. He and Alan had a wonderful time exchanging stories with Zinzan, but their enjoyment paled beside the excited reception they received at one of the Duffy schools that Mainfreight sponsors. They were welcomed in Maori by the school's kaumatua. First was Zinzan, who hardly needed an introduction, and then 'the man who writes books' and, much to Bruce's amusement, 'a man from the education department'. Zinzan was the first of the Books in Homes' 'Heroes', travelling the country selling the message 'It's cool to read', handing out books at Hero Assemblies, reading to the pupils and talking about the magic of books and dreams — and about rugby of course.

Bruce Plested had not needed a call from us to get Mainfreight involved. Like Nate Smith and so many of the leaders of the companies who became our sponsors, his reasons were a mix of personal, philanthropic and business. He had seen a television documentary on Alan Duff talking about Maori, their past and future. It struck a chord. Bruce had grown up in the 1940s in Auckland's Grey Lynn, then a staunchly working-class suburb, with a large Maori whanau living in two houses over the back fence. He called Alan, saying he understood Alan's desire to do something to help Maori and agreeing with him that the best place to start was among the poorest and most disadvantaged. Alan told Bruce about my first fundraising dinner. I was having another. Bruce should come.

Bruce and Mainfreight had already formed a relationship with Bairds Road Primary in South Auckland, where the company is based. When people ask what business gets from such sponsorship, Bruce's response is that he did not do it to get something out of it. Nevertheless, it is an important question. Bruce believes he can show shareholders that Mainfreight ends up with more in the bank by caring for the community, and that involvement in programmes like Books in Homes is good for the staff as well. He is justifiably proud that the first kid from Bairds Road Primary to earn a university degree now works for Mainfreight. Bruce made Mainfreight the biggest sponsor of Books in Homes and an integral part of the programme.

It took a long time to raise the money we needed to get the programme underway. Alan and I worked hard to find those first Gold sponsors who would provide the funds to get the programme started. We let the sponsors choose the schools that suited them — Carter Holt Harvey chose schools close to different aspects of their operation. This gave their employees the chance to get involved and to attend book assemblies. Often, the employees' kids were enrolled in those schools.

I sat on the phone at home and made hundreds of calls, and not just to businesses; I also tapped friends who I thought would like to support the programme. Many wrote later thanking me for such a gift. They formed close relationships with their schools, went to Hero Assemblies, handed out the books, and sometimes funded the school's side of the programme as well. One family described how they had not been expecting anything in return but their school had given them something special. The letters of thanks they received were full of drawings and information about the children's families and lives. It was like being welcomed into another community. The value of what they were getting back could never be counted in dollars. Another family who lived on an island had the whole of their small local school to visit. Duffy kids found a variety of ways of showing their appreciation. One school's violin group played outside their local Countrywide Bank, their sponsor.

There were other benefits for schools. In the still new environment of Tomorrow's Schools, sponsors could provide administrative help and budgeting advice to school boards. Rotorua North Rotary funded a 'how to' pamphlet, *Some Ideas for Raising Funds in Schools* by Ken Christiansen, that we sent out to all our schools. As the programme grew, so did the list of sponsors and supporters. Small businesses sponsored schools where their workers had children. A group of the Books in Homes office team banded together to fund one. The couple who ran the café where we went each morning for our start-up coffee became sponsors of a small school. For years, every couple of weeks, a cheque for $5 would arrive from the Hawke's Bay from someone called 'Bob'. Then one day Bob inadvertently included his address and we were finally able to write and thank him.

Books in Homes was launched officially at the end of March 1995, in a combined launch with Sky Network's new channel, Discovery. The Prime Minister, Jim Bolger, was in attendance, and it was a great chance for our Gold sponsors to be credited with being good citizens. It might seem strange to have a television company embracing reading but one of the things that consumed Nate right up until he returned to the United States was how to make learning better on the Sky channels when children spend so much time watching television.

Alan had imagined we might get ten schools to start. We had not ten schools but eighty, fourteen sponsors and eighteen thousand kids. I had been helped greatly by Riki Conway, a long time friend who has been with me in all kinds of roles and through many events in our lives. After cleaning up me and my house, she would join me on the phone, calling schools. She became an early member of our team.

The first books went out in August 1995. To begin with, we sent a catalogue to each school and divided it into sections according to age. That proved hopeless because kids who couldn't read were looking at their age group and thinking, 'Geez, better get that' even if it was totally inappropriate in terms of their ability. After a lot of consultation with teachers, we colour-coded the catalogue. When we had been going about a year, Carter Holt paid to have a copy of each book in the catalogue sent to the schools at selection time so the children had a chance to look at and handle the books before deciding which ones they wanted. Each child chose four and received two, and we tried very hard to give them their first choices. The display books went into the school libraries.

I chose the initial selection of books but once we were up and running I was eager to include those teachers and librarians who seemed to be the keenest to make the most of the programme. We'd lay out the books at Ashton Scholastic and gradually work our way through them until we had about thirty titles. Some teachers will tell you that they work their own form of selection when the display books arrive, or try to, pushing the ones they don't like (or approve of) to the back. But the kids aren't fooled. If they want them, they just reach right over the teacher-preferred ones. What they loved were the ones with a treasure box with plastic rings and necklaces; monosyllabic joke books were popular with the boys. Later came the *Captain Underpants* series. There are times when two children from the same family would pick the same book. But even when they're told, they often still insist on staying with their original choice. For so many of them, this was the first time they had the chance to choose something new for themselves. It was like Christmas. Staff at the first preschool to join, thinking along those lines, decided to wrap the very first books, to make the event even more special, only to discover that many of the little ones had never seen a wrapped present before and had no idea what to do with it.

In that first year, at two Hero Book Assemblies, each child received a total of four books from Duffy Heroes — sports stars, actors, musicians, television personalities. However, it was not long before there were chances to get extra books. The staff at Camberley Primary came up with the weekly 'Caught Being Good' award. Caught Being Good was not necessarily about reading, but it did place a value on books as a reward while reinforcing positive behaviour. It could be awarded for shutting a door quietly, stopping a bully or picking up a piece of rubbish in the playground. Then there was the bonus Budget Day Book for every Duffy child. Early in 1996 we had gone to Mr Bolger and the new Minister of Education, Wyatt Creech, and told them we wanted to put more books in homes. As a result, the 1996 Budget included a government grant of $250,000. In celebration, we gave every child an extra book. The 1997 Budget allocated the programme $900,000 over the next three years and then in 1998 the government announced it would invest another $1.5 million over three years in addition to the previous year's grant. We were the first privately run programme to receive a grant in the government budget, which pleased us enormously. However, philosophically we still wanted private sponsors to fund the majority. We didn't want to be, or even to be perceived to be, just another government-funded education programme.

Later I added the 'Caught Being a Good Mum', 'Caught Being a Good Dad' and 'Caught Being a Good Grandparent' awards for reading to the kids at school or at home. The adults received a book and certificate at an annual Caught Being Good assembly. Some found it hard to attend — they had bad memories of their own time at school. Most were very shy about being rewarded. It was only a few who had their whole whanau there to applaud them.

Stepping into classrooms, assembly halls and playgrounds carried pictures from the past for me too. I was no angel at school; I never got to be a prefect, win a cup or have a badge pinned to my chest. Instead I collected order marks — for talking in class, taking the stairs two at a time, having holes in gloves, being found loitering in dairies, doubling on a friend's bike, chatting to boys,

Alistair Guthrie, North & South

Reading to children at Tamaki Primary School, Glen Innes.

I was no angel at school; I never got to be a prefect, win a cup or have a badge pinned to my chest. Instead I collected order marks — for talking in class, taking the stairs two at a time, having holes in gloves, being found loitering in dairies, doubling on a friend's bike, chatting to boys, having more holes in gloves.

having more holes in my gloves. My mother was constantly in attendance at the principal's office. My parents made financial sacrifices to send me to Diocesan High School and it must have been particularly galling to have me always in trouble and, at one stage, suspended. A few years later I was a young parent with my own children at school. And then I was back in the classroom myself, spurred to action after hearing Germaine Greer speak at the Auckland Town Hall in 1972.

I went to hear her with an old friend, Lou, and Germaine turned our worlds upside down. She was so frank and strong and empowering for our generation, who had thought there was no latitude and that there could never be any equality in that husband/wife partnership — we were dependent and they were paying the mortgage. She was saying: 'Woman, sort your life out. Don't make it all dehydrated dinners and wet nappies. Your life is more than that.'

Lou's epiphany was contained in a short eight-word sentence. Germaine was talking about her brief three-week marriage and how it had got off to a bad start when the first morning her new husband asked her to get him a cup of tea and she replied, 'How about you get the cup of tea?' Today that sounds perfectly reasonable but back in 1972 it was still the wife's job. It had never occurred to Lou that it could be any other way. That little sentence made her see the world in a new light.

I had thrown away my qualifications when I had my first baby, thinking that would be it. I thought I would have the same deal as our mothers, continuing to vacuum and polish the silver and prepare five-course meals; and husbands certainly had that expectation, particularly husbands from private schools. You started the day in one outfit and then in the middle of the afternoon, before your man came home, you changed into something better. I realised I was slipping into that state Fraser McDonald called suburban neurosis. I was becoming depressed and finding it difficult to do anything around the house once I dropped the kids off to school. Instead I drifted into spending the family benefit on a growing collection of New Zealand furniture.

Germaine Greer was asking us to look at life from a new angle. She threw down a challenge: if you were unhappy and felt as if you were losing your energy and your choices and your life, then it was up to you to articulate the changes you needed and make them happen. It was an ignition point for us as individuals within that marriage partnership. It wasn't throwing everything away; it was standing up for ourselves and saying, 'Let's do this together. This is your life, this is my life, this is the kids' life. Write our own story.' Even though I had been reading about those things in magazines, and people like Kate Millett had been way out there before that, this time the message sank home. Germaine made it so personal for those who were there.

Afterwards, Lou and I ran down Queen Street shouting, 'We will do this! Let's change!' For Lou, that meant going back to medical school to finish the degree she'd abandoned for marriage and a family. I had left school at the end of the sixth form with university entrance accredited. There was little or no talk of going on to university for my sister and me. My father thought it was a waste of taxpayers' money; instead I should be earning my own. In the 1950s there were fewer women at university than there had been at the beginning of the twentieth century and my career options seemed to be nursing, teaching or secretarial, and then marriage. A couple of my school friends did go on to university but most went to secretarial college in Queen Street, the big smoke! So I went too, and did shorthand and typing before getting a job as a secretary in a law firm. In a funny way I thank Gramps for fantastic keyboard skills; no 'hunt and peck' for me.

In 1973 Allan and I had been married for ten years and had three children —David, Kate and Joseph. Unlike most of our contemporaries, we had never been overseas, apart from a short spell in Sydney when we were much younger. It was our turn now. The trip was one of those where you try and fit in everything, and in France I was shocked to find I couldn't navigate my way round Paris. I felt as if my brain had been disconnected. I was going to have to do something to reactivate it. That was when I went back to the classroom, first as a 'mature' student at teachers' training college and Auckland University and then as a primary teacher. I finished with an armful of awards; I even won my first cup at training college for the top student over three years. I carried it home in triumph, filled it with wine and drank a heartfelt toast to my family for their support . . . and was hideously sick. The inside was still generously coated in Silvo.

Although I ended up at a decile ten school, which was convenient for the family as it was just along the road from where my youngest Joe was at school, what I had loved in those three years at training college was my teaching sections at the South Auckland schools. The young kids particularly were so responsive. I remember standing in the middle of a wide-eyed group of Maori kids doing a lesson on eggs. I made one break by dropping it on the floor. They were astounded. It was really naughty to drop an egg like that and they'd never really looked at one in its uncooked state. It was the same when I was standing in front of a Books in Homes assembly. There were the same little kids, the same wide eyes, singing the Duffy song the loudest and clutching their Duffy books the tightest.

My move back into the world of education and paid work was a learning thing for Allan as much as it was for me. He would have expected me to behave as his mother did, so, while I trained all my kids to make a really good roast dinner, Allan also had to become extremely handy in the kitchen. I taught for not much more than a year before I was needed in a business we had bought, the publicly listed company, Walker and Hall Limited. However, that passion for and belief in education and the way it could awaken dreams and then help make them real stayed with me. It was that passion and belief for what Books in Homes stood for that made every dollar we gathered for the programme precious. I felt that any money not going directly into providing books and Hero visits was cheating the Duffy kids.

One of the biggest expenses for a programme like Books in Homes is overheads. Right from the start, thanks to the generosity of friends and sponsors, many were taken care of. While I finished decorating Craig Heatley's office, it made sense to stop fighting for room with the family Labrador at home and work out of his office. Then Trans Tasman, one of our sponsors, provided space in their building. After a couple of years we outgrew that and Bruce Plested gave us surplus office space at Mainfreight rent free. He also provided and paid for our power, phones, internet and postage and carried freight for us. Our contribution to Mainfreight, apparently, was loads of activity and a lot of noise. When Mainfreight moved to its new offices in 2006, Books in Homes went with them into a fantastic purpose-built area.

Staff costs grew, but slowly. I was in the fortunate position as chief executive of not needing to earn an income. None of the board members were paid in those first five years either and others also donated time and expertise. But by the time the first books were being dispatched it was obvious I needed permanent help in the office. I wrote everything by hand, as I was not yet conversant with computers. One of the volunteer helpers memorably introduced a university student looking for holiday work with: 'This is Susan. She's an angel.' She was, and was so called from then on until she left us eighteen months later for her Big OE. The office was a mix of full timers, part timers and volunteers, including Tracey Gieck-Morris and Craig Anderson. I was always conscious that people giving hard-earned money, discretionary spending, should have their contribution go where it was intended — straight to the kids. I kept the operation lean to maximise the programme and meet the ever increasing demand from schools to be part of Books in Homes.

One of the reasons schools were lining up to join, and that the government continued to support us financially, was the positive results Duffy schools were seeing. The principal of Camberley School had told Alan that in those first couple of years when Alan was providing books he had seen a marked decrease in the levels of truancy, vandalism and detentions, a new and improved attitude to learning, and a greater appreciation of reading. There was even an impact on the gang parents. Alan rang me one day to say, 'Chrissie, I've just been told we're both safe around Camberley!'

But we needed something more concrete than anecdotal evidence to show government, sponsors and schools in order to continue getting their support. We asked for the programme to be monitored and the Ministry of Education appointed Dr Warwick Elley, the Emeritus Professor of Education at the University of Canterbury, who for the next two years sent out questionnaires and visited schools. In their responses to the questionnaires many teachers said Books In Homes was one of the few good things to happen in their schools in a long time: there was better reading and book care, and parents were reading to their children and buying them books, particularly the book packs we started to provide for $5; behaviour improved and there was a marked reduction in damage to and stealing of school books now the kids had their own. Most satisfying of all, Dr Elley's report found that a year after joining, pupils' reading had improved by thirty five per cent. His results confirmed what we were hearing from teachers, children and parents in the hundreds of letters we received each week.

The stories we read and heard were wonderful and moving. A sponsor giving out the books at the end of a Hero Book Assembly said in amazement afterwards, 'They didn't hold the books, they hugged them!' Staff returned from visiting the schools to tell of walls of star readers, children who didn't let go of their new books all day and slept with them under their pillows, classes where they decorated boxes to take home and keep their books in, kids who hid their books at home under rugs or under trap doors in the basement so they wouldn't get damaged, or left them at school in the holidays to keep them safe. One child wrote to tell us, 'The books are lovely and gentle. They have not got ripped yet because I keep them in a secret place in the back room in my tree hut. I am a good reader already.' I remember a father in Gisborne who 'borrowed' some wood from the marae to build a special bookshelf over the fireplace. It was the altar to words for his family. Parents began asking if the school in the area they were moving to was part of the Duffy programme. Riki found a nine-year-old who had been in nineteen schools; Books in Homes was the only constant in his disrupted life. Just very occasionally the stories were darker — parents who took books away from children or, much worse, destroyed them as punishment.

My work life settled into a pattern. I found a typical day described in an old diary. There was the usual workday correspondence, phone calls and faxes, and kids' letters to admire. The most memorable was a wonderful book from Room 8 at Kaiti School in Gisborne which celebrated Norm Hewitt's visit. They wrote text, scanned photographs and ended by calling themselves proud Duffy kids. There was an accompanying letter from Keith Webber, 'proud to be a Duffy Principal'. At 12.30pm, I would take an hour off for fitness: 'I don't know, little has changed, nothing much off the estrogen roll, maybe a little less cellulite — but it is all hard work and a big effort,' I wrote. Jan was all action in the office posting out invoices for our August book accounts, Ang was onto the newsletter, Riks was drawing up itineraries for the Duffy Theatre tour, Tracey was cold-calling sponsors, Jacqui was home sick and Monique was typing up all my hand-written notes and letters. On the way home I had to do a supermarket call: chicken, salad and asparagus for dinner. No watching TV as John had the room at what felt like 110°C so I perched in bed writing up my day and reading *Driving Over Lemons* by Chris Stewart.

I enjoy a nocturnal hour or two of National Radio and that night I heard on *The Best of Brian Edwards* an interview with Sean Fitzpatrick, ex-All Black captain. Extraordinarily he talked of his work with Books in Homes and he was very complimentary of what we did. It was a great end to the day.

I found it hard to get out of the office and so my school visits became much less regular, but each left an indelible impression. One of my first was to a school without a hall, not unlike many low-decile schools. I talked to them out in the sun in the playground instead, about life and books and what books mean. I had one of my very first books from my childhood with me. I was

*Bellbird Corner
on the way to the
tailing yards.*

so enthusiastic about how the rabbit got its ears, but still I knew I wasn't reaching them. Afterwards I asked the staff what would really hold the children's attention and make a difference. The teachers' reply introduced another aspect to the programme: none of the children had had the chance to see live theatre and the school and parents couldn't afford to take them. This conversation was the genesis of what would become the ASB Duffy Theatre. The originators and performers of the first play about the adventures of Duffy, Byron the Bookworm and other crazy characters were Justin Lewis, who would go on to co-write, direct and produce *Krishnan's Dairy*, Ross Brannigan, Rachel Nash and Tracey Collins. Every year since every Duffy school has been enthralled, amused and delighted by another riotous performance in which books help Duffy escape his current predicament. Rave

letters arriving at the office left no doubt the players were on the kids' wave length: 'My favourite part was when Duffy puts his hand into the toilet and pulled out the pig snot.'

Sometimes I was lucky enough to find time to visit some of our most far-flung schools. On one occasion, John joined Angel and me for a trip around East Cape. We travelled in convoy, he in one of his fantastic classic cars, (John and his motor always a hit with kids and teachers) staying overnight at small motels along the way. I soon discovered that the children from these isolated schools were thrilled that people were taking the time to come and see them. Another time Ang Radford and I flew to Kerikeri, picked up a car and drove north to Te Hapua, celebrating the wonder of Northland as we went. Because we were staying overnight, we stopped at the Mangonui butchery and bought a big piece of sirloin and a bottle of wine as koha for our hosts. We were welcomed with a powhiri in the school hall. Judith Aitken, then with the Education Review Office, had already told me that she had been to many schools but at Te Hapua she had sat and cried, and I was conscious of that as I went in.

It was one of those beautiful old school halls with a high vaulted ceiling like an old wooden church and with incredible acoustics. They had school chairs for us in the middle, parents round the sides and the children up front so we sat in a sea of space. It was a wonderful powhiri. The school song was about being the furthest north school in the North and I found myself doing a Judith Aitken, tears spilling down my face. I felt inadequate and ashamed with my response to the welcome; my 'kia ora' and 'tena koutou' were halting, and my song in response was muted and ordinary.

After the children had gone home, we went across to stay at one of the two school houses with the principal and his wife, who was also a teacher. The first thing she did was to put our beautiful piece of sirloin that we had been stroking in anticipation since Mangonui in her freezer; she had made us a lasagne. We opened the wine and as we sipped I could feel the steak getting colder and colder. They talked about school life in Te Hapua and how when Matiu Rata died and was brought home for his tangi the kids were mesmerised by what they saw: people arriving by helicopter, walking around talking on mobile phones and press and TV everywhere. It was not at all like a local funeral. It had lost the familiar essence of homecoming and the quiet and gravitas they expected.

As Books in Homes grew, one of the challenges was not just to find the number of heroes needed to head out to the Hero Book Assemblies held at every school twice a year, but also to find people who could take the time needed to travel those distances. Air New Zealand was extremely generous but many of the smaller rural schools were hundreds of kilometres from the nearest airport. John and I knew a helicopter pilot called Prickles de Ridder, who would do a whole circuit of Northland schools transporting a Hero, for free. He would also treat a couple of kids from each school to a flight to the next school. The further north you went the more it was like a magic carpet ride for the children. One of them sent us a long letter after flying with rugby player and Books Hero, Dallas Seymour, from Awanui to Te Hapua. It was the first time he had been in any kind of aircraft and, unable to believe he was in the sky, he wrote that his thoughts 'were running all over the place . . . It was like sightseeing at the Cape [Reinga], instead of looking at the sea you were looking at the land. I had butterflies in my stomach from the time I left . . . I felt too excited to talk to anyone except look out the window. The view below could almost be seen as if we were a flying camera looking through the eye lens where everything appears very small. The people below looked like ants and the Aupouri Forest looked like long blades of grass.'

Most of the time visits went smoothly but once in a while I would be caught by the unexpected. On a trip to a Hero Book Assembly at a Northland school with one of TVNZ's best-known Maori broadcasters, Hone Edwards, Hone had read *Romunga's Cloak* in his wonderful voice and, true to style, stopped at the most exciting part and left it for the children to finish. We were invited to stay for a cup of tea afterwards. I thought the staffroom strangely empty and wondered where everyone had gone. On the way back in the plane Hone told me one of the staff had organised a boycott to protest this rich Pakeha woman coming to hand out largesse. He was furious. It had never occurred to me that anyone would doubt the sincerity of my intentions.

There was a time when I did feel out of place and out of my depth. Once again it was at a small school, this time in a Maori settlement on the East Coast I had visited earlier with John in his classic car. They rang and asked me to go down and open the new addition to their library. I didn't feel right; I cannot speak Maori, which is integral to all events in these schools, and I told them that. But they still wanted me to go.

So I flew to Whakatane, where the first thing I did was go straight to The Warehouse and, not sure how big the school was, buy about 100 small Agee jars with screw top lids. Then I drove up the coast, realising on the way that I was wearing pants and that for formal occasions on the marae you wear a skirt. At least I was in black. By then I was feeling really apprehensive. I arrived with all these clinking jars at a school like many others around the East Cape, opposite a beautiful gleaming white chapel with the graveyard laid out neatly beside. I stood outside the lychgate. I could see the kaumatua on their sticks in front of the school. This was certainly an important event. I could hear the wonderful voice of the girl calling me in. After many speeches in Maori it was my turn and the only te reo I had in reply was 'Tena koutou, tena koutou, tena koutu katoa'. Then I talked about the jars, the 'Can-do' jars I had brought them.

I told them I thought most people lacked confidence and that it is one of the hardest things for us to gain. Confidence comes from achieving success. It doesn't need to be something big; milestones in little things can grow it. You fill your 'Can-do' jar with everything you can do — I can ride a bike, I can read chapter books, for example. You write each of them down and put it in the jar and then when you are reflecting on things and thinking you are useless, you get out your jar and go through all those things you can do and your Can-do jar invigorates and reinforces your confidence and gives you the energy to go and try something else. That was why I took the jars. I thought the idea would click with the children and their parents.

Instead it was horrible. When I finished people moved without comment to serve the food and drink. I drove back to Whakatane thinking that I had tried to put energy into dreaming and I hadn't got it right at all. I felt I should have stuck to my original gut instinct. I wasn't the person who should be doing that there. It was beyond my mana. I wasn't Maori-speaking and I wasn't a celebrity. I wasn't anything. I had felt isolated and lonely. They wrote a beautiful letter of thanks but that feeling remained with me.

Brendon O'Hagan

The programme itself kept expanding, not just in the number of schools and sponsors, but also in depth. We knew that the books on their own would not be enough, which was why the Hero visits were so important with their message of 'It's cool to read'. The same applied to the Duffy Theatre and the different forms of Caught Being Good. Then there was *Tikity-boo!*, an annual anthology of writing and pictures by children from Duffy schools which developed after Warwick Elley noted that if we could get more resources it was a natural progression to go from reading to writing; they were logical partners. *Tikity-boo!* was sponsored by Carter Holt Harvey, whose chief executive, Chris Liddell, was doubly committed because he had started school in a tiny village in the Ureweras where his father was a forester. He was distressed to see how the school had changed and how its decile rating had dropped after the local mill closed. He thought Books in Homes was the best community investment the company had made. Every child in a Duffy school received a copy of *Tikity-boo!* There were also the book packs parents and families could buy for $5; they contained a book, a magazine and either a bookmark, poster or door hanger, and they sold in their thousands. We commissioned two bilingual books in Maori and English and would have done more if their progress had not been so fraught with difficulties because of dialectical differences.

We started annual touch tournaments, a great way for teachers, parents and kids to get together, have fun, build a sense of community and talk about the programme and the different ways they implemented it in their schools. The first year, Wellington, conforming to stereotype, had to postpone until the next day because of a hurricane warning. In Auckland I escaped the office to cook hundreds of sausages on the barbecue line, pass out drinks, chips and fruit and generally have an excellent time. Jonah Lomu was the great hit that year. I gave him a thank-you hug and easily fitted under his armpit. Once a year there was Apple Day when, courtesy of sponsors, some seventy-five thousand Braeburn apples were distributed for children and teachers to

crunch through. McGregor's in New Plymouth made us packs of Duffy sunflower seeds which we sent out to all the schools. In some areas you can still see their big golden heads over the top of the corrugated iron fences as they continue to self seed and spread. Guy Fawkes Day each year began with a bang with a special School Leaders Assembly. Local secondary students visited their closest Duffy school to talk about their own achievements and dreams for life. And at a special end-of-year assembly the annual Mainfreight Duffy Award for Excellence in Attitude was presented to a student in each Duffy school. By November 1998, seventy eight per cent of all decile one primary schools were in the programme, some fifty six thousand children, and there were a growing number of schools on the list waiting for sponsors.

Principals and teachers had talked about the differences between children arriving at school already familiar with books and those who were not. For those who had no contact with books, it can be four to six months before they understand basics. I decided to extend the programme to the pre-school siblings of Duffy kids, and the board agreed. This new branch was called Kids at Home — KaH. By June 1999, two hundred and sixty two of the two hundred and eighty two schools then part of Books in Homes had registered as KaH founder schools and Penguin Books was contracted to supply fifteen thousand books for two- three- and four-year-olds for the first year. The aim was to introduce the pre-schoolers to the world of books, how to hold them, turn the pages, recognise words, colours and numbers. They received their book on their birthday from their Duffy brothers and sisters, giving the older children the chance to be heroes to their younger brothers and sisters — writing a birthday card and giving them a birthday present. With the book came bookmarks, information about libraries and a Pumpkin Patch sponsored t-shirt with the KaH character created by Dick Frizzell, who had already re-designed Books in Homes' main logo and the Duffy character in return for a dozen bottles of pinot noir. Duffy kids regularly reported it was difficult to get their little brothers and sisters out of their KaH t-shirts.

1999 was a big year. It also turned out to be my last with Books in Homes. In no particular order, there was the Duffy song and CD that went out to every Duffy school. Called *Read About It*, it had music by Jan Hellriegel (one of New Zealand's top female singers and our full-time accounts person) and Dave Dobbyn, with words by Jan and Toi Iti. When it was recorded for free at Stebbings Studio some of the country's finest musicians came along to add their magic. The staff and I were in the chorus. The singing quality was variable. I was wildly out of tune and I bet this will remain the first and only time I am recorded in a music studio. The tune was memorable, the lyrics inspiring:

> I'm going to read my way around the world
> Jump on a dream and go real far
> I'm a Duffy kid so I'm a star
> And I read about it.
> And when I tell my story then I
>   know I have the words.
> And when I tell my story, then I
>   know I will be heard.
>
> *Chorus*
> Going to read, read about it
> I'm a Duffy kid and so proud of it

You can do it. Nothing to it.

I can help you if you want me to.

Tall as a totara Duffy kids will

   read around the world.

If you want to know what makes thing go

If you want to know how the flowers grow

If you want to learn how to be the best you can

You just read about it.

And when I tell my story then I

   know I'll have the words

And when I tell my story, then I

   know I will be heard.

It was an instant hit with teachers and pupils and some schools soon put actions to it. It was sung with great heart and pride at the party we threw at John's Classic Car Museum one night in early August 1999. We were celebrating one million books going into New Zealand homes in just four years. It was a milestone and we hung a banner across Auckland's Queen Street to skite a little and to encourage yet more sponsors. We had set ourselves a millennium target to give twenty thousand more children the opportunity to join. We sent a Duffy's Millennium Scrapbook for each child to fill between September 1999 and August 2000 along with a disposable camera donated by Kodak. In November 1999 Mainfreight trucks carried 'Duffy's Pictorial History of New Zealand, Aotearoa — A Millennium Poster', one to every child and one for each classroom. I arranged for schools to send in completed diaries to the National Library and they are now deposited in the Alexander Turnbull Library in Wellington. In the Books in Homes office we hung a shield sent from Alan's founding school, Camberley, carved by six pupils under the direction of master carver Matt Edwards with the words: 'Tinopai Puka Puka — It's Cool to Read'. With sixteen more schools signed on to begin in 2000, the programme now encompassed three hundred schools, sixty three thousand Duffy kids and it was still expanding.

I announced my decision to leave in December, at the turn of the century. There were a number of reasons. Books in Homes had the respect of parents, educators and the government. In 1998 the programme and its co-ordinator had been awarded the Multiserve Education Trust National Service Award after being nominated by three of our schools. The staff took silly photos of

Sponsors were happy, the kids were switched on to reading and books, we were growing at a good rate and we were well funded.

Quantum Fields from Rambandit Valley. Spittle Hill is in the distance at left.

me with my medal for our regular newsletter. The organisation had fine management structures in place thanks in large part to my fellow full-time volunteer, Craig Anderson. Sponsors were happy, the kids were switched on to reading. We were growing at a good rate and we were well funded. For six years I had committed the majority of my time to the programme while working hard. I wanted more time with family and friends, and to keep up with my role on the board of the Salvation Army, which involved fundraising for them too. And then there was my golf, which had definitely been squeezed and was suffering for it. The other reason for my departure was a divergence of opinion on a project promoted by Alan Duff.

Alan was great as the founder and front man of the programme. Certainly he could ruffle feathers, and did, but people and the media took notice of what he said. He used his fortnightly newspaper columns to help keep Books in Homes before the public. It was priceless publicity for an education programme that was more than fifty per cent privately funded. In 1999, Alan rang me about a book he wished to write on Maori heroes. He wanted to fund it in part through Books in Homes and to give a copy to every Duffy kid. We had about $2.2 million in the bank, held in readiness for the next round of

books. In addition, teachers had been telling us that the children needed atlases and dictionaries that they could own and I was keen to do something about that.

Although I thought *Maori Heroes* was a good idea, I didn't think it right for Books in Homes unless it included heroes from all New Zealand cultures. We had been very staunch that the programme was for every kid in decile one and two schools. The dollars given to Books in Homes by sponsors were given with the understanding that the programme was for all kids, regardless of ethnicity. Other projects such as *Tikity-boo!* and the Millennium Scrapbook were both paid for entirely by Carter Holt Harvey. The Duffy millennium history posters were sponsored by Carter Holt Harvey and Soar Printing. However, the board of trustees, while having some misgivings, voted to underwrite Alan's book up to $100,000. Craig Anderson and I disagreed and abstained from the vote. In the end a government grant of $300,000 towards the book was not sufficient to cover the purchase of sixty five thousand copies for Books in Homes and the programme had to cover the balance.

Alan and I are very different people, both strong characters with strongly held opinions. Despite the inevitable differences that arose occasionally, we had worked well together since we joined forces. For much of the time he left me to grow and run the programme, trusting me to hold tight to the principles and goals we had established. I counted him as a friend. The split when it came was hard and hurtful for us both and it took time for those feelings to ease to the point where we could start to talk again and re-establish our friendship.

Once the news broke that I was leaving, letters and parcels from Duffy schools began arriving. The messages were simple, warm and heart-felt. Oranga School, near the Mainfreight office, put together an enormous book of artwork and handmade cards. I got a packet of bookmarks. On the back of one with the hand-scripted message 'It's good to read' was a note: 'I would [heart shape] to thank you for your effort to get books 4 us. Your hard work is greatly appreciated by all of us and we are very sorry to see you go. Good luck with your next venture. You can do it and keep the Duffy spirit.' A glitter-covered card said, 'Thank you for working so hard for five years and all for nothing. We appreciate all your hard work and we think your wonderful.'

That little phrase 'all for nothing' has become double-edged when I read the latest national literacy statistics. One in five young New Zealanders are still leaving school unable to read and write to a level that allows them to fully operate and participate in today's world. I am distressed to see that drug, anger and violence problems still exist around schools in some of our founding areas. The programme has been running for over ten years. In June 2002, it had put two million books into the homes of Duffy kids; four million by the end of 2006. In 2007, the school year opened with four hundred and ninety six schools and ninety five thousand pupils in the programme. I thought the day a kid got their first book they would never forget that feeling and they would pass it on to their kids in turn and their kids' kids. I believed that putting books into homes that didn't have them, instilling in those children a love of reading and writing, would give them new dreams, new ambitions and the key to access them. I realise the programme is only one influence on those it is directed to, but I really believed it would bring enduring change. If not, why were we doing it?

I stepped away into the new century intent on spending time with John and my family. I vowed I would not raise another dollar. But even as I was relishing the thought of this change in pace, a delegation of principals from Auckland's Glen Innes and Point England area had me in their sights. What they had to tell me changed my mind. Instead I began work on a project to address the problems facing another neglected group in low-decile schools — the most gifted pupils.

John and me with Ed, Snow, Midge and Pearl above Camp Stream with Mount Torlesse behind.

CHAPTER 3

The young

and gifted

In the files at the office of the Charitable Trust for the Gifted Kids Programme (GKP) is a letter from one of the first pupils reflecting on what the programme means to him: 'GKP is an *excellent* place for learning because it permits challenging activities, abstract ways of learning and way of looking at things. It also involves a lot of working with computers, which I enjoy, and working to your strengths.'

This was a boy who, his mother said, would be sitting outside the principal's office if it wasn't for GKP. Instead, his passion and enthusiasm for Gifted Kids was such that he never missed his one day a week of the programme, no matter what. He was there even when he was sick, wrapped up, lying on the couch, but there, not wanting to miss a moment. When I think of Gifted Kids, David is someone who comes to mind.

On the rocks at Castle Hill.

About the time I resigned from Books in Homes, Clive Sharpe at Tamaki Intermediate, a Duffy school, sent me a booklet just released by the Ministry of

Mark Smith

Raking freshly cut meadow grass ready for baling.

Too many people think giftedness is the preserve of the middle class or the well off. Their picture of a gifted child places them in a private school uniform in a big car with a violin case on their lap, being driven to music lessons.

Education that dealt with the issue of educational support for gifted children. Clive wanted to meet and talk.

The subject was not new. There has always been a small group within the education system interested in fostering the most talented and specially gifted, despite the overwhelming and prevailing orthodoxy that all children are gifted; that to pick a few and give them special attention is elitism. Cream, supposedly, always rises to the top. There were principals in the decile one and two schools I knew through Books in Homes who sometimes worried that too much of their time and resources were going on picking up and supporting the at-risk children at the bottom of the academic tables. It takes enormous energy to look after their needs and they were aware that while this was happening the really bright and smart weren't being supported or stretched so they could make the most of their abilities. One of the galvanising moments for me was the story a Northland principal had told me about one of his pupils. She was twelve and among his brightest; she was also pregnant. He was so disappointed; he felt he had personally failed her, and that if that enquiring mind died it would be such a waste. I found myself thinking about gifted children more and more.

At the time there was no funding for pull-out classes for gifted and talented pupils and many principals felt quite desperate. The schools that did have pull-out programmes were reliant on the enthusiasm of a teacher who was interested in gifted education; if they left, replacements were hard to find and the programme often languished. Teachers' training colleges then barely covered education for the gifted.

At Books in Homes Craig Anderson, Tracey Gieck-Morris and I had begun to talk about what we might do for these children, who were also at risk. This was more of a problem in the low-decile schools in low socio-economic areas, where there was an obvious meltdown with kids who were gifted. They were full of potential but there was no focus on developing it. They felt alienated, frustrated and often found it easier to be naughty than clever. Their lateral answers to questions in class provoked murmurs of 'Is this guy for real?!' or 'You're weird'. If they were biddable, they were used as teacher aides, or taken out of classes to work in the library or in the lunch room, to do the dishes and ring the bell. They were used to show visitors round, to promote the school. It was almost Dickensian in practice. When they were in class, if they finished their exercises long before everyone else, they were simply given more of the same. Some adapted to their situation and coasted through their early school years, only to arrive at secondary school without the time-management skills to cope with much more demanding work and schedules. Dr Roger Moltzen, chair of Gifted Education at Waikato University, argues that this is a form of abuse: 'Gifted children assume extra responsibility for others. They need to wear a Red Cross sign that says, "Stop. I have given enough".'

It is generally different for gifted children from middle class and wealthier families who have a much greater chance of having their potential recognised and nurtured. Higher decile schools are often better able to identify gifted children and promote them, and their families can afford to pay to get them the help they need to develop their talents. At the time, there was one organisation in Auckland offering programmes for such children, the George Parkyn Centre, set up by Rosemary Cathcart in 1995. She was well known in the gifted education field and had experience working with children who had been identified as gifted. We wondered whether we could do something together. Craig, Tracey and I went to see her set-up in Dominion Road and visited one of her units in a South Auckland school. But what we saw didn't fit with what we had in mind. We decided to go it alone. We took our idea to the Duffy trustees, arguing that it made sense to base this new venture inside what was now a smooth-running programme, sharing any overheads in common. The other trustees disagreed, wanting to concentrate on the at-risk kids targeted by Books in Homes. All this became academic when I left Books in Homes at the end of 1999. Then in the new year Clive Sharpe contacted me with a challenging, 'Come on, Chrissie. What are you going to do about this?'

Gifted kids play to prejudices. Too many people think giftedness is the preserve of the middle class or the well off. Their picture of a gifted child places them in a private school uniform in a big car with a violin case on their lap, being driven to music lessons. Combine that with the suggestion that they get special classes, or that the government provides greater support, and you attract that accusation of elitism. People don't believe (or it never occurs to them) that giftedness exists in schools in low socio-economic areas and among children from Maori and Pacific Island families. Unfortunately, that negative perception turned out to be true of a few teachers in those schools as well; we were told more than once that a decile one school couldn't possibly have a gifted child on its roll.

Yet the more Craig and I read about gifted children and talked to those with an interest in them, the more I began to see that a programme that targeted lower socio-economic groups would have even greater impact than one for the higher socio-economic groups. Give a gifted child in a low-decile school pride in their talents and pleasure in what they could achieve with them and they would not be the only ones to benefit. Their brothers and sisters, their friends and their community would realise that knowing how to read and write, to master maths and science, and to do what you are good at to the very best of your abilities, was cool.

We sat down with Clive Sharpe, who had a proposition for us. He was already contracting a teacher to run an extension class for his gifted pupils at Tamaki Intermediate one or two days a week. He wanted to move it to the next level and had decided Craig and I were the people who could make that work. He had a falling roll and a classroom to spare which he would make available if we set up something for the gifted kids in his area. The Tamaki region contains relatively affluent suburbs as well as large tracts of low income and state housing. It is as culturally diverse as it is economically. There were twenty three schools within this catchment area, ranging from decile one to decile ten, but the majority were designated decile one and two. I could hardly refuse. It was time to begin hunting the sponsorship dollar once more, the thing I'd promised myself I would not do again. This time I enlisted the help of Jack Hodgetts. I first met Jack when we were on the board of the Salvation Army and everywhere I had worked with him I saw his incredible energy and commitment. He had retired by this time, and claimed he was too old to help, but he completely understood the potential benefits of a programme aimed at the gifted young in less advantaged suburbs. He headed out into his extensive business network to ask for funding . . . and came back disheartened.

The preconceived ideas about giftedness and elitism, and the misconception that it was the preserve of the middle class, made finding money for a privately sponsored programme much more difficult than for Books in Homes. There was an arrogance among many of the people we approached for funding. They did not believe a child could be Pacific Island or Maori and gifted. Jack also found that the business environment had changed. Many of the corporate leaders he knew had handed over to a new generation. There were different attitudes to philanthropy. There was also a strong feeling that, as the highest tax payers in the country, if there was a need then the government should be paying for it. Jack said he would help in any other way. He got us paint at a good price, pews and a second-hand oven. The three of us set about redecorating the classroom Clive had given us and the space Craig and I had rented in downtown Auckland for a gallery we were preparing to open to promote twentieth century New Zealand decorative and applied arts. The GKP office would be located there, tucked in beside the gallery.

I was convinced of the importance of branding GKP. One notable aspect of the existing units we had seen had been the lack of differentiation from their surroundings and the paucity of resources. We had to do better than that. We wanted a place the children knew was special and different from the moment they entered. Tamaki Intermediate was being refurbished, and Clive had offered to do our classroom as well. The school colour was blue but I wanted something vibrant, stimulating and warm so I chose chilli red fabric panels instead. As well as the usual cupboards, shelves, tables and chairs,

I brought some couches and bean bags from home. It still looked bare so Craig and I covered the walls with contemporary New Zealand art from our own collections. The kids would be surrounded by Pat Hanly, Dean Buchanan and Toss Wollaston until they had generated enough work of their own. The classroom was well stocked with layers of resources, including the daily newspaper.

We knew the quality of the teacher is always of paramount importance in any form of learning. We advertised and were incredibly lucky. One of the people who had been helping us was Robyn Young, who worked with Rosemary Cathcart, and who applied and became GKP's first teacher. Meanwhile Clive talked to the other principals in the Tamaki region to find out who was interested in sending pupils to the new programme. I was particularly delighted to see the principals from some of my Duffy schools, Anne-Marie Biggs from Glendowie Primary, Rod Bright from Panmure Bridge and Cyril Nevezie from Stanhope Road, unreservedly embrace the idea. We ran sessions at the schools to help teachers recognise kids who were gifted. We were really glad that we did because there was so much confusion

about what a gifted child was. We found when we asked schools to put forward their gifted children, they would choose the ones who talked the most, the linguistically strong. This really disadvantaged the brightest Maori and Pacific Island pupils, who were less verbal in class.

A number of characteristics are common to gifted children. Many are obsessive — about perfection, an idea, or doing the right thing. They learn much quicker than their peers and tend to remember what they've learned, which makes revision and repetition painfully boring. They often have a much larger vocabulary than their classmates and see ideas and concepts in a more complex and abstract way. They relate to and seek out adults and older kids rather than those of their own age. They have a long attention span and can also concentrate on a number of things at once: they may not appear to be paying attention but will still know what is going on in the lesson. They often become passionately interested in single or specific topics. They are intensely curious, constantly asking questions, and have a vivid imagination.

There are also less positive characteristics, the result of frustration and feeling different or unaccepted. As a consequence many gifted children decide to turn off, to stop playing the game. The irony is a gifted child may be the class non-performer. A lot of children told us that their learning started at three o'clock when they walked out the school gates. They can also be afraid to take risks, reluctant to try something new in case they cannot do it or get it wrong. They are often labelled as problem children and sent to psychological services and special needs teachers. One of the brightest children to go through GKP arrived with a huge file from his school and all the classic indicators for ADHD; his principal had a gut feeling he was exceptional but no one had been able to get him to keep still long enough to find out. We told him everyone thought he was bright. 'I am bright,' he said. Well then, we said, we need you to stop moving long enough to show us. He told us that as a small boy he loved electricity and he couldn't wait to start school so he could talk to his teacher about it. But he realised very quickly, within a few sentences, that the teacher didn't like him. He was too bright for her. So he decided to be naughty, because that was another way of getting attention. The programme was the saving of him, and his stressed family. His solo mother was at rock bottom; she didn't know what to do with him. She was so relieved that we believed her. Her father had always said her son was gifted.

As well as looking at gifted children's potential, you look for what they have missed in the preceding years of schooling. The most obvious is poor reading and writing skills. Swinburne University in Melbourne tested nine to fifteen-year-olds with IQs of 130+ and found that forty per cent did not reach the norms expected for their age in numeracy and literacy. They were like gruyere cheese with large learning holes which, as they go on through school, become harder and harder to cover up.

Four schools decided to put forward pupils for the programme. The selection process began with teachers picking students they thought fitted the gifted profile we had given them. We used ten to twelve criteria that made the process transparent and fair and covered multiple skill and talent categories, and the schools also sought the parents' agreement beforehand. We asked the children to bring any work or projects they had done by themselves at home, independent of school. We first met them when they came to the unit for a morning and did maths, wrote an essay and an exercise in creative interpretation and finished with a twenty-minute one-to-one interview. At the end of the day we sat round the table and decided who would be accepted into the start-up programme. Up until that point no one had looked at the PAT (Progressive Achievement Test) results which the schools sent with the children. We didn't want our view of them to be influenced ahead of time. What we found was that almost all those accepted had PAT results consistent with being well above average. The 'maybes' often didn't have the best PAT results but there was always something magic about them.

At the beginning of the fourth term of 2000, fourteen kids aged eight to twelve started GKP, attending for one day a week. That first day was enormously exciting. Tamaki Intermediate welcomed the newcomers into their school with a powhiri. The kids arrived full of anticipation, eager to be there and find out what this experience would bring them. One of the first things they had to do was to write a mission statement, which still stands:

'We are here to expand our opportunities and to have fun learning. We are here for better challenges and to make the right choices. To be passionate about life and to make friends with children of similar abilities.

'We are here for a better education and we are here to succeed. We will achieve this by respecting and appreciating each other. By being part of a team and supporting and encouraging each other. By having a good sense of humour. We will believe in ourselves and have confidence in what we do.

'We will share our thoughts and strive to succeed. We will enjoy life as it comes and we will NEVER SAY NEVER!'

Once a week, Tamaki Intermediate loaned us their school van and Craig and I took it in turns to pick up those who needed a lift from their contributing schools. Over time we got to know not just the children but also their families and friends, their lives. Their GKP day often began on those trips. Discussions might develop out of issues raised in the news. For instance, should New Zealand police be armed? I asked for arguments for and against. One young Malaysian boy thought they should: If you've broken the law, you've done it wrong and you're shot — summary justice. A young Maori boy whose father was in prison disagreed: Sometimes you just get it wrong. His dad was really neat and really cared for his kids and still loved them. Another topic for discussion was 'Should money grow on trees?' Some kids had plantations of trees and the money was freely available for everybody to harvest. It was all about sharing. Others thought, no, such a tree should have mighty walls around it. People must work hard for their money otherwise they don't value it.

The first end-of-year assembly was a revelation for everyone. In many low-decile schools, teachers and boards of trustees are stretched to breaking and the surrounding communities tired. School involvement is patchy at best. It is not that they don't care; it is just that there is a level of exhaustion in their lives. GKP broke that pattern. Parental involvement, support and participation were constantly remarked on by teachers from contributing schools. Parents often spent time at the unit to see what their children were doing and they were encouraged to call and talk to us any time they liked. They took up the offer, even the shy ones. Our end-of-year assembly was packed with the children's parents and extended families, whose pride in what their children were achieving was palpable. The children's delight in such parent pleasure and approval shone back. The families' generosity was represented by their traditional way of saying thank you, and it came in abundance. At the assembly

In The Shearing Shed

During the 2006 shear.

Top left: The shearers wear lambskin moccasins.

Top right: At Castle Hill we machine shear only for dagging, crutching and bellying. At our main shear in September the shearers use hand blades. When you blade shear the fleece comes away all in one piece and is then thrown onto the sorting table.

Opposite: The shearing shed's grapple and wooden wheel for lifting bales to the upper level are still in use a century on.

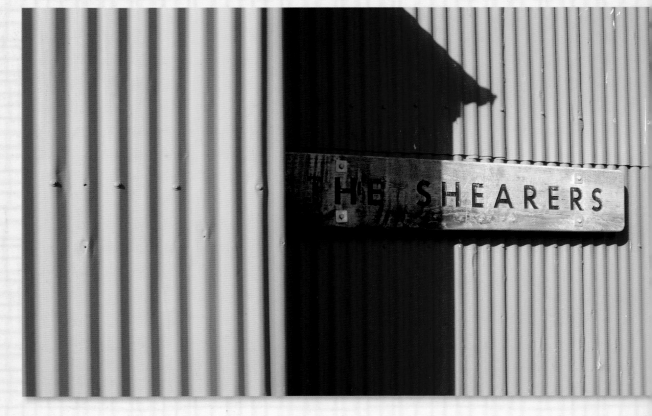

THE SHEARERS

From top left: The dogs help me pen sheep for post-shear drenching; throwing the fleece onto the sorting table; loading bales onto the waiting truck from the shed's upper level; the shearers and I take a break; post-shear pre-lamb drenching with vitamins. My technique has improved since this photograph was taken.

and at other functions, we used to have to layer the food, leaving dishes on shelves until the first plates were empty. There was always food left over for the staff to take home.

Not all families had been sure about the Gifted Kids Programme before it started. In fact, our insistence on using the word 'gifted' in the name of the school had many critics and we came under heavy pressure not to use it. I was surprised to find people in gifted education used the term among themselves but censored it when talking to the general public. Some parents, particularly Maori parents, were worried about having their child labelled as gifted, about singling them out from their brothers and sisters and from their classmates. They didn't want them to become braggarts or to rise above their position. They allowed them to come with the proviso that they monitor the effects. But it wasn't long before they began to see how beneficial it was for their kids.

Very occasionally it was a child who didn't want to be singled out. Anne was accepted on to the programme but didn't want to leave her friends. Then she started to hear about what the others from her school were doing with us. She called. She had changed her mind. But by then all the places were taken and she had to wait two terms before one became vacant. Anne was one of five sisters. They all had wonderful singing voices, church quality. The family would open and close our assemblies at Tamaki with a waiata and Anne's father became our kaumatua. When the time came for her to move on to high school, we tried to get her an Endeavour Scholarship to St Cuthbert's. Sadly, we were unsuccessful.

The 2001 school year opened and another key teacher joined us, Julie Mills, as the GPK Programme principal. In Clive's words she was a crackerjack teacher; he had received a call from the principal of her old school asking how we had managed to lure away his 'very, very, very best teacher ever'. One of Julie's tasks outside the classroom was to increase the roll. By the end of the year, we had seventy five children in five classes of fifteen and thirteen contributing schools. Although GKP's primary concern had been for gifted children from lower socio-economic groups, unlike Books in Homes it was never intended to be exclusively so. As word of its positive effects spread among teachers and parents, higher decile schools in the Tamaki region contacted us wanting to join. The result, a mix of children from very different backgrounds who would normally have nothing to do with each other, broadened and enriched the programme. Those new connections spread to weekends. Children who learnt chess got together and took themselves off to competitions around Auckland. Until then, so many of the decile one and two children lived within a triangle formed by school, church and supermarket, their life locked into that grid.

A day at GKP was very different to the other four days at their contributing schools. First, the teacher worked with smaller numbers; there were never more than fifteen to a class. We provided structure and created an environment to allow them to pursue the things that interested them, to see where they fitted in society and to accept their differences. Surrounded by like minds for the first time, they were free to show the emotional intensity so many of them feel. They were introduced to Shakespeare and had lessons in Italian and chess. A year eight student reported, 'In my life rivals are rare. In chess at GKP they are a dime a dozen.' Another said, 'It's so cool coming here because kids laugh at my jokes.' They learned thinking skills, and strategies to attack and solve a problem. Over the next couple of years this developed into the highly creative and effective Mental Edge which focuses on the three C's — critical thinking skills, caring thinking skills and creative thinking skills. Julie introduced them to Habits of Mind, which was new to New Zealand then and had come out of research done by Art Costa and Bena Kallick at Harvard University. Professor Costa describes it as 'the characteristics of what intelligent people do when they are confronted with problems, the resolutions of which are not immediately apparent'. The sixteen habits include persistence, thinking flexibly, striving for accuracy, taking responsible risks, applying past knowledge to new situations, thinking about your thinking, gathering data through all your senses and finding humour. There is always a lot of laughter and giggling woven through GKP learning.

We gave them all notebooks to be used as Ignorance Logs. They would write down every question they could think of about something they were working on. Then they would work through them, and as they did the 'why' questions would emerge. The questions got better and better, developing higher and higher levels of sophistication. Overlaying a lot of our learning was the mantra which said that you know what you know and you know things you don't know, but there is also stuff you don't know that you don't know.

It was all about enquiry. We brought in experts in all kinds of fields to talk to them and let them ask yet more questions. Early on, HSBC, one of our major sponsors, brought the head of the bank for the Asia Pacific region to see one of our classes. He told them his life story, talked to our kids, and went away incredibly impressed. Another visitor was Ross George from Direct Capital Partners. He set the kids an exercise in business choices: if you bought a company would you chose the most profitable or one that was less profitable but had a better reputation and company culture for the people who worked for it?

All learning operated on multiple levels. One example began with the reading of a sophisticated picture book, Laurence Anholt's *Leonardo and the Flying Boy*, which is based on Leonardo da Vinci, his inventions and creativity, seen through the eyes of a street urchin, who, with his friends, steals the artist's flying machine to test fly it. The teacher read it to the class and then they went and made their own invention, or compared it with someone else's, like John Britten's. Britten was keeping his own ideas book when he was twelve. They looked at why he was like that and how it could apply to them. Then they were invited to follow any tangent they liked — for instance, finding the inventions they considered the most useful in the last hundred years. They interviewed people, looked through books and the internet, and created a timeline for them. But more than that, they also considered philosophy: after all, the children in the story had stolen the flying machine.

This was the kind of higher order thinking and discussion gifted children are passionate about. Craig and I used to pinch ourselves, almost unable to believe that we had these children and their potential for twenty per cent of their school year. It was an enormous responsibility and we were determined to do the very best for them.

When Craig and I weren't on van duties or joining the class for some of their activities, we were preparing for the opening of the Anderson Fernyhough Gallery. It was arranged for 12 September 2001 and the inaugural exhibition had works by the carver Harry Watson. On the morning of the twelfth we woke to images of the September 11 attack on the Twin Towers. New Zealand, like many other countries, was transfixed by the disaster. We didn't know what to do. Should we go ahead? If we did, would anyone come? I called Sir Tom Clark, founder of Crown Lynn Potteries, who had agreed to open the gallery for us. We must, he said, go ahead. People did come that evening and Tom marked the tragedy with a minute's silence.

The gallery was one of those ideas that seemed good at the time but on reflection was not fully thought through. Someone would need to mind the gallery and Craig and I had not considered what it would be like to sit all day waiting for people to wander in. It was a job far too solitary and sedentary for either of us. Our exhibitions were sometimes based around work for sale but just as often featured objects, photos and ceramics from our own and others' collections which were presented together with curatorial lectures. It was another form of learning and dissemination of knowledge. I put items in for sale and then — in classic collector pathology — found I couldn't part from them. Red stickers would be hastily attached. But perhaps our biggest mistake was not to put higher prices on the work that was for sale. People walking through, seeing items listed at $40 or $70, came to the conclusion that what they were looking at was not of great value and so didn't buy. We stopped advertising; if people found us we were happy for them to look around. Craig and I kept our Crown Lynn pieces there as we turned from a commercial gallery to something closer to a museum exhibition.

At the start of term two 2002, we opened a GKP unit at Tikipunga Primary in Whangarei. New units always required money — approximately $55,000 to set up and about $130,000 a year to run — but most of all, they needed the right teacher. Over the years many teachers applied to GKP but we were always looking for someone special. If we couldn't find that person, the unit didn't open until we did. In Whangarei we had the good fortune to acquire an outstanding teacher, Michelle Parsons-Sim, ex-Army and a former teacher in Singapore, where special schools and programmes for gifted children have been running for at least twenty years. Every GKP teacher showed courage in stepping outside the system to join us, living up to our motto to 'go beyond the known'. At that time teachers lost their registration if they were more than two years outside the education system and one of my first tasks was to petition the Minister to change that. But taking that step to join us also opened opportunities to them; for instance, Julie and Pam Hook, who joined GKP in 2001, started their own business when they moved on from GKP to work as private consultants to schools and the education ministry.

While we were setting up our classroom at Tikipunga, I had the good fortune to meet a man who had a gifted child and had always been interested in giftedness. He made very good furniture for schools and got us furniture at a discount, which became part of all our classrooms. He saves the overruns and offcuts from his main orders for GKP, which has added to the colourful and informal look of our rooms. My personal contribution to Whangarei was an enormous blue couch which was delivered on the first day to the children's surprise and delight. Michelle had seen it in a shop window and I had overheard her say that it would look fantastic in the new room.

We took a group from Tamaki GKP north for the Tikipunga opening. Among the parents was Kim, a thirty five-year-old who had never crossed Auckland's harbour bridge. Someone had loaned her a mobile phone and as we crested the bridge she called her mother, 'Mummy, you'll never guess where I am!' Kim was one of many parents who wanted more for their kids, wanted what she had missed out on.

It would be difficult to talk about the opening of the Whangarei unit without talking about one of the families, the Cottons, who were very supportive. Levi Cotton, their eldest son, led the karakia for the thirty children who were starting GKP. Within weeks, the family was involved in a car crash in which their daughter was killed and the three sons, including Levi, were very badly injured. When I heard they were in the Starship children's hospital, I took some of my granny-kids to visit them. I had talked about the Cotton family and Levi, and the granny-kids decided we should take them some toys and that they would loan them their PlayStation until the boys were well enough to return home.

Once Levi was out of hospital, he didn't get back to school for some time, but he did return to GKP. He felt it was the only safe place to come to while he was recovering. Our connection with this school and his family continued. When John died the family and the Tikipunga kaumatua, TK, drove down to the funeral. John's coffin was draped in a korowai (feather cloak), a mark of love and respect from Riki, her whanau and their iwi, Ngati Te Ata. The Cotton family encircled it and the lovely wooden interior of St Mary's in Parnell filled with their karakia of farewell. It was their way of saying thank you for our family's support.

Tikipunga turned out to require an extra level of commitment from the school, the parents and children, at least in the beginning. We were made very welcome by the school and staff, and the principal in particular was so supportive of the concept that he was one of the only ones prepared to put his neck on the block to get the programme into Whangarei. However, there were teething problems right at the beginning. Tikipunga was a decile one school in

an area with gang associations and there were kids coming to GKP from schools right across the decile range and throughout the region. Some kids from the primary school threw rocks at the windows of our classroom. They told the outsiders to 'fuck off our patch or we'll do you'. The GKP's parents became slightly apprehensive. It prompted the beginning of our inter-class and inter-school strategy. We ran an open door policy — any teacher or class could visit at any time to see what we were doing. We made sure the GKP kids went out into the playground and mixed. It helped that we had some children from Tikipunga Primary in the programme. Things soon calmed down. Some schools were gutsy to have our programme and parents were gutsy to send their kids. They did it because they all saw how it worked for the children.

A Night of the Notables was a project which became part of every units' year. The children pick a well-known person from history, research everything they can about them and then make a presentation to their teachers, classmates and parents. The first year at Tikipunga, Michelle organised a town crier to announce each child. They put the most amazing amount of work into their characters. A ten-year-old girl chose one of the female pharaohs. For part of her written presentation she researched hieroglyphics, created a wonderful display of pyramids, looked into the diet of ancient Egyptians and then made platters of authentic Egyptian food. There was a Churchill who spent the night chomping on a cigar, and later played the saxophone, and a beautifully uniformed Florence Nightingale. In the spirit of the night, I dressed in character too. I went as Mary Quant with an asymmetrical haircut, haven't-slept-for-a-week eyes, a purple mini dress and black boots. Apparently it was a sight both memorable and notable.

We began to hear stories about the programme's effects. A couple of weeks after Tikipunga opened, a mother came up to Michelle in the street with tears in her eyes. She wanted to thank her for the wonderful day she was giving her son. Four days of the week she could not get him out of bed to go to school. But on Tuesdays he was up at six in the morning, making his own lunch, packing his bag and running in the school gate to GKP. Another of the pupils was a young Maori who was cutting himself. He had become a real concern for his school and social services had become involved. But at GKP he displayed none of the disruptive or violent behaviour that he did at his main school. A mother reported that her daughter's favourite saying used to be 'I'm bored'. 'Not any more. She is constantly up to something new and looks forward to each subject.' Another parent was excited there was something available for his son who 'thinks outside the square and needs encouragement and nurturing, not squashing'.

The GKP children came with a range of abilities and interests. GKP gave one nine-year-old with a passion for IT the time and opportunity to create his own computer game. An eleven-year-old boy, now alive to the pleasures of learning, happily spent two weeks of the school holidays in the library researching and then making a fantastic book on World War II; it was a subject that captured his interest and an achievement of which he was justifiably proud. Parents constantly told us of the changes they saw in their children. When we started out we thought the main gain for the kids would be in intellectual growth. Although that has been the case, the main benefit has turned out to be in their social and emotional development. One example that has always stuck in my mind was the twelve-year-old who had never been invited to a birthday party. At GPK she clicked with another girl. They were both learning French and would call each other and chatter away on the phone in French. It was like a gift to her worried mother.

The impact on families could be great. Some made enormous sacrifices. Because Tikipunga's catchment covered a huge area of Northland, some pupils had to travel for more than an hour. Parents were getting up at three in the morning to milk and then organise car pools for the kids. If a parent brought them from somewhere like Ruawai, they generally stayed in town until the end of the day to take them home. That was a huge commitment for farming families.

Sometimes it made parents look at themselves. Pupil turnover is common in low-decile schools where some have up to forty per cent roll turnover in a year. One mother had a child who had been to five primary schools by the time he started GKP; she came to realise she had to let her son settle down. Inspired by the changes she saw in him, she applied to university and began a course in early childhood education. A Fijian family put aside a special area in their house and each week when their daughter came home from GKP she would sit and tell her brothers what she had learned. Often brothers or sisters of pupils on the programme would try to get in but many either weren't gifted or they were too young. At Tamaki we started a class of six-year-olds but there were issues: they found it difficult to settle in the one-day programme when they were so little; it was like coming into a class of strangers each week. We set a lower age limit of eight.

For some children and their parents, GKP proved a godsend where the child had become school-phobic. There was the six-year-old who arrived at a new school and when the teacher got out the reading books she eagerly put up her hand and announced she'd just finished the third *Harry Potter* book. The child was told those weren't the kinds of books they read in school. She was given very basic school readers to take home for practice. Her parents became frustrated. Each morning they found her under her bed crying. Their small daughter had turned off school. They had lost their happy girl. They took her for intelligence tests, where she scored in the very top percentile. Armed with that information, the parents went back to school and were told tests like that were not valid within the school. They watched their gifted daughter consciously decide to dumb down. She was in one of our first intakes of six-year-olds. Her parents came to us directly and at that point we suggested they look for a school that was more accepting of gifted children.

Learning continued outside the classroom, and covered a wide range of experiences, from the intellectual to the artistic to the physical. We took them to the theatre at night. For virtually all our children it was their first time, and they were mesmerised and transported. They got to write, shoot and edit their own television show and movie and went to poetry readings at Borders bookshop. Sue Lusk, a friend of mine who is an Italophile, came twice a week at lunch time to teach Italian. The end of the year always culminated in a lunch at Vivace, her daughter's restaurant. One year the kids were seated between the crew from *Luna Rossa*, the Italian entry in the America's Cup. One of the boys, mimicking what he had seen in movies, clicked his fingers to call over the young waitress. He said something to her and the waitress blushed. Sue asked what he said. The twelve-year-old had told her in Italian, 'You're one hot chick!'

They went on a visit to a glass studio to learn about stained glass. Then they designed and made a glass pane using what they had learnt, which combined a whole range of learning along with the more obvious creativity. Their research showed that the ingredients in different colours affected how expensive the colours were. Knowing that, they then had to develop a business plan that took that scarcity value into account. This was an exercise they did prior to our annual work-experience week. It gave them some background knowledge of what makes businesses tick and enabled them to compile a series of questions to ask the companies they visited.

In talking with the children I was constantly surprised by how little understanding there was of business and work in their homes. Indeed, many of the kids came from two or three generations of unemployed. As a number of the kids were with us for three years, they got to experience three work options that covered a wide range of professions and industries: logistics with Mainfreight, law with Simpson Grierson, tourism with Queen Street Backpackers, design-to-retail at Pumpkin Patch, publishing with Scholastic, engineering with Tonkin & Taylor, electronic media at TVNZoom, auction houses with Webb's Gallery and architecture with Jane Aimer Architect. I discovered it is much more complicated arranging to distribute fifteen children around a variety of locations when parents don't have cars. We had to prevail on the time and generosity of

our family and friends to cover the logistics of transporting them.

The Tamaki class went to Wellington — train one way and plane back — where they met their local MP, Clem Simich, and then lunched with the Speaker of the House, Jonathon Hunt. In two days we crammed in as much as we could, spurred on by the children's excitement and interest. Back in Auckland they faced and conquered their fears on the rock climbing wall at the Millennium Centre. And in the Intelligence in the Wild course we really hit the outdoors to give them a huge range of experiences. We had them abseiling from the highest pine tree, and making camp ovens and cooking on them. They constructed stretchers out of branches and erected bivouacs. Everything had to be made from scratch, just as if they were in real jeopardy in the bush. We provided mountain bikes for a cross country ride and found that some of the kids from the decile one schools had never seen or been on one. The accompanying fathers were kept fit running beside them to hold them steady.

We set up an alumni programme at the University of Auckland, made possible by the then Vice Chancellor, John Hood. With the exception of a couple of kids, there weren't any children with parents who had tertiary education. We arranged for a university visit and some of the fathers from Tikipunga brought children from Whangarei down to join the Auckland classes. The university provided a barbecue and university students buddied-up with pairs of our students to show them through various departments of the university. Then we had a game of touch on the quad followed by radio host and author Justin Brown, of *Rugby Speak* fame, compering a university challenge. The best thing about the afternoon was that the people in the PR office of the university who organised our visit met the parents to talk about university life and the opportunities it brings. It became an annual event. We had more fathers attending the alumni afternoons than anything else we did.

John often came with me when I visited GKP units and so came to know the kids. He offered his new Classic Car Museum as another learning opportunity and turned it over to us as a classroom for a week. Although he was ill, as each class came through he would take them round in small groups, talking quietly to them about the cars and their engines. They loved their day there and so did he. I dedicated my end-of-year speech at the 2003 GKP assemblies to him. By then he was very, very sick and I was spending most of my time caring for him. As a result, for the first time I did not get to all the gatherings out of Auckland and had to ask the principal teachers to read my speech for me.

In it I told the children how John also had been a gifted kid like them, how he had asked the why questions, was curious, had weird and wonderful ideas and passions, walked and talked early, played the piano, thought outside the square, was quick with his answers and sometimes found it easier to be naughty than clever. He was a complicated person. I told them how hard it had been when he had his stroke and lost so much of that gift they have in common. How he had to struggle to think, to have ideas, to carry on conversations, to find his way round the house. I told them he would want them to know that while he might have done some things better, he could have done worse, that he thought the secret of life and happiness is to give it a go, to give it your best shot. He sent them a message about new adventures, quoting the German poet, Goethe: 'The moment you definitely commit yourself is the moment providence also moves. All kinds of things occur to help you which would otherwise not happen. A whole stream of advantageous events flow from your decision. They bring all kinds of unexpected chance meetings and material assistance which no one could have foreseen. Whatever you can do, or dream you can do, begin it. Boldness has genius, power and magic in it. To make your dream come true, begin.'

Several more GKP units had been opened: the Waikowhai Unit in Mt Roskill and Rata Street in Wellington in 2002, and Rotorua and Wainuiomata in 2003. The one constant through everything was the ongoing search for funding. It was an expensive programme to run and I worked on never having less than one to one-and-a-half years' funding in the bank. When you fundraise you are relying on other people to dream your dream; it filled much of my time and once classes were over Robyn and Julie also joined me. I had my network of contributors from Books in Homes and some were prepared to help here too. The difference, as I discovered, was that rather than dealing in $4 units for books we were talking $1800 for a full scholarship to keep a child in the programme for a year. To begin with funding was split between the contributing school, the parents and sponsors. If parents could afford to, they paid the full amount. Many could not. We asked for what they could afford, with a nominal base fee of $5 for each day attended. Sometimes even that was beyond a family's means. When we were feeling the pressure financially, I'd set myself goals and announce them when I arrived in the morning, to keep me honest: I am not going to leave the office until I've found $12,000, I would say.

I told the private sector and business people I approached that they knew from business experience the highest return came from the best or the scarcest product or resource they produced. If they believed, as I do, that education is at the heart of a society, that it represents the future wealth of the country, then investing in New Zealand's brightest minds will be the wisest of investments. I am shameless about asking for money for causes I believe in. But for some of the others it was a new experience. Julie remembers to this day the time I wanted her to replace me at a meeting I had organised with one of our best supporters, John Todd. He had asked me what I needed. I wanted her to ask him for $2 million. Her eyes opened and her mouth probably did too. She looked appalled. 'I can't do that!' she said. I reminded her he was the one who had encouraged us to keep up the momentum and to grow and spread. Already there were demands to open units in Christchurch and Invercargill but no funds to do it. John wanted to see teachers with qualifications in gifted education throughout the education system as well.

Julie went home and spent a large part of the evening practising asking

'The moment you definitely commit yourself is the moment providence also moves. All kinds of things occur to help you which would otherwise not happen.'

Cloud spilling over Porters Pass — I call it my 'Lake Lyndon Curtain'.

for $2 million while watching her expression in the mirror. I told her she had to believe in it. She couldn't blink. When she got to John the next afternoon she managed to say the magic sum. There was a small silence and then, while she was still clutching the table, he said, 'I'm unable to respond. I've never been asked for $2 million.' He confessed he was clutching the table too. I was proud of her. I'm not sure I could have done it. We didn't get the $2 million but John did give us a significant contribution.

We were also back knocking on the government's door for financial support. Trevor Mallard was now Minister of Education. I went to see him with Julie and gave him a bottle of Cold Duck which I said was a bribe. He had been a great supporter of Books in Homes and he appreciated what we wanted to do with GKP. He had opened both the Tamaki and the Tikipunga units and Wainuiomata was in his electorate. We achieved a first for gifted education in having the ministry contribute towards GKP's teachers' salaries. We also won the Ministry

of Education's Professional Development contract called The Gifted Edge, a programme developed by Julie Mills and Pam Hook for teachers and parents in all our contributing schools. It included workshops, one each term, run in Auckland, Wellington and Rotorua. It informed teachers about the needs of gifted students so they have support in their main school. This was in addition to the enormous amount of feedback and material that each unit sent back to the contributing schools with their pupils.

Some mainstream teachers took it up with alacrity; others were not so enthusiastic. Principals were universal in their positive response. They talked about their gifted pupils being 'role models for their peers and our hope for the future', but only as long as those talents were encouraged to flourish, which was where they gave credit to GKP. They told us they had seen 'a growth in confidence, self-esteem and achievement in all the children' attending. One of Gifted Edge's main objectives was to increase the number of teachers qualified in gifted education. This became imperative in 2005 when the ministry made it mandatory for all schools to put in place a strategy and educational programme specifically for their gifted pupils. The other significant part of Gifted Edge was parent workshops that provided families with ways to understand and cope with what were often very demanding and difficult children. Parents made sometimes Herculean efforts to attend. They found, like their children, comfort in being among others who understood the joys and tribulations of parenting a gifted child.

Pam Hook had joined us to work on a number of fronts. Apart from teaching one day a week at the Waikowhai Unit, she was working with Auckland University to develop a programme to research and evaluate GKP and our kids. She was also developing programmes for gifted Pacifica people with Dr Airini Airini. However, it was her fourth project that consumed more and more of my thought and energy: Pam was working on a proposal for a new full-time school for gifted children. After all, they were gifted seven days a week, not just the one we had them for.

The push for a full-time school did not come from us. It was driven by the parents and their children. Every time their kids left our unit parents would ask, 'What now?' We held three meetings packed with parents and children in the Classic Car Museum. At the first meeting there was standing room only and over four hundred children. The interest was overwhelming. Parents from all walks of life wanted choice — another suspect word in education circles — for their kids. At the second meeting we split parents and children and asked both groups to write down the kind of school they wanted. At the third meeting we presented their ideas collated, their dream school, one they had designed, one they thought would be right for them.

For more than a year, with support from others in GKP, Pam worked on putting together a detailed, cogently argued proposal for a junior high school for gifted children. The final document filled a hundred pages. One of the salient arguments on which the application was based, was the statement in law that says every New Zealand child is entitled to an education appropriate to his or her needs. This very legality was being thrashed out in newspapers at the time. Parents of disabled children were arguing that not all of them

should be mainstreamed. For some it was totally inadequate to their needs. We believed our kids were no different.

However, the ministry's one-size-fits-all attitude became increasingly apparent when we applied for a full-time gifted kids junior high under Section 1.56 of the Education Act — Designated Character School — which covers special interest schools like kura kaupapa Maori and Catholic schools. At the time one other school had been established under this section, former Christchurch mayor Vicky Buck's Discovery School, to which any child could apply and where there were individual contracts between teachers, parents and children, covering what and how they would be taught. I thought I might find a supporter there, but Vicky Buck too talked about the concept of a gifted school being elite.

An indication of what we were facing emerged at our first meeting with the minister and ministry in Trevor Mallard's office in 2001. We arrived wearing t-shirts in black with the silver initials GKJH — Gifted Kids Junior High. We presented Trevor with a shirt along with a pile of requests for the school from the parents and children. One woman from the ministry told us we would be facing an uphill battle because, apparently, 'it would be just like Auckland Grammar' — too elite. Letters to newspapers asked querulously, 'Isn't ability grouping elitist and undemocratic?' On another occasion Mallard argued that you can easily tell Maori schools and Catholic schools and their natural constituencies. I said, somewhat irritably, 'Well, for goodness sake, do gifted kids have to have pointed heads or something?' To try to ease what was becoming a tetchy situation, and one that was not looking good for us, I sent him, the prime minister and other senior ministers a Christmas box. Inside was our own version of *The Twelve Days of Christmas* along with a bottle of bubbles to celebrate the money and the junior high they were going to give us:

> On the first day of Christmas GKP gave to me . . .
> One kete from GKP
> Two Lateral Thinkers
> Three Creative Challenges
> Four Thinker's Keys
> Five Gifted Units
> Six de Bono Thinking Hats
> Seven Budding Artists

Eight Enquiring Minds
Nine Gifted Musicians
Ten Young Entrepreneurs
Eleven Future Problem Solvers
Twelve Gifted Kids Going Beyond the Known.

I am not sure now that was the smartest of my ideas.

In the end, our application for more money and for the junior high were turned down. What was so extraordinary was some of their objections to the full-time school. First, we were not allowed to talk about gifted and talented. We had to employ a lawyer to find an acceptable alternative for such 'inflammatory' terms. The woolly solution was 'a school environment which would allow children to flourish'. Because it was to be a publicly funded school, we couldn't concentrate on the lower deciles as we had originally with GKP. Instead we would have to take ten per cent from each decile. Next was the ministry's concern over how the students would get to the school. What would we do for a bus? And lastly, they said New Zealand was not into junior highs for years seven to ten. Since then three or four junior highs have opened and we constantly run across extracts from our application which these new schools have used.

The failure to get government and education ministry approval for the Gifted Kids Junior High was one of the most devastating blows I've ever experienced. The GKP parents and children and all the staff were bitterly disappointed. I don't like letting any fight go, and it was especially true of that one. We had put in almost two years' work, and the support and money of a lot of believers, just to get it to that stage. It was what our parents and students had asked for.

Secondary school is especially hard for some of them. One of our teachers kept in contact with the very bright boy who had arrived with a huge file and full-blown ADHD. He was hard work sometimes but GKP had positive results and he really loved it. Now he was in secondary school, and she wanted to know how he was getting on. His class teacher told her he was difficult and when it got too much they just tied him to his chair. None of us could get the image out of our heads.

I guess, too, the ministry's treatment of our day programme had given me some underlying trust in their belief in us. That year they had given GKP a significant grant from the Contestable Fund, more than any other similar education group. We were taking state school pupils out of their classrooms and into ours for twenty per cent of their school year. Yet not once did the ministry ask to see what we were doing or visit our units to see our programme in action. Even though they knew me from Books in Homes and who our teachers were, I found that extraordinary and I still do.

I had withdrawn from the day-to-day business of GKP once it was plain John had little time left. After he died, I tried to go back, but it was no longer the same. I had expended a huge amount of energy in those final months caring for him and in our campaign for the junior high before that. But neither could I let go completely. We organised a trip for the Tamaki kids and some of their parents to the Army Museum at Waiouru. They were looking at aspects of war. It was the first time I had gone away with them since John died; he used to come to everything with me. The kids absolutely adored the museum's pounamu wall and they loved getting dressed in the combat gear from different eras and branches of the army and then exploring the museum to find out about the people their uniform represented before reporting back.

We stayed in a ski lodge in Ohakune, empty except for us. It was my birthday. The parents and teachers organised the kids and gave them one hour to write a song for me and a rather eclectic selection of props in which rubber

Jack Cleaver, Snow's son, breaking in Tempest. The horse came with the chattels when I bought the farm. He remains my $100 unbroken horse.

Propped up is this two-windows-and-a-door pitsawn timber cottage from the mid 1800s. I shall have to wait until the exchange rate drops and the wool price rises before what I affectionately call my New Zealand house is restored and ready to display my kiwiana collection.

gloves came to star prominently. The kids also made gifts with whatever material they could find. I had no idea about any of this until they sat me down to begin my party. I couldn't stop smiling. The next day we visited a King Country sheep station to see sheep dogs working. I watched, never imagining that one day I would be working with them myself. Later, while we were having tea at the homestead, the Maori fathers gathered the boys together and did an impromptu haka on the lawn for their hosts and for us. It was a fantastic and moving act, all the more so because it was so unexpected and spontaneous.

In August 2004 I moved to Castle Hill and a few weeks later I wrote to the GKP staff and to Trevor Mallard letting them know I was formally disengaging from the programme. I had quickly come to realise the station was not something I could do, nor would want to do, part time. It would need total commitment if I was to make it work. The big Rural Delivery mail bags brought cards and letters and photo albums from kids, teachers and parents. They told me we had started a very good thing; we really had changed the face of gifted education. Although there had always been a small group hammering away since the 1940s, the only ministry focus on gifted education had been a small handbook issued in 1972 and updated in 2000. Then at the beginning of 2005, the Ministry changed the National Administrative Guidelines to make it mandatory for all schools to have processes in place to identify and cater for the gifted and talented within their school.

I believe what GKP did with our public profile and our decision to use 'gifted' in our name, even though we were criticised for it, was to help push the needs of the gifted back onto the ministerial agenda. There was also a

Night-time hare hunts keep these pests down and are a huge amount of fun.

whole area of professional development now, answering John Todd's call to pepper-pot schools with teachers who understood gifted. We might not have taken it as far as we had hoped, but we had definitely stepped up to Clive Sharpe's challenge.

CHAPTER 4

A bitter beginning

In July 2004, just before I took possession of Castle Hill, I had spent an evening at Inverary Station at Mt Somers, on the road between Christchurch and Queenstown. I first visited Inverary three years earlier with my brother Malcolm and sister-in-law, Gill, when we had been doing 'Station-to-Station', visiting and staying at a number of high country sheep and cattle stations. Before we headed off for the next farm on our itinerary, I somewhat recklessly promised our hosts, John and Anne Chapman, I'd be back for shearing. I failed to keep that promise.

Then, out of the blue, Anne called and asked if I would fly down from Auckland and speak to a dinner group. I was happy to, and I talked about education, Books in Homes and the Gifted Kids Programme, as they expected. Then I told them I was soon to be a neighbour and why. Those rural women nearly feel off their chairs with mirth. Or maybe they were amused at the idea of my pre-enrolment at Lincoln University to do a Diploma of Agriculture.

In the station's old Roadman's hut before it was restored.

Mark Smith

Or perhaps my optimistic enthusiasm for the front page of the weekend's *New Zealand Herald* that talked of farm fields being 'paved with gold'.

In Auckland, an old school friend organised a farm-themed farewell lunch with a quiz on the side. Wendy and her husband run about thirty five ewes and a ram on a lush paddock out the back of Manukau City. Among other things, they also keep a few hens. Wendy told me the Castle Hill hens would need one of their wings clipped to stop them flying round my garden. She had me pick up one of hers and practise. It felt weird but I told myself I'd better not flinch in front of my mates. 'It doesn't hurt. They don't mind at all,' they said encouragingly. Wendy had laid out all kinds of antique farming tools and equipment which we had to identify. I had never seen most of them before — ear tags, castrating implements, things to shackle stock. I thought the drench gun looked like something you'd use as a douche. I felt even less prepared for my new career.

I sent an email to the new farm manager outlining my hopes for the station: 'Our vision for Castle Hill Station is to achieve excellence in High Country farming performance, to be sensitive in our custodianship of Castle Hill's unique environment and to add value, through diversification and wise development, to Castle Hill's remarkable nature and iconic landscapes.' 'Okay with you?' I finished.

I had decided to give it five years, to restore the station, work it hard, turn it around and get it producing income — something, it transpired, that had rarely been done before. It had turned a profit when wool prices had been good, particularly in the 1950s, and in more recent times owners had made good money selling surplus winter feed to the coast, but it had been a farm that could only sustain an owner-operator. By takeover time, realities were beginning to push their way in to my dream. The moving and set-up costs were proving much greater than I anticipated. As well as paying for a whole lot of plant and machinery I didn't want, problems had emerged while making a few alterations to the homestead where I was going to live which would require additional work to put right. Builders and trades people were playing pass-the-blame or failing to return calls. The first stock had been bought — two bulls from Kakahu for over $11,000 — and the farm manager was getting price lists for fencing materials with a warning to hold on to my hat. The good news was we had sold some steers, two-year rising, which I hoped would make the works' five-star criteria and fetch the $50 premium. I even had a chap up to look them over. His 'eye-chrometre'

said a few were the required weight but the rest were not quite there. So it was off to the general killing yards and an average price. The manager had also discovered we had lambs that had been born out of our season, the offspring of rogue rams up the Cheeseman. Perhaps, I told friends, some ram may ride over the Torlesse and find me. I felt slightly off balance and out of control, and besieged by payouts.

I arrived at Castle Hill after a stern talking-to from my daughter Kate. At dinner just before I left Auckland, she reminded me that the mother she knows has always been an optimist. I was not to lose that now. I was to put that great positive energy back into my life. The following weeks further eroded my usual confidence and daily strip-mined my supposedly inexhaustible optimism. The farm manager and I were failing to develop a good working relationship. I had asked him to come up to the homestead each morning to go through the day's work and also to review progress. I asked what he was doing. He was feeding out silage and hay in the snow and break-fencing the winter feed. Okay, I said, I want to come with you. His employment contract made it very clear I wished to be fully involved with the farm, not a city sightseer, a cheque-signer. I would be living there at least eighty per cent of the time. I had no idea what he should be doing but I explained that I had to learn from the bottom up and actually doing the work was the only way I could do that.

We headed out. The farm tracks were muddy and deeply rutted. We had terrible trouble moving the electric fence in the turnip paddock. We were using three single wires for the break fence and moving it almost every day, allowing the stock controlled access to the feed. The bitter wind was constantly at us, pushing us around. I started to understand the meaning of the term wind chill. It was so cold that after the first time I didn't want to go out again. A picture in *The Press* that week showed me leaning on a fence post in my new red check farm jacket, smiling brightly into a gale as snow flew past on the horizontal and the limestone rocks behind faded into the mist. Just out of frame my son David's kids, James, Emma and Grace, and his wife Julie were being towed up the hill by David on the farm quad bike to ski down onto the flats.

Brendon O'Hagan

I'd wanted a special place for the granny-kids when they came to stay, and found the perfect space above the garage. It was big, open and unfinished and I had it lined, painted and carpeted. I bought four beds with roll-aways and made them a dormitory. French doors at one end opened to nowhere; they were locked securely and the key hidden to stop fearless granny-kids doing death defying leaps onto the drive below. In a trunk I kept nine fat stuffed monkeys — one for each of them. They adored it. They loved the chickens first and then the dogs and pigs. The offal pit was a real hit and James was mad about the tractor. Now at the back door that leads to their dormitory there are sleds for snow time hanging on the wall with Swannies, gumboots tumbling and tilting underneath. It's there on hand for whenever they come.

The first of the major farm work began. Fencing was the greatest expense to start and it has remained near the top; for the next three years fencers would be working somewhere on the property. Once I began really looking at the farm, the fences were the first thing I noticed and, even to

The bitter wind was constantly at us, pushing us around. I started to understand the meaning of the term wind chill. It was so cold that after the first time I didn't want to go out again.

an untrained eye, it was obvious they were years old. There were a lot of traditional Merino fences — a few standards and posts and a bit of barbed wire. Some leant to the wind, some were propped up. Gates were not swinging properly and pretty soon we had cattle and sheep on Highway 73 and in neighbouring Castle Hill Village.

Good fencers are a rare breed and they are to be treasured. You have them working for you, then you let them go. You recommend them to others in the valley and then find you've lost them just as you reach a point where you can no longer manage without something somewhere being fixed. I was really lucky to find Geoff Rogers — also known as Bucko — who was just back from riding steers on the rodeo circuit in Australia. Geoff is a fencing expert, which was really important as I had no idea about the things you have to take into account when putting in fences, such as how to move stock; and how the position of gates is pivotal when doing that. We needed to stop the stock getting onto the road — if a car hits an animal, it is the farmer's responsibility. The other priority was the most broken-down fences and the area on the flats, the most valuable part of the farm. With a 28,000 thousand-acre spread you can afford to have huge paddocks but once you are down to ten thousand acres it is vital you reconfigure and reduce paddock size to make it work. DOC was also ready to start putting up the first boundary fence and Geoff was contracted to do that.

We went out with Allan McKenzie of Nature Heritage to view the Hogs Back and adjacent Thomas Bush areas and discuss the fencing plan which would separate the DOC land from the station's. On the way the truck got stuck, destroying more farm track, and the steep climb brought on an asthma attack. I was rapidly discovering I had picked a place to live that contained almost all my major allergy triggers: grasses, horses, dogs. Fencing of the vast Serengeti-like deer block was also underway. We were dividing the existing paddock into two more, with a race planned to the yards which were yet to be built. I would need to think of names for the newly organised paddocks.

All farmers with spreads of any size name their fields. Naming your paddocks is practical. If someone's doing top dressing or spreading lime or fixing irrigation you have a map and you can say, 'You go to Ed's Glory or to The Lucerne.' I had no idea of most of the existing names at Castle Hill because there was no current map of the farm. I found a framed hand-painted sketch of a work programme done in the 1950s and another pencilled on a piece of Pinex. I carried on with the obvious ones — Plenty (on the lower slopes of Mt Plenty), The Rocks, Enys Block (after the Enys brothers, who farmed here from 1864 until the late 1880s), and then Emu, Thomas and Whitewater for the streams that run through them.

It was fun to think of apt names. You might take a distinguishing feature, like Ghost Flat near Ghost Stream, Land's End because it is the farthest paddock, the end of the property, and Montana because although I've never been there I always think of great plains. There is emotional context: Chrissie's, Homestead, Pig Paddock, Whitehorse, Tatters Field, July (for the month I paid for the station), August (the month I moved in), Rob's because he was right there at beginning of negotiations, Giffney's because Colin was the one who first told me about Castle Hill and suggested it might be the farm for me. Frizzells' had a double-barrelled reason, first because it was spending time with Dick and Judy in Hawke's Bay that had first made me think of farming, and then because they were there to help me move in to Castle Hill. It was only afterwards that Dick discovered another reason: thirty years earlier the farm had been owned by a Frizzell.

Eager to make myself useful, I took my first trip in to the stock and station agents in Darfield with an order for fencing materials. Geoff had given me a list that included items I'd neither seen nor heard of such as Hayes wire strainers and gudgeons. There were three local stock agents at the time: Pynes up a side street, Wrightson's on the main road and CRT. I got to know CRT early because they had a good deal with Genesis Power and so my electricity bills came through them. It was a new shopping experience. I was looking at, though not yet purchasing, the Airtex shirts and moleskins and other classic pieces from the farming wardrobe. At this stage I was still more Zambesi-ish in style. It did not take me long to understand the practicalities of that South Island clothing. You need a collar you can turn up to protect the back of the neck when mustering. Same for the layers — you're always peeling off the Swanndri, then the jersey, the shirt, down and down, and then putting it back on again as the temperature drops in the dying day. Vests are practical because they allow you to work with your arms and hands free.

It took me longer to accept bulk buying. Purchasing lavatory paper in packs of twelve, huge tins of Nescafé Classic and buckets of Persil felt like running a hotel when it was just a house, and for one most of the time. Then there was the slight unreality of the method of payment. Money doesn't change hands. It is not even like using your credit card: they send you an account but they've already deducted their costs and commission and what you've spent from what you've earned from the stock or produce you have sold through them.

There was no progress with the farm manager. I was less and less welcome to help with the day-to-day jobs. He failed to introduce me to the stock agents, and was reluctant to answer my questions or to pass on the kind of knowledge I needed to be able to help. It was the absolute opposite of everything I had hoped for in this new enterprise. I found life on my own hard enough. I missed John terribly, and that was one of the reasons I chose to do something so totally different from anything I had done previously. This failure in communication also meant failure to better understand each other. Among the rubbish and broken equipment I had discovered traditional old dog kennels and tin-topped benches and a hen coop. Returning from a visit to Auckland I found them piled up about

Tailing

Tailing lambs is a major annual task. We set up mobile tailing yards around the farm, and it's hard work. In front of The Limestone, top centre, is the 2006 tailing gang: Terry O'Loughlin, Daniel Urquhart, John, me and my stock manager Snow Cleaver.

to be burnt. He saw them all as rubbish to be cleared away; to me they
represented a precious part of our past that should be saved and restored.
He stopped coming up to the homestead and I stopped asking him to.
I needed some convivial company and a bit of advice. With her usual
impeccable timing, Anne Chapman rang and suggested I visit and stay for
the night. I drove down to Mt Somers via Methven and Primo E Secondi
Café and Collectibles where I fossicked. The owner, Maria Trengrave, has
my kind of gear, and there's nothing like finding a small kiwiana treasure or
a bargain to cheer me up. Anne was warm and welcoming as always. We sat
in the snug and I talked to John Chapman and to the managers of White
Rock Station in the Rangitata Gorge about the fundamentals of a high
country station like Castle Hill.

John gave me access to all his farm notes and files and helped me come
to understand that hills were tilted flats and should be treated like that,
particularly if they faced north. Even though he had been farming his farm
for forty years, he was still trying new things, always aiming to improve.
He was very free with what hadn't worked as well as what had. He was
also interesting about how things had changed for farms like ours. He
said that in the 1950s, in the halcyon days of high wool prices, they'd have
general hands, musterers, shepherds, up to five or six people, working on
the station. Now in the 2000s, despite running twice the stock, a semi stud
with very sophisticated record keeping and stock analysis, they only employ
one manager and one shepherd and there had been no real improvement
in return. I remember meeting the elderly woman from Surrey Hills at the
Chapmans place who told me that in her time there would be a thousand
people at a field day, and that always included the Minister of Agriculture
and local MPs and, more often than not, the prime minister. Today, she said,
there may be three hundred, of whom a good portion are selling grass seed,
and there is not a government minister or MP in sight.

In the morning, as always, Anne insisted on bringing me breakfast in
bed, served on a practical old-fashioned breakfast tray on legs. While I
ate she sat and talked about her mother and father and the farm and went
through her book of traditional high country recipes for any I might enjoy.
I learnt a lot and left with ideas, booklets, references and a revived spirit.
I'd driven the unsealed Lake Lyndon road there and back, even though it
was closed. The locals did it all the time but I felt very daring.

*Early morning return
of the hoggets from
Plenty to McLeods.*

The first big date on the Castle Hill farm calendar after I arrived was shearing in early September. The gang had been organised and set up in the old shearers' quarters which doubled as backpackers' accommodation. I had never seen a backpackers close up — very basic, with an overflowing septic tank belching by the back door. It brought back memories of the 1960s when Allan and I had rental houses in central Auckland in the old and as yet ungentrified suburbs of Grey Lynn, Eden Terrace and Ponsonby. There was one backpacker in residence when I bought, a young Frenchman who had paid for three months' stay upfront. During the day he went bouldering on the limestone rocks and at night he completed academic papers which he posted back to Paris for marking. I decided he would be the last paying guest until I had done up the buildings and determined how I wanted to approach the tourism side of the business. I took down the backpackers sign by the road.

Shearing was my first opportunity to see an integral part of a sheep station's life and to get to know the contractors involved. Kate and Rob were down with their children, Will, George and the twins Alice and Jack, as was professional photographer Jae Frew and his family. Jae headed for the woolshed one morning with his camera and was told by the manager he was not to go anywhere near the shed. He would not explain why but he did not want any of us over there. I told him the photographer had my permission to be there. I had no intention of being shut out. I would march in and stand next to the rousies or shearers, watching, listening and asking questions. I made scones, though they had their own cook, and took them over for the morning tea breaks. After they finished for the day, I took beer to the shearers' quarters. At night they sat crammed in a small room set up like the television rooms I'd seen so often at Salvation Army hostels. Rows of old chairs backed along the walls and big Wattie's cans for cigarette butts dotted the floor. Their clothes hung around and above them. They smelt of fleeces during the day and at night of socks still wet.

I loved the woolshed, the way the pens were made of black beech saplings, the noise and rowdy music, the neat curves and sweeps of the rousie's broom as it kept the floor round the shearers clear, the way the fleeces opened and spread as they were thrown onto the table for the wool classer to grade them, and the crunch of the wool press. I had my first thrill of ownership as 'Castle Hill' was stamped on a wool sack with 'Merino AAA', thinking, that will help pay for some bills. And I really loved the wonderful hoist mechanism — the big wooden wheel with its cogs and gears, great blacksmith-forged iron grabbers and old rope that for the last hundred years had turned the wheel as you pulled down, lifting the bales up to the top floor. There they were lined up and then dropped out onto a truck: it gave me a sense of production from my land. I kept wool samples from that first shear. They nestle in envelopes marked with their class, like Merino AAA — seventeen microns, a memento and my first learning tools.

September, and there was still snow on the Craigieburn and Torlesse ranges and all the way down to the highway. When one is fresh from wet and windy Parnell, snow blanketing the ground outside your door and snowmen on the lawn built with the granny-kids was like living inside one of the Christmas cards my mother's family used to send from England. The snow fell in all kinds of ways and weights — a dump, a blizzard, a sprinkling, a dusting, the last two quick to melt. There were unwritten rules of survival for high country travellers which, if you were lucky, you found out before you needed them. In winter you try to travel with a full tank (to keep the heater running if you get trapped by snow or ice), a strong torch, a thick blanket and some whisky for internal heat. I also made discoveries of my own. Creeping back over the pass one night through heavy falling snow taught me you can't drive in a snow storm with your headlights on high beam. They made it impossible to see. The local road contractors have an obligation to keep the main highway open in winter and in my first two years at Castle Hill there were no road closures of any length before the snow plough had it cleared. In bad weather they used to sit at the top of the pass. I found their presence reassuring.

The station tradition of taking guests for picnics or sunset drinks started soon after I moved in. While Kate and Rob and the granny-kids were still with me I took them down to the old stock bridge over the Porter River late one afternoon. It was a favourite place I liked to go by myself. The banks along the track are studded with wonderful shell fossils. In the beginning I thought it might be part of a favoured greenstone route and the shells the remains of a midden. I found out later this was one of the first areas John Enys took possession of because he was so enthralled by its geology and botany. The mountains around Castle Hill are made of greywacke, a dark, coarse grained sandstone that began life as sediment eroded from granite mountains along the eastern edge of the southern super continent Gondwana, between two hundred and twenty five and two hundred million years ago. Fast flowing rivers washed the sediment down to the sea where it was deposited along the margins of the land. That greywacke is the base rock for the limestone which emerged a mere twenty to thirty million years ago in shallow seas when most of the continent of Zealandia (New Zealand) was submerged. Constant movement of sediment on the sea floor trapped and preserved marine life. Over time that sedimentary limestone rock and its cargo of tiny shellfish and other sea creatures was pushed up to form the fantastic hills and rocks of Castle Hill basin. It is their remains that so excited John Enys and that I could still see.

Down by the river large gnarled willows crowd and lie over the top of huge limestone rocks that lean against each other. The stock bridge was an amazing structure, built by the owners in the early 1900s. Made of wood, it was suspended by huge iron lengths like halyards that tied back to big hooks in the trees and land-bound rocks. Decades of use had covered the base and sides of the bridge with mud and dung and consolidated limestone. The coating was so thick it fooled you into thinking you were on solid ground. In truth it was no more than rotten planks held together by limestone and mud.

As we made our way down the track we noticed some peculiar rocks below, white and not at all like the grey surrounding limestone. I reached the entrance to the bridge last. Merinos, thick with wool, lay in a pile. There were more in the river and along its banks, all gleaming white and very dead. The water was running red. When we recovered from our shock the questions began: how and when had they died, and why did I know nothing about it? Later I found out what had happened and what it was called — a smother. The track down to the bridge was very narrow. The farm manager had brought a big flock of sheep to the top and then, instead of taking them down and across the bridge in lots, he started to push them down on his horse. The track surface is almost like scree and a couple of sheep slipped and fell. You only need a couple to tumble behind the others and it sets up a domino effect. More and more fall on top of those further down and you end up with a smother. It shouldn't happen, but from time to time it does.

At the end of this one, one hundred and twenty eight sheep were dead. He had told the farm advisor but neither of them had told me. And nothing had been done to clear them.

They could not be left there to rot. Wool takes a long time to break down in water and things decay slowly in the high country climate. They were stinking and fetid, thick with flies, and polluting the river. I had to employ someone to reopen and widen the track so we could bring the tractor down to bury them and repair and widen the old stock bridge so it was safe. Added to those costs were the losses. To this day I don't know which sheep they were, the best of the flock or not, pregnant or not, but they were covered in wool, so I lost that.

The whole episode had angered and shaken me. The bills continued to arrive and I felt that my ignorance only served to disadvantage me, as did my status as a wealthy Auckland widow. My bank balance was behaving

Sheep feeding on balage during the big snow of 2006. Their hooves didn't touch grass for over two months.

like high country temperatures — freezing or below. The manager remained difficult, angry and rude. I retreated to Auckland again for a few days.

At the same time, letters began to arrive from people who had read about my move in the rural and local press. Some were wonderfully supportive. A woman who had done what I initially planned and bought a farm in Hawke's Bay told me, 'You have one of the most pretty farms in a fabulous area. Look after it and it will look after you. Good luck and remember to follow your own gut feelings . . . It's not easy knowing nothing, but look and listen, the wise heads all around have reasons for "doing" things. But don't be put off by conservative farm talk — Canterbury has heaps of it . . .'

A man wrote from Tirau, waiting for the sun to rise. He had bought a farm on the spur of the moment and left his stressful city job a month later: 'Many colleagues thought I was a nut case. The day I moved to the farm it snowed, quite a change for an Auckland city boy! I did wonder if my choice was wise. However, I must say that moving to that farm was the best thing I ever did. It was truly a different experience. I had never crutched a sheep before, did not know much about Romneys, less about teeth etc of sheep but I was quite certain it would work out.' The locals had their doubts, he said, but he learnt fast and 'had a real ball'.

His entrance-level ignorance sounded about the same as mine. Not only did I not know what a wether was and kept calling all cattle cows even when they were bulls. I also didn't know that sheep had no top teeth. There was a pile of letters with requests to walk, tramp and orienteer across the farm. It was no good hiding in Auckland. I had to go back.

There was snow on the tops, green peeking through in the fields, and blue skies to welcome me. I spent some time the first evening trying and failing to email from my new laptop. The whole of the valley must have been online checking stock prices. This is another reality of remote country life — the old dial-up system, connection at exasperatingly low speeds and constantly being disconnected. City friends, used to broadband, become enraged and wonder how farming families can put up with such dismal service. I decided to start tidying up around the house and garage and down in the farm compound. There was so much mess. It was like decades of exterior dust. Every morning the curtains opened on a day differently beautiful to the last. I'd load the pickup and drive it over to the rubbish pit. I also wasn't paying Geoff and the fencers to tidy up after them, so any old standards or posts or waratahs that could be used again needed to be sorted and put aside and the rest collected to be taken to the pit to be burned. On a farm, cleaning up never finishes.

Phil from The Burn, where the Frizzells and I had spent our very first night, rang to see if I wanted to go to the Sunday morning market at Riccarton. I recognised the people who ran it; they were sponsors of Books in Homes. I started to go regularly. I'd wander the stalls, maybe buy a little bit of kiwiana, and look for fresh vegetables and good fruit to make into jams so I could indulge and improve my home-making skills. Slowly I got to know the roadside stalls as well, who had the best potatoes, apples, plums, and the man who in asparagus season put an old chest freezer at the front gate with the bagged green spears and honesty box inside. I'd come back laden, intoxicated by the way the produce tracked the seasons. I had food for an army and only myself to feed. In my dream of country living, good local produce, loving preparation and slow cooking were all part of this rural life I'd chosen. Colin Giffney sent me a recipe for Le Gigot de Sept Heures, noting that the French use hogget. Now I was on a farm, I could do the same.

There was often a man selling free-range eggs at Riccarton. I started buying his eggs even though I had inherited hens with the farm, an assorted number of Black Orpingtons, Leghorns, New York Reds and others. There was an old hen house and run but the hens had become almost totally free range and wild. They laid their eggs anywhere but in the laying boxes. The hen house needed to be cleaned and the hens rounded up. Then I was told they had lice and wouldn't be good for much longer.

Some people say fowls lay for ever; others reckon you knock off their heads after year. I went to Riccarton to consult. They recommended a fresh start and that I buy Red Shavers because they need little care and are good

The Witches of Springfield, Gail and Caroline.

layers. I bought hen pellets and eagerly awaited my first harvest. The laying boxes remained empty most of the time. I fed out more pellets. How could ten hens produce only two eggs? Then I'd find a huge cache of eggs in the grass or under a shed. I learned you are not meant to let them out after you've fed them in the morning until later in the day. That way they peck-peck and then lay in the boxes before they get to range free.

My difficulty is that I can't bear to keep things locked up. So although my egg numbers have increased greatly, I still hit piles of old ones when I'm out on the mower. I love the hens. I love the way they greet me with cupboard love when I go in to feed them. I don't clip their wings either. They don't get up as far as my garden but it's a different matter for the manager's house and garden: I'm filled with admiration for Castle Hill's current stock manager, Snow, and his tolerance for free-range hens that wreck his garden and crap by his back door. He is also very forgiving of the rooster. While I enjoy hearing its early morning calls, romanticised by

distance, it is crowing right outside his bedroom window.

I was keen to get stuck into something I knew I could do and was good at, and that was restoring and doing up old buildings and structures. First on my list were the mailbox out on the road and the pigsty. I advertised for a handyman/builder who could maintain the house and farm: hang a gate, fix fencing, tidy up and restore the historical buildings and generally be another person about the place. One I could work with. My sister had friends who said they might know of someone. Meantime I went in search of a particular paint. I remembered seeing red farm buildings on the Panama to Alaska Rally with John. I loved the way they looked, and the old tin shed at Castle Hill was still red oxide and fitted really well into the landscape. With the help of Stewart and Jess Gunn at Brooksdale, on the flats out of Springfield, I found a supply of ten-litre pails of Red Ember. You could apply it without undercoat and put it on any way you liked. My kind of paint. We would use it on the pigsty and letter box and

Castle Hill had extensive deer herds and I've kept them on. Deer prices were appalling when I bought the station and the advice was to get out of deer. Three years on, our Red Deer herd is vastly improved and we are buying in new stock.

simultaneously do the stables and little red shed.

With perfect timing, I had a call from someone interested in the job. Keith Cross had lived in the area for thirty years after moving here from York in England. He and his wife, Christine, had originally come to New Zealand for some mountaineering. He was just finishing work on Jack's Hut at Arthur's Pass for DOC and doing a university course in Classics. He heard things weren't great at the station and that I was looking for help. I suggested he check the work I wanted done and talk to the manager about some of the idiosyncrasies of the station. If he was still willing, I was keen for him to start as soon as possible.

I decided I should go to back to Auckland until matters were resolved with the manager. There had been an intolerable meeting with him and me and the farm advisor, who had recommended him, to try and resolve matters. It had failed completely and I could see no way to redeem the situation. I gave him notice and asked him to be gone by Labour Weekend. I would not return until he had left. I felt I had made a mess of my first and most important decision. I clung to the words of an Auckland business friend: your best loss is your first loss. That appealed to the optimist in me. I would learn from my mistakes.

Keith picked me up at the airport. I had my granddaughter Grace with me. The manager's house was empty and, despite the fact the stock appeared to be scattered to the farthest corners of the farm, I felt an enormous sense of relief. Keith was still orienting himself to the place and it was obvious we needed more help while we waited for a new manager. 'Don't worry,' he said, 'I'll help you, bonnie lassie.' He rang round his mates. Simon — one-eyed musterer with a poppy in his hat — was the only one not busy. So it was me and Dad's Army, all over sixty, shaking Coke bottles full of stones to move the stock, instead of the bark of sheep dogs we didn't have, on a farm with bad fences. We'd start each morning up at the house with a cup of coffee and a plan for the day and finish with a much needed whisky or two. I had only been back a day when there was a call from Castle Hill Village to tell us our cattle were loose on the nine-hole golf course. Keith put me in Christine's car to herd them while he ran backwards and forwards on foot. We cobbled together the broken fences with waratahs and No 8 wire.

*Old fence posts
on Longspur.*

It was time for a bit of fun, time to meet some neighbours. My friend Betsy Benjamin had promised to organise something when I first bought the station. We put together a guest list. It included some people she knew, and the Chapmans and Gunns and others I'd met through Anne and John. Jo and Mark Acland made the two hour drive just to be there. It was a great party. I discovered no one dreams of coming to a high country dinner or a barbecue or drinks without bringing contributions — potato salad, apple cake, whitebait and zippered cold-bags of beer. It was an early example of the high country generosity that has become so familiar to me.

There's a pleasing lack of formality when people get together. They tend to hang out in the kitchen, which helped as I was not used to cooking a meal and serving drinks at the same time, although John Fernyhough was never much good at that. At the end of the evening people always do the dishes, which I appreciated. There were gifts of welcome too. The guests from the valley brought me supplies of evening primrose oil and cod liver oil and super-rich cream for dry skin. I thought they were getting at my middle age. No, they cried, it's to save your skin. My hair has always been dreadful, probably because I've dyed it since I was twenty-eight, cursed with the family trait of greying early. Even though I was now buying the most sophisticated conditioners — top dressing for the hair — they couldn't counteract underground limestone. The hard water, combined with the dry and freezing climate, was also affecting my skin. I appreciated their thoughtfulness, glad to find I wasn't the only person whose skin reacted so badly. I'd always looked after it too. Face the day every day was the motto, and I saw no reason to change now I was down on the farm. I still put on my makeup and red lippy and always wore a hat.

The night of the party, Jo Acland had brought me a big bunch of glowing red tulips. In Auckland I was used to seeing them with their heads lying on the table by the time I waved my guests goodbye. This was obviously a better climate for flowers, or they grew them stronger here. For a week they stood proudly upright in the vase. I liked the attitude. They say adversity makes you commit more to a place. My brother and others were telling me to stop saying I was 'going broke in paradise'. They were right. I thought of Kate's words to me only a few weeks earlier. I was not going to let recent circumstances beat me. I would engage my optimism again.

The century-old Roadman's cottage alongside State Highway 73 was one of the first I restored.

Below: The Roadman's before work began.

Moving cattle in autumn
2007. I'm riding Tarndale,
the latest of my several
experiments with horses.
He suits me well.

CHAPTER 5

Dad's
Army

At the end of October, Rob Hellreigel, Colin Giffney and I sat down with the farm advisor to discuss a master plan for Castle Hill. When I took possession, the station was carrying six thousand and sixty eight stock units: sheep, cattle and deer. I had lost eighteen thousand acres to DOC and according to the advisor, the ten thousand acres that now made up the station could not support that number of animals. DOC had suggested four thousand as the new carrying capacity, but four thousand stock would not pay a manager's salary and give me a cash return. The farm was not sustainable without development.

The advisor suggested four options. The first was to complete the deer fencing and share-farm deer that were owned by an investor. Next, to renew pasture on the front flats through winter feed crops and fence off more paddocks, as well as creating a lane across the flats to avoid having to move stock along the main road. The third option was to subdivide the Longspur, Broken River and Whitewater blocks with cheap electric fences which would increase the number of

Hay-making on the flats alongside State Highway 73. Building up our winter feed was a crucial element in improving our productivity.

paddocks and allow better management of stock and pasture. And, finally, to do more over-sowing with seed and fertiliser on flats and hill blocks. Each of these options was designed to bring a return that would be significantly greater than the capital invested in them.

Whichever options we took, I was smart enough to know that the fencing had to be done. But I was worried about expenditure. I knew that while the previous owner had not done much to look after the fences and gates, he would have been vigilant about putting on fertiliser. People up and down the valley also assured me he had. I felt confident I could leave a major fertilisation programme for a year to eighteen months. In retrospect, I don't think that was wise. The climate in the Castle Hill basin depletes the soil very quickly and my decision to do no more than maintenance fertilisation led to the need for massive capital investment in 2006. I suggested to Rob and Colin that the best option for a quick return would be to begin on the flats, fencing and renewing pasture and planting winter feed. I knew the previous owners, the Bradleys, had supplemented their income selling surplus feed. The idea appealed to Colin, who was beginning to ask about generating cash flow. We would start working up the flats: spray off the brown top and then fertilise and sow lucerne, turnips, kale, rape and annual rye.

Winter feed is a two-year programme after which you put the fields into permanent pasture. Up past Castle Hill Village was another big paddock where the previous owners had put in the first year of winter feed after spraying to get rid of a heavy infestation of broom, a plant introduced by

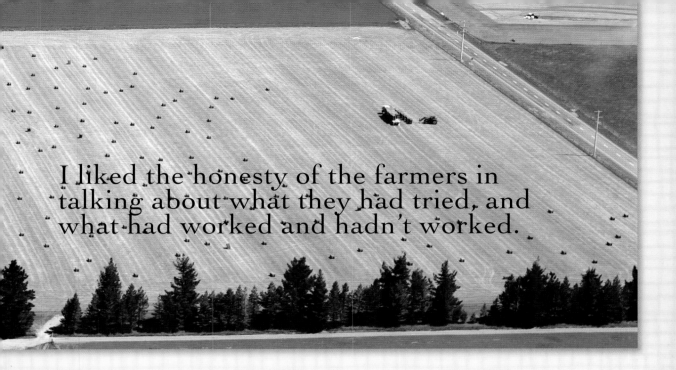

I liked the honesty of the farmers in talking about what they had tried, and what had worked and hadn't worked.

the first European settlers and now one of the high country's most invasive weeds. Before I could sow the second year of crops, I needed to clear the paddock of the broom killed by the previous year's spraying. This was not the fine delicate bush people usually associate with broom; the plants were so old the woody trunks and branches I was throwing into the back of the truck were as big as those of small trees. Once the block was clear, we sprayed and then planted the second year of turnips, kale and rape. Where the ground became too steep to plant, the paddock remained in natives and at the very top up by Longspur we used a helicopter to spray the broom there. What has been disappointing is that after putting this block into permanent pasture, certain areas are once again thick with regenerating broom.

Our talk of feed and pasture was timely. I was only just back from the annual Grasslands Conference which had been held in Ashburton and I was being told farming was all about 'nutrition, nutrition, nutrition and genetics' or the three 'Fs' — 'feed, fertiliser and fences'. Grasslands seemed a good place to start learning. I was particularly impressed by the field trips. I liked the honesty of the farmers in talking about what they had tried, and what had worked and hadn't worked. And a lot hadn't worked. They'd say, for example 'on this southern face we planted certain grass types and they just didn't take'. These were farmers who have been on farms fifty to sixty years and were still experimenting with the new and different, looking for improvements and telling others the results. One of them was John Chapman at Inverary. Down on the flats we looked through

Moving a mob of lambs across the Porter River.

a research block put together by seed merchants with plots of various grass combinations. The talk was of diploid and triploid and it was all beyond someone like me who in the past had confined my work with grass to digging out paspalum from the lawn at home in Auckland.

It was on one of the field trips that I had a really fortuitous meeting. Emily Crofoot was staying with the Aclands at Mt Somers Station during the conference and had been told to look out for me. She introduced herself. It seems that my black leather pants and leopard print hat set me aside from the other more conservatively dressed farmers. Emily and her husband Anders own Castlepoint Station in the Wairarapa, where Anders says he mainly looks after dead things — inanimate objects like tractors and machinery — while Emily looks after the animate, the stock. They are Americans, and much of what I was experiencing as a woman from the 'outside' starting in agriculture was similar to what Emily had experienced moving to New Zealand. We shared stories and laughed and Emily proved a great person to talk through

some of the challenges I was facing. We discussed prioritisation, staffing, the role of advisors, and thinking through my role as 'an involved owner' who, at that stage, would not be on the farm one hundred per cent of the time. We talked about the importance of finding a balance between being involved and having input and giving a manager the space to carry out their work. I felt Castle Hill was very much my baby and there were instances where I tended to micro manage.

The search for a new manager had not taken long. Andy Bitmead, who was working at neighbouring Cora Lynn Station with the joint owner, Paul Jarman, a man who has a great reputation as a farmer, applied for the job. Andy was different in every way from the previous manager. It would be his first time in charge of a farm but he was familiar with the area and its characteristics and he was keen to prove himself. He and his wife, Jo, and their two small children would move in just before Christmas. Renovating and refurbishing the manager's house, and fencing its garden, became a priority. Dad's Army and I were also busy managing the stock as efficiently as we could. Simon, Keith and I spent a lot of time moving stock so paddocks were grazed and then rested, grazed and rested. It was difficult to muster the sheep beyond the flats. We had to move them without dogs, Simon on the farm quad bike and Keith and I in trucks and on foot, plodding across the tussock in all weathers. Herding with our arms and voices, we loaded about seventy wether hoggets I'd sold onto a stock truck. They had not fetched a great price but at least it was a return.

My memory of that first winter and early spring was of perishing cold. The locals told me it was mild, hardly a winter at all. The surrounding ski fields of Porter Heights, Cheeseman and Craigieburn opened and then closed. There was not enough snow to make more to sustain the runs.

However after mild Auckland the conditions were like nothing I had ever known. I remember my shock the first few times I went to open a gate and my fingers stuck to the freezing metal; and then the agony as I peeled them off. The days were usually spectacularly beautiful, the white hills cut in to blue blue skies. But the air was freezing, especially when the wind was up. I noticed it particularly when feeding out, pitching hay from the back of the Land Cruiser to eager animals. I kept buying more and more thermals and gloves. But the gloves made me clumsy. I'd take them off and then they'd be dropped or one would get lost. I bought mittens so I'd still have some dexterity but they were as cold as no gloves at all. It was better to forget about gloves completely and fumble around with numb fingers. I used to catch sight of my hands and hardly recognise them as the work and weather took their toll.

We were now under pressure to get several things done quickly. I also wanted to make up for what I felt was time lost. We were having ongoing problems with stock getting onto the main road or escaping to tramp all over the nine-hole golf course at the village. Early one morning, just a day after we had rounded up loose heifers in the Porter River, I went down to the compound and came face to face with our bulls milling around by the diesel pump. They had broken through one of the feeble gates. There was no one else about and I didn't think this was the time to try mustering with stone-filled bottles and flapping arms. There was only a short driveway between them and the road. While I was trying to gently sweet-talk them back to their field, a young man drove in to the yard. He had seen my predicament. He had his dog with him and together we herded the bulls back and wired shut the gate. It was one breakout too many. I moved Geoff and his fencing gang to work exclusively on the fences and gates along State Highway 73. The potential liabilities and losses were becoming too great. I also realised I had to have a working dog.

John Chapman said he had an old heading dog I could have. Moss had had rickets when he was young so he was not a good looker but John was sure he would suit me. Keith and I went down to Inverary and watched Joe, the shepherd, put Moss through his paces on some flat paddocks and I thought he looked fine. Back at Castle Hill I told Keith I was going to work him. There was a flock of Merinos in the block up by the limestone rocks so Keith and I and Moss started there. I had a piece of paper with the whistles and commands and he would not respond to any of them. I said, 'Out of it,'

and the dog sat down. I walked forward a short way and said, 'Come back,' the command to go right. Moss roared out to the left and started pushing the mob round. I began shouting 'Get out of it,' which turned out to be the command for 'go further out'. He had the sheep going round in circles and no matter what I shouted I could not get him to stop. There were tourists up on the rocks and they could be heard laughing. Finally Keith, with his Yorkshire accent and male voice, yelled and brought him to attention. Each time I tried working Moss, the same thing would happen — the dog would ignore my commands but respond immediately to Keith's. I tried lowering my shouts to a bass but the dog still wouldn't react. I pouted, admitted defeat and gave him to Keith, who kept him on the back of his truck while he was building. Eventually the dog went to Keith's daughter down on the flats south of Waimate, where I guess her husband is now in control of Moss. The experience put me off working with a dog and it would be a year before I tried again.

The laughter from the rocks was a reminder that from now on there would be greater numbers of people wanting access to the farm. Castle Hill has long been a favourite for tramping clubs. Trampers come all through the year, their visits both calendared and spontaneous, as individuals and by the scheduled busload. From time to time I received photos showing what the day had been like for them. I was invited to join an annual trek up Prebble Hill. The fishing register opened in November and stayed open until March. Occasionally I'd return home to find a bottle of wine or a fresh trout by the door. The army is another of the regulars; the station is used

Using the 90hp Massey to load lucerne baleage onto the Penrose debaler before feeding out.

for orienteering and map-reading courses. Soldiers were dropped off in small groups and were next spotted running along State Highway 73 with guns and knapsacks. I thought I might barter for some army fatigues in exchange, but the nice commanding officer said the army was not in favour of giving its uniforms to civilians in case they were used in an attack against them. He brought me a pack of army rations instead.

During my first year, I also had numerous requests from tourist companies who wanted to take wealthy overseas visitors across the station. The tourists paid big money for such excursions but OSH regulations preclude any kind of payment to the farmer because if money changes hands and there is any kind of accident then you, the farmer, are liable. Despite the huge amount of work that had been done and continues to be done on the tracks around the farm, they are fragile. They wind through hillsides and gullies, cling to steep shingle banks and cross rivers and streams where the safest path is always shifting. Springs run through many of the tracks, breaking them up over time. Many four-wheel drive cars and vans can not cope with the conditions safely; neither can the drivers. At the same time you are trying to manage your stock and protect them, especially in certain seasons such as lambing. We had a lot of tour companies through that first year and they promised to make a donation towards the roads' upkeep, but none of them did. Like the surrounding high country people, I came to the conclusion that it was not worth all the risks and that the wear and tear on the farm roads was an additional expense I could do without.

Keith found another person to join our Dad's Army, Anthony Hamilton, an ex-farmer and seaman and a general handyman. Keith's years working for DOC and renovating houses had given him numerous contacts in the building trade: plumbers, painters, electricians, sources for cheap metal and hardware, and people who made second-hand tables and recycled joinery out of old floor boards. When you've lived somewhere for any length of time, you build up a group of tradesmen, handymen and others whose work you know and trust. That was what I had been used to. But then I moved to the remote high country and knew no one at all and no one to ask, at least for the first couple of months. Now I was getting to know a whole new group.

Home baking

SCONE RECIPE

3 CUPS OF FLOUR
6 TSP OF BP
75 GRMS OF BUTTER
PINCH OF SALT
TAB OF SUGAR
HALF A CUP OF DATES
1½ CUPS OF MILK

SLICE IN THE BUTTER ADD THE MILK WORK QUICKLY COOK FOR 12 MINUTES ON 220

CMF '05

Country people need hearty meal breaks. I enjoy making scones for the shearing and tailing gangs. They've become my signature dish. I painted the scone recipe painting for John as a birthday present. My raspberry jam and quince jelly recipes are at the back of the book.

'Clappo' was the plumber, and not always reliable, but every so often he would turn up with a piece of pork or a chicken and put it in the oven to cook for a labourers' roast later. Wayne was a great electrician who could wire in the most obscure places, and like many in the high country had other businesses. He took photographs and DJ'd at weddings and taught ballroom dancing. Owen was a builder and worked with Keith and me on the restorations. There was Griff, a local lad and truck driver who helped Pete, the contract bulldozer driver. Griff was always in black with a black hat with a feather and had some rather interesting acquaintances. He was also the biggest 'Steptoe' around and thought I was a river of gold, with my clear-out and clean-up attitude. One of the positives of my move from the big house in Remuera to Parnell had been the accompanying focus on getting rid of clutter. It seemed a world-wide phenomenon because when I sent John's and my antiques to Christies in England to sell, prices except for the highly academic pieces were low, acknowledging the over-supply there. Despite advice to the contrary, I may have done better selling in New Zealand.

Anthony set up sawhorses from bits of plant and machinery and we started work on repairing the fencing for the pig pen. I had inherited some milled larch with the farm which was stacked by Castle Hill Village. I'd load up the red Hilux and then tool back down the highway with tea towels fluttering from the protruding ends. Anthony showed me how to saw perfect lengths for the sides of the fence. There was a concrete block pigsty but it was disintegrating. It needed a totally new roof and I was the corrugated iron roofer. Then I finished it — and a pair of Zambesi trousers — with three coats of Red Ember paint. I thought it was the loveliest sweetest smelling pigsty.

Pynes called to say they had two weaners for me to pick up. I'd bought one, Keith and Christine the other. In Darfield I found a huge stock truck with two little pigs wandering round in the back. I spread some sacks on the rear seats of my trusty Prado with more than 200,000 kilometres on the clock and they screeched and protested all the way home, just like the days when I used to sing to my kids. I turned up the Slim Dusty CD that was in the glove box when I bought the car. He was singing, very appropriately, about the girl with the calloused hands.

At the farm I popped them into their new home. I'd been told to keep the pigs out of their paddock and on the concrete slab in front of the sty for the first few days. Next morning everything looked fine. I decided to call them and all future pigs Hamilton and Nelson. That way I hoped I wouldn't feel too sad when it came time to turn them into chops, hams and bacon. The following day they were lifting up the concrete with their snouts. Simon, who'd kept pigs before, came over to have a look and returned with a length of wire, wire cutters, pliers and a concrete block that he placed in the middle of the slab. He sat down, sharpened one end of the wire and, grabbing them one at a time, pushed it through their noses. Then he tied it off and trimmed the ends. It certainly wasn't the neat ring you see in nursery rhyme books, and was my introduction to the first of many uses for No 8 wire. The pigs sulked, but they didn't rip up the concrete any more.

I don't like waste or throwing out food but with the pigs it felt slightly more legitimate. I began a collection of pig buckets. When I was by myself, they were almost on starvation rations because I couldn't produce enough waste. In the school holidays, when the family was down, and once the Bitmeads arrived, they were grunting happily through two and more buckets a day. Sometimes people from Castle Hill Village gave us their food scraps and later we were very fortunate to have the Cheeseman ski field ask us to take theirs. Their alternative was to pay to have it carted away or to dig a huge rubbish pit somewhere in the Craigieburn forest. It was a good example of a symbiotic relationship.

Judging when Nelson and Hamilton were big enough to kill was a bit like the witch fattening up Hansel and Gretel. It is always the greedy one who is first for the slaughter. When the time came, I absented myself from the coup de grâce. After the pig was shot the carcass was placed in the bucket of a tractor, its thorax slit and then it was taken across to the old cast iron bath by the killing shed. The bath had been filled with water and a fire lit underneath. Once the water reached 70°C, two lengths of chain were laid across the bath and the pig lowered in on top of them. The chains were used to help turn the pig as the hot water loosened the bristles which were scraped off with a knife. Then it was lifted out of the bath, butchers' hooks were inserted through the hocks and the carcass was hoisted up so the entrails could be taken out. Male pigs are always 'loaded', so the penis is removed first, otherwise it sours the meat. Sow's meat is generally considered to be more tender. The guts went to the offal pit and the carcass to the Fromm family, who've owned the butcher shop at Oxford for generations. There it was turned into wonderful little packages of whatever you wanted. Keith came back with an enormous amount of recently dissected and bagged pig — bacon, hams, roasts and chops — which precipitated the beginning of my ever increasing number of freezers. Now I had my own bacon. I'm a bacon fanatic and I could hardly wait for the first taste. To my surprise and disappointment I didn't like it. It was not the streaky bacon I was used to. This was real bacon — thick-sliced meaty rashers. It took me many breakfasts to get used to it, and then to like it.

I had spent time getting quotes for all the work now underway. I was discovering that the high country practice is to pick someone and then stay with them. It is the longevity of the relationship that is so important. Sometimes in the city you don't give yourself enough time to know contractors because there is always another option. I rather liked this other way of doing business. Country suppliers' ultimate asset is their integrity and fairness and the fact they are not gouging anybody. It was almost insulting to suggest they could cut their prices or costs any further.

Meanwhile, Keith had started renovating the manager's house. Having learnt basic skills on the pigsty, I elevated myself to builder's apprentice. Occasionally, Anthony also lent a hand. Having haunted second-hand and demolition yards for years, I was the one sent to find or collect whatever materials were needed. One day I headed back from Placemakers in Christchurch with my purchases heaped high and hanging over the end of the truck. By the time I got to the flats at the start of Old West Coast Road it was pouring with rain and the tape holding the mountain of goods was melting. There was a long way to go before I even began the climb over Porters Pass. I stood forlorn at the side of the road with nothing to bind the precarious pile. I had forgotten one of the country driver's basic rules: always carry rope. Luckily I was saved by a real country driver.

The manager's house needed a lot of work: new carpet and lino, a covered porch-way at the back door, Batts for insulation, replacement doors and windows, a deck, a good coat of paint and a washing line. There had been a passage linking the back of the old limestone cottage to the manager's house. We separated them, blocked off The Limestone end and made it into a manager's office. Then we fenced the house and garden. Lastly we needed firewood, one of the fundamentals of high country living.

Providing wood is the station owner's responsibility; fires burn continuously from March to November most years, sometimes even longer, consuming fuel at a great rate. The fire heats not just the house but often the hot water too. That winter I bought $2000 worth of firewood, resentful at having to pay for larch and pine when I was surrounded by it and only needed someone to cut it.

Although still at Cora Lynn, Andy Bitmead was coming up regularly to establish a work programme. This was underpinned by the farm advisor's plan but Andy was keen to put his own mark on it. We were in the process of selling stock, partly to earn some income and also to reduce stock numbers and bring us into line with the somewhat arbitrary limits set by LINZ. After a morning with Andy inspecting the winter feed and hay paddocks, I joined Simon at the old cattle yards further up the road. With the help of a man from Wrightson's we were to tag steers before sending them down to 'God's flats' to finish fattening. The yards were grim, built in about 1940 and in a very bad state of repair. They sat, or slumped, on a slope at the bottom of the quarry paddock. Huge rotten gates hung off broken hinges. We had to run the steers through the race twice: once to put tags in their ears and then again to board the stock truck. It was a battle that lasted all afternoon. Cattle and humans were soon up to mid shins in mud from the springs above and the winter thaw.

My job was to herd the steers through the two high-fenced holding pens and then into the race. Each time I drove another group forward into the next pen or the race I was ready behind the massive gates, pushing with all my might to stop the steers turning and rushing back the way they'd just come. They charged noisily along the narrow race until slowed by the sharp angle that brought them to the crush. Up until then I thought a crush was an adolescent passion. This was a mechanism designed to grip the cattle's necks and hold their heads relatively steady. Like everything else it was broken, no more than a stump that had been extended with a makeshift piece of iron. As the crush caught them and clamped their necks they bucked and looked extremely out of sorts. Tags were punched into each ear, one giving the herd number, the other the individual cow number. The French Charolais were the most ill-tempered, the Herefords slightly less put out and the lovely Black Angus perfectly peaceful.

The stock truck backed in and we propped up the high-sided loading ramp with railway sleepers, waratahs and stumps. Then we began pushing

Snow and I at the cattle yards. I am pouring on drench and he is injecting copper to counteract the very low copper content of Castle Hill's soil.

the steers through the pens and race again, up the ramp and into the truck. Just as the driver was climbing back into the cab, a piece of corrugated iron dropped off the cattle shed roof and cut his finger. That was it. We would be reported to OSH and this would be his last time on Castle Hill. He would not collect stock from us again. But, I protested, constantly covered in plasters, it's a mere scratch. I ended the afternoon with an aching back that lasted for several days.

New cattle yards were in the development plan but this meant they had to move up the list, and I began looking at designs and building materials. I enumerated for Colin what I now saw as the capital investment and development for the rest of that financial year. Apart from fixing the manager's house and tidying the farm sheds, it would be getting the fences and gates in order, making sure there were troughs or a water source in each paddock, growing the healthiest of winter feed and building the combined cattle and deer yards.

A week later I was helping Simon and my brother Malcolm nick the ears of thirty Merino rams to take blood samples. For someone who hates needles and anything to do with cutting and blood, despite everything I had gone through with John, it was difficult work. The samples were sent to Lincoln University to be tested for the foot rot gene. The ram is the main determinant of how susceptible a lamb will be to foot rot and once we knew the results, we could make some decisions about whether to cull any of those whose grades indicated a high likelihood of producing offspring with foot rot. Foot rot, like cold sores, is a virus. It is activated in the right conditions: warm humidity and wet pastures. It cripples the sheep and causes considerable pain. In the worst cases, they drop to their knees to reduce the hurt, restricting their movement and ability to feed. They become skinny, unable to produce milk and therefore unable to feed their lambs. A lactating ewe is said to need the equivalent of five litres of finely cut grass each day.

The Merino wool auctions were underway at Pynes in Christchurch, the last year they would be held there. Although wool prices were down, this was my first big sale. I could hardly stay away. It was very different from the furniture and art auctions I was used to. Everything moved at speed. The buyers, mostly from overseas with the main ones from Italy, Australia and China, yelled and screamed their bids and the auctioneer up on a pulpit-like stand repeated the figures in a monotone, bringing down his gavel every couple of seconds. You had to be quick to get down the prices. From our first clip of ninety bales, I was looking forward to finding out what our best three bales of finest wool — 17.7 micron with vegetable matter of 0.4 (very clean) — would bring. Somehow a mistake was made and they were left out of the auction. To add insult to injury, four bales of our 18.2 micron did not reach reserve.

The budget prepared by the farm advisor had estimated $10,000 for shearing. The actual cost was more than twice that. The wool had been predicted to sell at $7.30/$6.50 a kilo. The auction prices were very different — an approximate average of $6.60. There was no way I would get the return the budget had indicated. Driving home on Old West Coast Road I could feel pricking behind my eyes. It had been a while since I felt incipient tears. It was more usual to suddenly be caught by overwhelming tiredness. I would pull over and sit on the side of the road knowing no one would recognise me and stop to ask what was wrong. Then I would weave my way home, switch on all the lights, turn the electric blanket up high, put on 'Redemption Song' and poach a couple of eggs. Maybe I'd sit dully in front of the TV for a short time, mentally chastising myself for not reading, and then head to bed. After years of married life and sleeping on the left-hand side, I experimented with the right.

Work, Dad's Army and the weather were my salve. The first couple of seasons, each throw of the weather dice filled me with excitement, gratitude, dismay — all iced with the knowledge it couldn't be changed. I started to take my morning toast out to read the rain gauge on a fence post beside the house. Then at least I would be on a par with the locals, who always seemed to be able to quote how many millimetres they'd had the previous night. Unused to living in a place with four distinct seasons, I thought the spring extraordinary after the bleakness of winter. It arrived with imperceptible changes, teasing almost, as the snow melted and fell again. Lulled by an extended period of fine weather, I dug and planted a herb garden in front of the limestone cottage. Two weeks later it was covered in snow and the tender seedlings beneath did not survive. In winter and early spring, the landscape was perfectly manicured. Then within a melt, the living things underneath broke free. All the weeds started to appear: thistles and briars, borage on the river flats, barley grass in the sheep camps on the ridges, and digitalis, known as shepherd's loo paper, which by summer stood two metres' tall. That first spring we had a particularly bad weed infestation; any disturbance of the soil stirred them to life.

Seasons change like moods, and change moods. Spring has always stirred in the loins and brought an involuntary smile. I had the equivalent of what I now know as doe fever. I'd be driving and thinking, 'How come I feel so warm and happy and embracing?' And then I'd look out the window at the haze of bright green buds like fists about to open, the sheep in the station paddocks up to their bellies in clover.

Spring, while exciting and satisfying for the farm, reminded me I was alone. Friends told me this was the time to treat myself, to open a bottle of fine wine and cook a great meal. I loved the sentiments and understood the reasoning. I might even get out my recipe books. But too often I would poach an egg instead.

The other comfort was my growing circle of friends. Jess and Stewart

Gunn in particular regularly invited me down for a meal, to watch their
two kids at the local school's sports day, or just to hang out. They'd call up
and say they were having a few people over for drinks and why didn't I join
them. Mostly you changed your boots and went as you were. Then one day
I arrived to find the drinks were on the chiffonier and the other guests had
changed a lot more than their boots. After that it became a bit of a joke.
When they called I'd make sure to ask if the drinks were on the chiffonier
or in the pantry. Gillie and Tim Deans are another great family who run an
open-door policy. Farming people have children, and they are very tolerant
when you turn up with four under three. 'Bring 'em in,' they say. Everyone

adopts that welcoming way. If you have friends with you, then they are part of you and they're welcome too. I got to know the Deans when Gillie rang me not long after I arrived to introduce herself. She knew what it was like to come to a new place. She was interested in art and knew I was too. Dinner parties and lunches at their place are always stimulating affairs.

By this time I was desperate for some help around the house. I was used to having someone to clean up and organise me in Auckland and I had not come down to the farm to do housekeeping again; there was enough to clean up outside. First I asked around. Next I put an advertisement in the *Malvern News*. When it was published, two digits in my phone number were transposed. I shrugged and forgot about it for a couple of weeks, until the phone rang. It was Caroline Hawkins, asking about the job. Such initiative and perseverance — it was hers. And so arrived the first of the 'Witches of Springfield', the 'Witch' here defined as in the *Concise Oxford*; 'a fascinating or bewitching woman'. As well as cleaning and washing, Caroline would bake favourite recipes like gingerbread cakes or cook lunches for whichever contractors were working on the station. She was horrified there was no recycling on the farm; everything was going to the communal rubbish bins at Castle Hill Village or to the pit. I had bought huge plastic containers to store the dry feed for the pigs, hens and dogs. One evening I found them in the garage with beautifully hand-lettered signs. 'Plastic — remove lids, wash and squash.' 'Glass — do not leave caps on bottles.' Newspapers and magazines were to be flattened and form neat piles on a shelf. Every so often, she took them home for her local recycling collection. As time passed, more of her talents emerged. She's a dab hand with hammer and nails. She rearranged the garage, built cupboards, and put up shelves with mitred corners and boards to hang a farm's hundred keys.

Keith and I continued to traverse the farm to tidy up after Geoff and the fencers. The rubbish pit became a familiar destination, not just for fencing detritus but also for the endless loads of rubbish. It was not just from our restoration work. There was rubbish dumped everywhere and anywhere. The sheds were filled with generations of the broken, the maybe-it-will-come-in-handy again. I felt more confident driving across country with someone beside me, although I'm not sure I can say the same for Keith. Over the next year, when he was with me he was constantly hitting my left knee to remind me to take my foot off the clutch. Like applying the brakes going into a skid, many of my natural instincts were not just wrong but dangerous. It was Keith who taught me to approach a hill straight on and not try to drive up or down it on the diagonal. I used to hang at the lip of a steep slope, not quite ready to trust that going straight down with a fully engaged clutch in low gear would keep us safe. I learnt how to use the four wheel drive and to keep pressure on the accelerator light if I lost traction in muddy or slippery ground. He taught me to read the landscape and to be aware of red tussock, which meant it could be boggy. In that first year we did a lot of work upgrading the tracks out the back of the station. Castle Hill is criss-crossed by a multitude of springs and the water table is constantly changing. Before Pete began putting in culverts, we ran the risk of getting stuck and so tended to drive out the back in pairs so that if one truck got into trouble there was another there to pull it out.

November and December were busy months. We had winter feed and pasture to sow and while we weren't aerial topdressing, we were spreading lime and fertiliser on the flats by truck. We were making baleage and hay. December began with a weekend visit from my former Gifted Kids' colleagues Julie Mills and Pam Hook, who had been warned to be prepared to work. The Roadman's hut was next on Keith's list, once he had finished at the manager's house. The Roadman's was small — two rooms and a lean-to added later — and in very poor condition. It had become another of the sheds where people dumped or stored everything they didn't want or didn't know what to do with. We cleaned out crates of old brown quart beer bottles, wire-wove beds, kapok mattresses and an amazing variety of other junk until there was just broken-down bare rooms with holes in the floor. We kept some pennies and long tongs made out of No 8 wire, a mouth organ, old cigarette papers and a few bottles which all sit on the mantelpiece now. The people who stayed there clearly lived modestly; I found no sovereigns.

The station's development plan had included deer. At the time of the purchase, I had been in two minds about whether to keep them. There were four generations of Scottish Reds roaming an enormous block: stags, hinds, weaners and fawns all in together and interbreeding. They had not been rounded up for eighteen months and therefore had not had TB tests.

I learnt how to use the four-wheel drive and to keep pressure on the accelerator light if I lost traction in muddy or slippery ground.

Cattle muster beneath the station's limestone rocks. The lines on the hill are made by sheep. We use horses on Castle Hill because not all the farm has tracks. They are quiet — and when you're riding you're free to concentrate on the stock, and not the steering wheel.

To get them off the farm would be difficult. The deer block was well along a tired farm track that crossed over the braided Porter River. Its flow varies enormously so you can never be sure which ford will be safe. I did not see how a stock truck could reach them or how we could take them out to another paddock on the Torlesse Range. We obviously couldn't shoot them all. We then looked at keeping them as a way to put some diversity into the farm's production. Surely, the reasoning went, prices for velvet and venison could not be down at the same time as wool and meat prices. Unfortunately they were; venison and deer velvet had not just gone down,

Cattle in the lee of the limestone escarpment of Prebble Hill.

they had collapsed. However, I like deer. I particularly like the idea that they need minimal attention; an annual TB test, a drench and a draft at weaning time. I also enjoy the occasional venison meal. I could see no acceptable way of removing them from the farm, so I decided to keep them. The farm advisor, who had become rather adept at spending the wealthy widow's money, came up with what he thought a fair price. The herd was categorised and tallied, although how that was managed in an area the size of a small game park eluded me. They became part of the inventory of stock and machinery that I did not see before it was signed off. I ended up paying more than $39,000 for two hundred and thirty four deer.

I was moaning about it to my old boys' network over a few beers and whiskys at one of our regular Friday night 'staff meetings' when they suggested they had just the person to give me some advice. 'Just the person' arrived, looked at the deer and suggested that if we put up some netting and a length of calico to stretch like a wing against a fence, we'd capture the deer before they realised it. Then, he suggested, the only other thing we needed was a small pen-like structure made with plywood. I looked at them leaping ten feet in the air, and at the stags with huge, ten-pointer antlers, and wondered how those would work with curtain material. I was not convinced. We wandered further into the 'Serengeti'. He thought the deer looked very pale. It must be that they had Johnes disease, a wasting disorder that is highly contagious. I checked the Lincoln Technical Manual that had sat on the dining table since I arrived, ever ready to be consulted. I looked up Johnes, not easy when you think it is spelt with a 'Y'. It was very bad.

Next day he came with gun and suggested culling the really sick looking ones in the hope of halting the disease's spread. After the third knock-over, I became really uneasy. This was madness. We were choosing them on little better than a whim and a pale coat. We needed solid information before there was further carnage. We took samples from the intestines and livers of the three we'd shot and sent them to the vet to be tested. There was no evidence of Johnes disease. It had been a bad experience and I wanted another opinion. Keith told me he had a friend from Oxford who'd recently sold a deer farm for $2 million. He came to have a look and made much better sense. One piece of advice was that I needed to put chains and padlocks on the gates by the Porter River immediately. If I had fencing gangs going in and out on their way across the farm, it would only take someone to slip up once shutting the gates and the deer would be out.

Just days later, while I was in Auckland, Keith called. The deer were out. They had gone deep into the bush way up the back of the station. Unlike sheep and cattle, deer are totally undomesticated. You can see in their eyes they are still wild. They are intelligent, fast and suspicious and don't muster easily. Keith called a mate with a helicopter and with a few foot soldiers, and after a lot of hard work, they finally got most of the deer back in their paddock. Three years later, shooters are still knocking over tagged deer in the back gullies out by the Emu Block. The cost of that exercise in retrieval was over $5000. That put their price up to $44,000 and I still hadn't earned anything from them. It was a very expensive lesson on how you should do things immediately you're told. There's a saying that the difference between a good farmer and an average farmer is three days. A couple of months later I had a call to ask me to a meeting to discuss local progress in controlling TB. My herd still had not been tested because they had yet to be brought in to the yards. I thought it best not to turn up. I needed to do something about the deer first.

There was tailing before Christmas, another job for contractors — a musterer and a tailing gang. I had two of my granny-kids, Will and George, with me and we went to watch them bring the ewes and lambs in to the tailing yards. The musterer was bringing down the mobs from Prebble and Gorge Hills. It was extraordinary to watch his dogs going round the steep sides to mop up the sheep while he stood some distance away directing them with whistles. Everything would be going well and then a dog would go the wrong way and the musterer would start using 'f' language, deeply shocking the kids. Once the mustering season was over in New Zealand, he worked as a builder in England until the next season. Working between hemispheres is common practice today. Some of the other farming contractors do fencing in the United States in the off season. A number of our local shearing gang shear in Italy in the abattoirs and in Norway in their seasons and earn lot more money than here. Tailers might also do shearing or drive tractors and haymakers. They all must multi-task and be multi-skilled to survive.

The tailing was accompanied by loud music booming from the tailing gang's trucks. They used a huge wheel with docking cradles shaped like shin pads set around its rim. It was the first time I had seen this kind of setup. Big beefy guys stood beside it. The first one lifted a lamb onto the cradle and clipped an ear; left for a ewe or right for a ram. The wheel turned and the next man sizzled off the tail with a gas-fired blowtorch and tossed the tail into separate ewe or ram piles.

The head of the gang was doing the mulesing, a practice to stop fly strike, one of the cruellest things that can to happen to a sheep. Using blade shears, he cut off the folds around the anus of the ewe lambs, removing the wrinkly skin characteristic of Merinos. The smoother scar tissue that results has less wrinkles and less wool to trap faeces that can encourage fly strike. Every now and then he'd pop a roll-your-own between his lips, stop the wheel and sharpen his blades on a stone. New Zealand Merino farmers no longer use mulesing after the international animal rights group, People for the Ethical Treatment of Animals (PETA), began a very effective campaign to stop US stores carrying clothing made from Australian and New Zealand Merino wool unless the producers had contracted to no longer use mulesing.

The mulesing man also put rubber rings on the balls of the ram lambs to neuter them. Then they became wethers. He gave me a lesson so I could help and although I was slow, holding up the production line, I learned to reach up, pull and twist down, flicking on the rubber ring and making sure it was pushed up firmly against their stomach. The most important thing was to get both balls down. We also injected with B12 and I sprayed antibiotic disinfectant over the scorched tail and mulesing. Conversation was very blokey. There were lots of jokes and games, like naming countries and songs beginning with each letter of the alphabet, to help keep everybody alert. I managed my tasks on the line well but I had nightmares about the mulesing. Sometimes I thought the cuts rough and deeper than needed, and as I was standing next to him, the bleating of the lamb and the cutting of the flesh got into my head; I can still see it three years later. This was enough to make me stop the practice on Castle Hill, regardless of the fact that when I contracted to New Zealand Merino I could no longer use it. That year I didn't see any of our Merinos with fly strike, nor the next. In 2007 we had half a dozen because the spring was hot and wet and humid, ideal conditions. We managed to save three of the sheep by using our blade shears to cut around the affected area which was then sprayed liberally with Maggo; but they still don't look strong. It takes a lot to recover from flies in the belly. Unless caught in time, they eat the sheep from the inside out.

The days in the tailing yards were long, and for the first time I was experiencing concentrated manual work where, as part of a production line, I needed to keep up with everyone else. I used to wonder why country people stopped at 10 o'clock and again for lunch. I'd come from offices where morning coffee and lunch, if you had it, was quite often taken at your desk. I soon realised that the physicality of farm work meant you needed those breaks to recharge. And I learned a lot over a mug of tea: what other people were doing, what other farms' lambs were like, prices at the last clearing sale. Contractors are like a mobile farming section of the newspaper. They travel far and wide. I made sure to provide good morning teas, great, well-filled, white bread sandwiches and slabs of fruit cake, because by the time they reached us they had been on road since the first lambs were on the ground in July. In our valley, we were almost the last on the circuit. You need to look after your contract workers because word gets into the pubs and is passed around. If there are choices, you want them to pick you when you want them and not when it suits them. These are real worries as the number of tailers and shearers is shrinking rapidly.

I threw a big thank you Christmas party for all the contractors and others who had worked on the farm since I took over. They told me it was great to feel part of the re-birth of such an amazing place and brought me a beautiful bouquet of pink and white flowers, a difficult thing to do when there are no flower shops for tens of kilometres. Keith presented me with a knife, a Kershaw with 'Bonnie Lass' engraved on it. Every farmer needs a good knife to hang from their belt. I keep mine in my truck. I went up to join the family for Christmas in Auckland and was back at the farm on Boxing Day. Andy and family had moved in and the old shearers' quarters had a new occupant, Harry White, who was straight from Lincoln University. He wanted a job from Christmas through to March or April before finishing his helicopter training and then heading for England. He would work with Andy around the farm.

On New Year's Day there was lunch for the
locals and some of the family. Kate and I hired
a spit and Rob roasted an annual draft Castle
Hill hogget. There were many people I wanted
to thank for making me so welcome over the
last four and a half months. Christmas to New
Year is one of the busiest periods in the farming
calendar, but almost everyone came. It was fine
and hot, with licks of snow still sitting in the
gullies and basins along the tops of the ranges,
a perfect high country day. I felt at last I was
really beginning to get involved in the farm. I
still didn't know very much, but it was more
than I did a couple of months earlier. Working
with Keith and Simon, moving and caring for the
stock, had made me feel closer to the realities of
farming. Even if I was messing up, it was me that
was messing up. The first manager was gone,
Andy was now in place and Dad's Army had
been re-assigned. Keith and Owen could turn
their attention full time to the restoration of the
historic buildings.

There had been change upon change and
I felt I hadn't really found the rhythm yet. I was
dipping into some of the many things that make
farm life. I was used to going to an office where
I did pretty much the same thing each day and
I could predict what I would be doing during a
week. Now I was working in a place where
I might start off to move sheep and be diverted
by bulls loose in the yard. Or draw up a schedule
for the next six months and then the weather
would force a change. It was all approximate, all
things over which I had no control. Nevertheless,
I thought I was starting to see a pattern. My next
decision was a big one — whether to get out of Merinos, as many others
were doing.

*Every April we bring
all the sheep in for
their annual medical:
a pre-tup drench and
mineral boosters.*

Now I was working in a place where I might start off to move sheep and be diverted by bulls loose in the yard.

CHAPTER 6

A fresh start

Mustering across
the Porter River
with Midge.

I needed a new tractor; that had become all too clear during the reign of Dad's Army. The farm inventory included two Deutz tractors and as I like Deutz bubbles I thought the tractors should show quality. Instead one did not start below ten degrees and the other coughed and choked. I began writing to dealers asking for information. Tractors are expensive items and farmers take great care when they buy new ones. Everyone in this business wants to get the best for the least amount of coin. Warwick 'Waka' James at Benmore Station had recently been through the same exercise, and on his recommendation I looked at John Deeres and decided, with knee-deep snow in mind, on a 100 hp model, even though it was more expensive. The winter of 2006 showed it was worth every cent as we went through one of the worst snow storms in Canterbury for a century. I traded in as much as I could to cut the cash cost — two old tractors, a grubber, a broken-down trailer and the silage wagon. The last was probably a mistake.

In December contractors had been on the flats making baleage and in January we were cutting hay for winter feed. I'd been told Castle Hill has one hundred and thirty days of winter — one day for each kilometre the station is from the main south road, according to local lore. It is high and cold and needs a huge amount of winter feed. My first winter and spring had been atypical: because there was relatively little snow, the stock had been able find enough to eat in the ground and we only needed to feed out occasionally. The farm traditionally made silage, which is cheaper than baleage, but I disliked it.

Castle Hill's silage pit had become contaminated when it was left open during the winter. I could have had it cleaned out and started again but I was aiming for a model farm and I did not like the way silage pits looked, covered in ugly black plastic held down with tyres. I thought fields lined with baleage in long white or green wrapped rows, or studded with plastic wrapped 'lozenges', much tidier. I also had read that baleage contained higher dry matter content than silage, which meant it is more nutritious, a claim silage proponents dispute. Another benefit was that it was ready-packaged for sale, and I was hoping there would be enough for us to sell some. Andy was keen to do baleage and hay, which was what they did at Cora Lynn, but the drawback with baleage is that it is much more labour intensive to feed out and more expensive to make. After three years, I have begun to reconsider silage because it is a quarter the cost of baleage.

The new John Deere arrived — big, green, very high, and with a cab crammed with the latest technology: hydraulic seats, air conditioning, a heater, a CD player and an FM/AM radio that had the best reception on the station to keep you company as you work. I looked it over. I suddenly had memories of the big red quad bike John and I bought to use on Moturoa Island, where cars are banned. I had a short practice run in Auckland and then it was shipped north. At Moturoa I was demonstrating how to drive it to my thirteen-year-old son Joe when I roared into a post and broke my leg. I'd rarely been on one since.

Now the John Deere loomed over me, a vastly more formidable machine. Harry gave me a quick lesson in a big field and then I thought I'd take it for a little drive along the road to the baleage paddock to see if I could operate the tines well enough to pick up a bale. In the John Deere all the foot pedals are close together. As I reached the gate I saw a car coming and realised to my horror I could not stop. I roared out into the middle

of the road pushing every pedal I could find until it finally came to a halt. Terrified I had crushed the car and wrecked the expensive new tractor, I opened the cab door and took a deep breath. There was a startled driver but no damage.

Since then I have grown to love the John Deere. It is really comfortable, deliciously warm in winter and it turns well, as I discovered raking the lucerne paddock. But there are drawbacks. I find driving a tractor with so many gears and levers controlling so many different parts and positions — up, down, back, forward — like rubbing your stomach while patting your head. Even though you are surrounded by glass in the cab, you still don't have the same visibility as on the good old Massey, a more recent acquisition, where you are totally exposed to the elements but can see everything. I now drive the John Deere slower than anyone else — like a tortoise, which is unusual for one who has always been a hare.

The total opposite of the shiny new tractor was Old Blue. I had been driving the station's red Hilux but in one of the sheds there was a broken-down 1970s Land Cruiser which had been included in the plant and machinery inventory. I'd bought it for $1250, together with a spare motor we've yet to find. I turned down a number of offers for Old Blue, even though it was not going, because that vintage of Land Cruiser is one of *the*

high country trucks. I had it towed into Darfield, where South Terrace Motors gave it a major service and fixed the hydraulics and the brakes — as much as they could. When it was ready, Andy's wife Jo drove me down and was to follow me back in case it didn't survive Porters Pass. But the truck was going so slowly, no matter how hard I tried to make it go faster, that she was soon fed up with trailing behind. I told her if I wasn't home in two hours they had better come looking. Some time later, Andy was out talking to the fencers along the straight to the farm when he heard a terrible sound and then became aware of an awful smell. Old Blue and I appeared round the corner. I had driven all the way in four-wheel drive in the lowest of the gears, and probably undone some of the garage's good work.

Old Blue became my truck, full of idiosyncrasies: there were wires hanging out of the dashboard, the windscreen could be opened but the side windows never closed, you had to use the outside handles to open the doors, the springs were coming through the seat, there was no power steering, of

Housing dogs well shows respect for their vital role on a farm. The new Castle Hill dog kennels were built off the ground to keep the dogs warmer and to allow waste to be hosed away.

course, and it had the biggest thinnest steering wheel. To kick it into life, there was a black button on the dashboard which had to be held down for a count of thirty before the engine would turn over and fire. When tipping junk into the rubbish pit from its tilting tray, I would have to zip round and jam a block in under the rear wheel before it slipped backwards into the hole, and the hydraulics often stuck, which meant you then drove round with the tray up until they reactivated and you could lower it. It is sky blue, a very un-male colour, which is why I like it.

In the station's stock calendar, New Year means 'Father's Day' for the bulls. We only had five to put out to the cows and heifers, including the two bought at Kakahu just before I arrived. The sixth had to be sent to the works after it developed a swollen and crooked back leg which meant it would not be able to mount. Nevertheless, Andy was fairly confident the five remaining bulls would be sufficient. We would find out in May when we pregnancy-tested the cows and heifers.

Weaning also took place in January, separating the lambs from the ewes. I had been deafened by everyone telling me that Castle Hill was just a breeding yard for store lambs. Everything, apart from replacement stock, should either be sold to be killed or go to farms with better feed and a more forgiving climate to be fattened and finished before going to the freezing works. Andy was barely a month on the station, with no experience to prove otherwise, and so that is what we did. We brought them all into the sheep yards, drafted them off the ewes and trucked them out. It was also the season for another of what I think of as the 'Ds' of farming: docking, dipping, drafting, dagging and drenching. Drenching was definitely something I could help with. The sheep are penned in the yards and then twenty or so are pushed up a narrow race. You pack them in so they can't move and start at the back, pushing your way between pairs, holding them with your knees as you grab one round the neck, tilt its head back and prise open its mouth. Then, still holding them steady, you insert the nozzle of the drench gun in the side of the mouth and squirt in the drench full of goodies to keep them parasite free along with a host of vitamins. It was great work for my quilted thighs.

For the first couple of months drenching, my index finger keep getting in the way as I pulled their heads back and they ended up munching on it while I tried to insert the nozzle. Practice, while not making perfect, has definitely improved my technique. Inoculations were also hard to master. We were giving B12 and anti-abortion injections to our hoggets. Quite apart from handling the needle, not something I will ever be comfortable with, there's the difficulty of holding a strong writhing animal as you part its wool and inject it as quickly as you can. There's quite a technique to the way you flick in the needle to hit the right spot. Both Andy and I managed to inject ourselves in the process and finished the day with stiff and swollen fingers. Since then I have become really quite good at inoculating stock.

Merinos are not big sheep. You farm them for their wool primarily rather than their meat, and wool prices had collapsed. Australia had, and still has, tens of thousands of bales in storage. Ever since I'd moved to Canterbury I'd heard people talk about getting rid of Merinos in favour of breeds with a bigger, meatier frame, or moving in to beef and, on the lowlands, in to dairy. It was not a decision taken lightly. People like John Chapman and the Tripps at Snowdon Station said they had never wanted to get rid of their Merino stud, they were such lovely sheep to work with, but it made no sense any more. Whichever way they looked at it, it just didn't stack up financially. The loss of so much of the tops of the ranges to DOC in the tenure review process had further encouraged this shift away. (So had the influence of some overseas owners, who required their managers to look short-term to maximise returns.) Merinos are great scavengers and do well on the dry scree and limited vegetation of those altitudes, but in Canterbury they were almost becoming an endangered species. When everyone is abandoning something is often the time to stay with it, however, I did want to find a way to also have a bigger, meatier carcass.

I knew Paul Jarman at Cora Lynn had bought Dohney rams from the ex-All Black Richard Loe, who'd seen them first in South Africa. Andy was keen to try them at Castle Hill. A Dohney-Merino cross would give us more meat while maintaining the fine wool. It seemed a good balance and we bought six rams from Loe. We decided not to put any of the Merino rams out in May; instead we would put the Dohney rams over the top mob of ewes and the Southdown and South Suffolk (Black Face) rams would service the rest of the flock. I had also been reading and hearing about Perendales and thought we should try them as well for more lamb meat. They are good at surviving in cold conditions and great fossickers but Andy was not keen at all, foreseeing the extra work and complications in running three different mobs. Other people also tried to put me off buying Perendales, shaking their heads and warning, 'There's Perendales and Perendales'. People seem to have a love/hate relationship with them. One of the farmers down the valley refers to his as 'Prickdales'.

Despite all this advice, I went ahead and bought three hundred Perendale lambs from Quartz Hill and three hundred lambs from Stewart Gunn at Brooksdale. Stew's were delivered the Saturday the Blues were playing the Crusaders and he had painted them all with blue stripes. What I foolishly didn't realise is that you don't buy lambs because you have to feed them for a year before you can put them to the ram and start earning some money from their progeny. That is why people don't want to sell two-tooths, ready as they are to start producing lambs. At the time I was buying, there was a huge demand for Perendales. A major amalgamation of farms in the

Country cooking

MEAT-BEEF.

Eat

MORE.

1 Tongue and Cheek.
2 Blade.
3 Rib Eye.
4 Sirloin, Porterhouse and Fillet.
5 Spare Ribs.
6 Rump Steak/
7 Rump Roast.
8 Topside.
9 Cornercut.
10 Topside Steaks.
11 Thick Flank.
12 Flank.
13 Brisket-Corned.
14 Brisket-Rolled.
15 Shin.
16 Shin.

We're frequently cooking
outdoors, especially down
by the river, where we
picnic with neighbours and
visiting friends. Ross
Urquhart and I, centre,
share out the wine. The
Eat More Meat Beef
painting hangs on the wall
at Jess and Stew Gunn's
place at Brooksdale. Above:
Friends from Auckland at
the stock bridge over the
Porter River.

Lees Valley was underway and had I wanted to buy hoggets it would have been impossible; even the lambs I bought were very expensive.

Despite all the negative publicity, I really like Perendales. They are smart sheep with spirit and attitude, and I soon discovered the basis for all the Perendale jokes. They are no respecters of turn-of-the-century Merino fences. For Perendales, the grass is always greener in the next paddock. That is why they are my Westie Girls. I keep them west of State Highway 73, where we have done re-fencing and there is a much better chance of keeping them in. But I still haven't been able to drench them, they are so strong.

After buying the Perendales we made some rather strange decisions. First we culled our Merino hoggets, goodness knows why. It was definitely a mistake. Next I went off by myself to a sale of Merino ewes at Omarama, south of Twizel. I had already received advice from a young farmer who was no longer in Merinos about what I should bid for. I needed sheep that would transfer well from that lower, southern area up to Castle Hill. He recommended the Berwen Station capital stock, (the top mob, kept for breeding) which would clearly be much better than the annual drafts where they were simply culling the sheep. At the sale, I hated the fact that unlike antique or collectibles auctions, where I was knowledgeable, I did not know what I was doing. I bent down and pretended to look them over and condition score them, but it was all a front. Then I sat nodding at my agent, Craig Miller, and purchased four hundred and eighty five ewes for $60 each, having just sold my Merino hoggets for $56 a head. The Berwens were mixed age ewes — a few two-tooths, and four-tooths, six-tooths and full mouths. I thought that as they had already had lambs they would be practised at giving me a harvest. Unfortunately they did not do very well at Castle Hill and people have told me since that the conditions at Berwen are too different from the altitude and climate at this high country station. The stock finds it too difficult to adjust.

Several things had changed since Andy's arrival. I was now splitting my time fairly evenly between work on the farm and the start of the restoration programme with Keith and Owen. I was beginning to reach parts of the property I had not seen before. Andy was a great set stocker, much of it out the back at the foot of the Torlesse Range, and mostly with cattle. There were no horses and Harry was the only one who used the station's quad bike. We went out in the Land Cruiser and on foot. I was also establishing our boundaries with Nature Heritage and DOC. We were using GPS (Global Positioning System) to survey and map the station, a lot of it done in helicopters for DOC. Then we would walk the perimeter, staking the line. To begin with I completely underestimated the distances. Convinced we would be no more than a couple of hours, I would set out with a sun hat and maybe a bottle of water. It would often take an hour or more to reach where we were working. Once there, our route might take us up steep hillsides and through scrub-filled gullies or spring-fed bogs. The days were much closer to eight hours long. As a result I ended up eating everyone else's food, a trick you can pull only for so long.

Walking the perimeter made me realise how much the station was already under my skin. I had a slightly irrational reluctance to give up what I had come to think of as mine. I was constantly trying to push the boundary fence a little further up the Torlesse. But DOC was pushing the other way. While we were walking the Thomas Bush boundary near Castle Hill Village, they began saying that there were a number of people who felt they had not been given the chance to participate in the tender process when Nature Heritage, DOC and I were negotiating the terms of our partnership to purchase. Now DOC was telling me that it wanted more land and more access for this group. But if I acceded, when it came time for tenure review with LINZ I would have already traded all the land and access DOC wanted and I would have nothing left to negotiate with. I became so concerned with the ongoing talk about more access across the farm to the limestone rocks that I asked for and got a special clause added to my purchase agreement with Nature Heritage saying they would support me in my application for freehold when I went for tenure review. Three years on, I am no closer to what I was assured would be a speedy review and an unproblematic granting of freehold for those parts of the station that are still in Crown lease.

Now that I was learning more about what the farm and its stock needed, there were other reasons to watch the placement of the boundaries very carefully. There had been a few mistakes already. The first couple were while I was in Auckland and the old manager had been out with them. In one place he told them to bring the fence well inside the boundary, losing us metres. He said it was in case the black beech trees, through which the boundary ran, fell on the fencing. But that is not a problem with black beech. They are not tall trees, their branches are not prone to wind fall, and they hardly ever fall over. In another place, the fence that now goes part of the way up the north side of Hill 906 could have been left off entirely and the whole of that side of the hill grazed because the other side was precipitous drop off, a natural barrier.

I made an even bigger mistake when I allowed myself to be talked into giving up a valley where the aerial GPS showed the boundary going right down into a gully. It was a mixture of tussock and red tussock, which meant it was probably quite boggy, and I could see the fencers thinking, 'this is going to be difficult'. DOC was keen to keep the gully for itself and suggested giving me a smooth knoll instead. The knoll gave sheep little food and no protection from wind; they would have been much better down in the gully. But I was up against DOC and the fencer so I foolishly gave in. As I was to find out, the springs that dot the farm can be deceiving, bubbling strongly in winter and spring only to dry out and disappear in summer, whereas the wet land round the red tussock often never dries out. This matters on a farm where there is limited rainfall.

Fencing between the limestone rocks and the homestead, the manager's house and the compound was another issue. I wanted to ensure that there was a decent piece of ground between the boundary and our houses and buildings. Summer had introduced me to what I call the 'weekend warriors'. Their cars beaded the edges of the highway on either side of the entrance to the rocks and they took their path across one of our fields of winter feed. It was not unusual to have people wander right down to edge of the bank behind the house or the field behind the farm buildings, yelling if they saw you around the house or yard. It felt uncomfortable and invasive.

We laid out stakes to mark the boundary ahead of the fencing gang. There were times when the usual sounds of the farm — wind, the brittle burnt-off summer pasture underfoot, gulls, paradise ducks and the rise and fall of the skylark's song — were overwhelmed by the explosive thud of the post driver. The fencers were amazing to watch — they'd put a thick wooden post on each shoulder and then tramp up to the top of a really steep paddock smoking a roll-your-own and talking. Geoff ran between posts carrying waratahs, slim iron fence posts with three ribs, and a lot heavier than they looked. They took their post driver onto the most unlikely slopes and tight places.

They also had a new member on the fencing gang. One day a truck dropped a young guy at the gate to the old shearers' quarters where they were living during the working week. Craig had a beanie pulled down to his eyebrows over lank blond hair, trousers held up with a red kerchief and a sweater out at the elbows. He had seen Geoff's advertisement for another hand and hitched up from Christchurch. Not everyone would have considered him a good employment prospect but Geoff saw something in him and took him on. Since then Craig has become his best worker and heads his best team. Once, during the following winter, Craig's truck crashed trying to follow the fence line into one of those impossible places. I was determined not to start adding new wrecks to the landscape and sent them back with a tractor to bring it out. It took so long and it was so cold we became worried and went to find them with every beanie and mitten we had — and a few shots of whisky. They were half-way back when we reached them. It had taken a very long time to retrieve the truck and Geoff, driving a tractor without a cab, had a face frozen like an ice block.

2005 was also the beginning of a year of work on the old buildings. With so much needing to be done on the station, it probably seemed strange to some of those passing that I was spending time and money on old farm buildings rather than one of the three 'Fs'. But during those initial months, because I did not know anything about pastures or managing stock, I decided to tackle the things I did know and was comfortable with. One thing I knew I was good at was the reconstruction of buildings. I also believe in branding. Wherever I have been and whatever I've done, I have always placed great store on its power. Branding creates pride, and once you have pride in your surroundings, it empowers you to work in a much more positive and creative way. Doing up the buildings was just as important as fixing the fences and pasture in creating the Castle Hill brand. So, too, was saving and cherishing physical links to our relatively short past. I hate to see history falling over.

It was also true that in those first months people were saying dispiriting things about the place, about how Castle Hill was a difficult farm, always with the rider that 'she's on the tourist route and you'll do well on that'. One

of the diversifications that came out of the
loss of farm subsidies in the 1980s was the
move by some farmers into tourism and tourist
accommodation was part of my first business
plan for the station. It was in a prime location
— an hour from Christchurch international
airport and with a main road passing the gate,
with three ski fields in close proximity, rivers
where you could catch trout and wild salmon
in season, boulders to climb, caves to explore
and DOC reserves and parks all around for
tramping, climbing and mountain biking. But
tourism has its drawbacks. I met local farming
women who told me that eighty to ninety
per cent of the paying guests that sat down
at their tables were really nice and that they
learnt from their visitors while telling them
about farming life. But these were women who
did not want to farm, and there was no doubt
what I wanted most of all, and that was to
farm. Each day I arose hungry to know what
was going to happen out in the paddocks. As
the restoration work progressed, I began to
realise that for a woman alone it was too much
to farm and cook and serve and talk.

I thought we should start work on the
smallest and simplest of the buildings, the
Roadman's hut, which sat right beside the
highway and which I wanted to be able to
rent out to visitors. Besides, Geoff, the fencers
and Harry were in the shearers' quarters, and
the original limestone farmhouse, the gem of
the trio, would require specialist stonemasons.

Keith and Owen began taking off the corrugated iron sides of the hut
while they finished covering in the implement shed to keep the snow and
rain off the hay and my new tractor. The Roadman's was probably built
in the 1880s, and was one of a series of huts that were stationed along

the highways every twenty or so miles. It may not even have been there
originally, as a number of attempts were made to go over Porters Pass. The
road once turned and went straight up the valley, through what is now the
Korowai Reserve. Early road makers no doubt wanted to avoid crossing
the pass but the old route proved equally torturous. The construction of
the current road over the pass is a modern marvel of engineering and it

*Snow, the dogs and
I take a break after
four hours on foot
moving sheep.*

reminds me of the maps of the Panama to Anchorage Rally route, where little parachute symbols either side indicate the sheer drops beyond the tarseal. At some stage the Roadman's, as I called it, no more than one room with a lean-to, had another room added and became a musterer's hut and, eventually, a dry dump for rubbish.

Once Keith and Owen had removed the corrugated iron sheets, they began attacking the sarking and linings. I said I wanted to keep as much as we could of the old materials to retain the integrity of the building. I returned one afternoon after being out the back of the farm with Andy to find the whole thing stripped and held up by noggins. You could see right through it. They had found borer and ripped out anything with a trace of the tell-tale pinholes. I've lived with borer all my life so I sorted out all the pieces that could be put back in and saved the old nails where we could. I had them put back the old doors as well.

While it was stripped we decided to use silver paper and Batts for insulation, plywood for strength and then we put on macrocarpa tongue

Feeding out to the cattle in early winter.

and groove sarking. Keith had spent a lot of time restoring old buildings, first in England and then for DOC, and he knew the right craftsmen for the job, who use traditional tools and carved the correct kinds of profiles in the tongue and groove for the walls. We recreated the original multi-pane windows and top hung them as they would have been in the 1800s. There had been no inside lavatory and the most rudimentary of bathrooms; now it has a decent one of both. How jealous those early road men would be of such a warm and comfortable shelter, although in the snows of 2006 the pipes froze for two months. A contributing cause was my decision to hide the water tank out of sight round the back of the nearby Telecom shed. It did not get any sun there and even the water in the tank froze. People say that if I wish to avoid that happening again I will have to move it to the front, but I am reluctant as that would spoil the whole look.

I wanted the feel of the hut to be as close as possible to what the early owners would have known. There's an open fireplace and the furnishings are unpretentious and simple — painted pieces I bought originally for a bach at Haumoana on the coast south of Napier. Dick and Judy Frizzell lived there while they were building their own house and soon after they left I sold it in order to put more capital into the restoration projects.

At the head of the north-western bedroom you can still see initials carved in the sarking, probably by musterers. There are also names carved in the fire surround and on a slab of limestone that we found standing on the hearth. It now rests just by the entrance to the front door. There is no radio or television. People listen to their music and read or play cards or board games. It has an air of tranquillity and makes a great reading room and a place for a quiet whisky. Round the back of the hut, the old wood-burning stove leans against a tree. The long drop is still there and old railway sleepers form a bridge to nowhere. I found a photo of the hut with cows standing beside it in a pond of water in a 2004 calendar. I rerouted the water back to what is now the park, made a path of stepping stones to the front door from limestone I'd found, planted tussocks and fenced it round. Among the first people to stay there was an English couple. They thought it perfect; their only complaint was the lack of egg cups.

As the Roadman's neared completion, people began to stop or call to tell me they used to muster at Castle Hill when it was 28,000 acres, getting up at three in the morning to walk to the top of Castle Hill or Red Hill for the big annual muster. True to the web of connections which bind this area, the painter's wife, Rose, said her father had lived in the hut when he managed a road gang. She and her husband are a mobile version of the workers of her father's time. They travel between jobs and live in a bus. All they need is a place to park and a power supply to plug in to and they are self sufficient. Country workers can still make themselves comfortable in the most spartan of surroundings.

Locals began telling me they were really pleased I had restored the hut. They thought the old buildings were beyond recovery and had never imagined anyone would save them. It began attracting weekend artists

The Roadman's cottage

Built over a century ago, the Roadman's is one of several huts that were once stationed every twenty or so miles along the highway. Later it served as a musterer's hut. By the time I bought the station it was in a poor state of repair. We stripped it, strengthened it, redecorated it and we've turned it into a cosy little retreat.

THE HOME AND COLONIAL

who would perch across the road with their sketch pads. One time I met a woman taking photographs. She told me she makes miniatures of the huts around Canterbury and sent me a photo of her finished model of the Roadman's — a perfect replica the size of a matchbox. More recently I was given a limited edition, hand screen print from the late 1800s titled, 'On the West Coast Road, the Craigieburn Range, Castle Hill'. It came from John Rusbatch, whose father and grandfather had worked this section of the road and more than likely stayed in the hut. The print shows two coaches, drawn by five Clydesdales, and eight suited, hatted, bearded gentlemen passengers.

Life began to change in my first summer at Castle Hill as I came to know more people. I felt less isolated and lonely. With all the work being done around the farm there was an ever increasing group of contractors, tradesmen, and the occasional passing local up at the homestead for drinks after work each Friday.

The long summer twilight is a boon to the valley's social life. After winter when people go to ground, they are ready to socialise. At the Gunns' it is barely spring before the barbecue is wheeled out to the tennis court with its bare sides and dishevelled wire netting across the ends, the cracks through the playing surface like fissures after drought. There are kids in the Para pool and all ages on the court. Pet lambs and calves are alongside in the home paddock where they are being readied for the A&P Show. Summer's the season of picnics out the back of farms — rugs spread in the shade or by a creek or stream, bacon and egg pie, sandwiches, scones or biscuits, and tea and coffee made with water boiled in a thermette — and there is always fishing for those who like it. One day I went on a rare treat, a picnic with Keith and Chris up the Hurunui, one of the rivers that divide Canterbury. We stopped at all the deep holes Keith knew and he gave me my first lessons in fly fishing. It was a chance to start to see the proximity of farms and river gorges.

There were hare hunts that begin at dusk and are fantastic fun. We'd take a pickup or the Hilux with two or three guys on the back, usually sharing a gun, and maybe another in the passenger seat. I was often the driver because I didn't shoot. (I applied for a gun licence at the end of my first year at the station and later collected the paperwork from the police station in Darfield. I had to have two local referees and to buy a gun cupboard and screw it to a wall, shutting it with a double lock. I swatted up for my test and then decided I just didn't like shooting. It was the responsibility of holding a gun in my hand, of holding life and death. I have put it on hold for the moment, together with the 'big red smile'.)

In hare hunts you need a high-powered spotlight, plugged into the cigarette lighter on the dashboard, to find the hares. Once spotted, you keep it focused while the person at the wheel drives like hell towards the hare, and those with guns begin firing. I always hope as we're careening along that the person firing doesn't shoot through the cabin or through themselves. It is certainly something you do before you open the beer and wine. The dead hares are thrown in the back of the truck. Harry would pull off the tails to keep tally and take the carcasses back for the pigs. Some dogs will eat hare, others won't. Otherwise the hares are thrown in the offal pit.

It is more than just an evening's sport. It is vital to keep hare and rabbit populations under control. Hares, like rabbits, cause erosion and just four hares can eat as much grass as one ewe. The station's rabbit status is checked annually by Mr McGimpsky, the rabbiter, who brings his caravan and parks by the fertiliser shed. He then gets aboard his farm equivalent of a Vespa and with his dogs cruises around the fence lines, and on foot out the back, to estimate numbers and make sure they are not increasing. This year, 2007, he reported that our rabbit population is down on 2006. There doesn't seem to be his equivalent to keep track of hares although there are many more of them.

That year I had trips to Auckland for summer weddings and to Australia to celebrate a friend's birthday. Just occasionally I'd feel flat for a couple of days on returning from spending time with family and dear friends but it was hard to stay down for long in a place I was madly in love with. Aucklanders came visiting me, curious to see where I was living and what I was doing with my new life. Mostly city people, very few had friends or family in the South Island or in high country farming. There was, in those early days, some confusion about my role on the station. It took a while for people to appreciate that, while generous with my time, I was not on holiday. Now they arrive ready and willing to get their hands and boots dirty, to drive tractors, move stock, help in the yards, and feed the hens and pigs, rather than being entertained. They realise farming is my job.

The friendliness of the local people eased my loneliness after the first few months. Families are always getting together for dinners and picnics. From top right: Phoebe James, Lucy Gunn and Bridget James at Brooksdale; Jo Acland, Anna Guild and Mark Acland at the Guilds' High Peak Station in the Rakaia Gorge; with Stewart and Jess Gunn and their children Lucy and Fergus in the kitchen at Brooksdale. Dinner at Castle Hill with the Gunns (Brooksdale), the Smiths (Mt White), the James (Benmore) and the Hills (Flock Hill); as always the children entertain the grown-ups with a concert; John Chapman of Inverary Station, who has given such useful advice; in the mustering hut at Craigieburn Station with a local hunter.

High country mates

That summer was as capricious as winter and spring had been. Just as winter is particularly long at Castle Hill, summer is shorter than in most of Canterbury, and dryer. In January it could still be Swanndri-cold at the beginning and end of the day. Sometimes at dawn there would be thick cloud right down to the ground and time for another coffee or even a quick look at *The Press*, if you could manage to extract it from its tightly wound sleeve of plastic. It protects the paper not just from snow and rain but from its readers. At 8.30am there might be enough visibility to start moving sheep through dew-drenched pastures; fine flower and seed tops of the brown top glittering like crystals shot with red; sodden boots and trouser bottoms; spider webs hanging between bush and ground, each strand drawn in beads of water and light, fibrillating in the faintest movements of air; the night's moisture rising from the ground like smoke, sucked up into the rapidly warming day. An hour later the sun was like a weight above your head.

By February the land was noticeably drier. The paddocks out the back still held their green but the flats turned yellow and then ochre in less than a week. Gale force winds raised dust storms and crumpled caravans at the top of Porters Pass. I watched the Merinos in the paddocks across the road. They stood in dust coloured circles under a white sun, heads to the centre, each giving the next sheep a little shade. Or they drifted backwards and forwards like groups of sleepwalkers across fields of stubble that crackled like breakfast cereal.It was a worrying time for farmers. Drought conditions can damage the wool staple, lowering its value. I looked for rain and when even the smallest amount fell, I felt like celebrating though it was not enough to soften the soil.

Two of the older granny-kids, Will and George, came for the school holidays and went with me to the Sunday Riccarton market. We brought back boxes of fresh fruit and vegetables. Joe and Symmone and their kids, Leo and Chloe, and Kate and Rob and the twins were arriving over the next few days. I made sandwiches with farm bacon for lunch. George said, between mouthfuls, 'These are yummy and the view makes them taste even better!' Part of sharing paradise with my family and visiting friends was giving them a taste of the country, eating from the fields of plenty that I regularly drove through. New season's apples were piled in bowls and I was eating them morning, noon and night, each mouthful taking me back to Aunt Phyl and the Kumeu orchard. There was an expanding row of my home-made jams and chutneys on the top shelf of the pantry.

Midge outside The Limestone, the original homestead on Castle Hill.

It was hard to stay down for long in a place I was madly in love with.

While the Roadman's was being finished, I began plans for Keith's next project, the old shearers' quarters. It was a much bigger job than the hut, and would not be completed until near the end of the year. I justified the capital expenditure, telling myself it was being done for tourism. At first I thought it looked as if it might originally have been a railways hut or even a school building that had been moved onto the farm. I knew the two previous shearers' quarters had burned down but during the restoration, we found on the Pinex in the ceiling a pencil sketch of a man, alongside his name and the date, 1943. The local builders remembered him. Almost everyone who had seen the quarters told me it was too much of a mess to even try and renovate. Of course I did not agree. Initially I planned a conversion with four double bedrooms with en suite bathrooms and a kitchen and sitting room. I had the draftsman who had designed the station homestead draw up plans. But by the time I had council approval I'd changed my mind. I decided to restore it as it was.

It had been used as backpackers' accommodation and so I thought it would be perfect to accommodate family and friends who came to stay. There were three double bedrooms and two bunk rooms. The interior was Pinex and tongue and groove. We put on quarter-round beadings to give it a better finish, replaced the skirtings and fixed the doors and ceilings where there were holes. The old lavatories were replaced with new and the showers and bathroom area modernised. At a later stage we put French doors off the double bedrooms onto a new deck that ran down three sides of the building. By the back door we put a large wood box and a gas barbecue. Then I painted it white throughout and bought some swanky white linen, all of which made it rather out of keeping with its original role as shearers' quarters. So I re-named it Old Quarters and had to find alternative accommodation for seasonal gangs, like the shearers, down at the pub in Springfield.

There was a scramble to get it habitable in time for the first occupants in November — the crew of a photo shoot for Pumpkin Patch organised by my daughter Kate, who heads their marketing department. In order for them to have something to relax on, I bought two plump comfortable sofas for the sitting room only to discover they were too large to fit through the door. We had to break one of the windows. Despite this inauspicious beginning, Kate maintains it was their best catalogue because of the incredible beauty and variety of the locations they found on the station. Once they were gone, there was still finishing and furnishing to do and I wanted to keep it in period, as I had with the Roadman's.

There seems to be little love or desire for 1940s oak veneer chairs and tables and so a number of shops selling collectables and odds and sods have painted them or others have, or I've painted them. I never mind if they've lost some of their paint or one of the handles. They are practical, light and Somerset Maugham-ish. My regular trips to Christchurch to have my hair dyed always included an excursion through the second-hand and antique dealers in the triangle of High, Tuam and Manchester Streets, my favourites being Chris at Chaos Collectibles, Helen at Forget Me Not and my beloved Frank at Frank Cronin Antiques. I have been buying from Frank for probably thirty years as he has moved back and forth between Auckland and Christchurch. Frank is known throughout the trade as a really nice guy with an amazing eye for the unique and stylish, and as a proponent of the modest mark-up for a quick turnover. I always feel I am getting fair deal. It was from Frank that I bought the enormous mural that now stretches along one wall in the Old Quarters' kitchen.

I bought it several years ago when he was in Christchurch and I was still in Auckland. Every now and then I would call him to find out if he had new treasures and he would send photos of anything I thought sounded interesting. This particular time he said he had something a bit different but truly remarkable. He sent pictures. I bought it and had it trucked up. However, I hadn't quite sorted out the scale in my head and when the mural arrived I found there was nowhere it would fit so it went into storage, until we opened the Anderson Fernyhough Gallery. It was perfect on the large wall in the stairwell and everyone who passed loved it. When I left Gifted Kids, it went back into storage again until I bought the station. Frank had purchased the mural from the famous Christchurch fish and chip restaurant, Fail's, and it brings cries of recognition from old Cantabrians. It is a seabed scene, a mermaid at the centre surrounded by marine life. What I love about it is that the limestone rocks Castle Hill is so renowned for came out of the sea. Hanging a mural of life in the depths of the ocean in an inland high country sheep station is not as contradictory as it might at first seem.

Most of the rest of the pictures in the Quarters are scenic photos taken in 1950s New Zealand. For a long time I have collected early

My wonderful stock manager, Snow Cleaver.

White's Aviation hand-painted photographs, taken when White's was photographing emblematic scenes of the country. For the Old Quarters I chose South Island places: Arrowtown and the Rakaia, Kaikoura waves, Lake Matheson and early South Island stone bridges. An aerial of the royal yacht *Britannia* sailing up the Waitemata Harbour during Queen Elizabeth's first visit in 1953/54 is to remind me of my other home in Parnell. What I particularly like about the photos is their wonderfully individual quality. They were farmed out to a variety of painters, so there will be a number of versions of the same photo, of leaves in Arrowtown for instance. They took painter's licence — every house in Alexandra is shown with a red roof, which they clearly didn't have. My younger son, Joe, has an even larger collection of Whites' photos and he generously gave me some of his South Island photos to hang.

Once Old Quarters was finished, it became popular with my friends. It is also a favourite for locals, such as those who live at the foot of Porters Pass, who like coming to breathe our fresh air and stay a couple of nights. It looks east to the Torlesse, west to Craigieburn and the limestone rocks,

Old Quarters, the former shearers' quarters, renovated to create a place where friends and family can stay.

and straight ahead to Flock Hill and Mt Constitution. But despite all the positive feedback, there was a problem. Even as the Old Quarters was being finished I was changing my mind about being in tourism. I was no longer keen on the idea of having people I didn't know staying in the Roadman's and Old Quarters. I was so involved in the farm, I did not see how I could do both, even if I wanted to, and maintain the high standards I care about. There was also the experience of the pipes freezing at the Roadman's. That would not go well with paying guests.

In the meantime, I intended to go ahead and find the right people to restore the old limestone cottage, even though it would mean selling some paintings to fund it. I knew I could do it well and I hated to see it deteriorating. My brother, knowing how overworked my cheque book was as the huge bills for farm work continued to roll in, suggested I put the station on the market, buy a farm in Hawke's Bay and start making some money. A friend in Auckland advised me I would do much better investing in the property market up there but I was not interested in exchanging my hills for concrete and glass towers. Old codgers at a party for Harry's graduation from Lincoln University kindly told me that while they admired my pluck I would never make a go of it at Castle Hill. The country was just too hard.

Despite the occasional terror of facing piles of invoices on my own, when the biggest deposit in my bank account was my GST rebate, I was having too much fun to listen to them.

My brother . . . suggested I put the station on the market, buy a farm in Hawke's Bay and start making some money.

Old Quarters interiors,
furnished with gems
from my forays to
Canterbury antique and
second-hand shops.
The mural used to hang
in Christchurch's
famous seafood
restaurant, Fail's Café.

CHAPTER 7

Strategies for
survival

On Easter Monday 2005, my much loved Aunt Phyl died. She was ninety two and had reached the stage where everything was wearing out. On Good Friday I flew to Auckland when I heard she was deteriorating to join my mother and sister at her bedside. Aunty Phyl had been a lifetime reader of the Bible and had taken Sunday School for decades. There was a church directly across the road from the Knox Home where she was now living, and at six o'clock every Sunday night the ministers visited the home to hold a service. They were arranging the room and laying out the prayer books when I asked the minister's assistant if he could come and say a prayer with my aunt. He knelt by her bed and for the first time since I had been there her eyes opened. They had that fixed stare that looked to a distant unknown, but her lips moved as she followed the words of the *Lord's Prayer*.

The remains of the Tussock Block cattleyards.

Next morning I arrived early with a sixth sense she was ready and found her slipping away. Although I had watched her pain and prayed for the release

that comes with death, at that moment I felt a huge sense of loss and self pity. We have so few people who love us unconditionally, and I was running out of them. My eulogy at her funeral sounded like a *Country Calendar* episode as it recounted all the times spent with her on the orchard at Kumeu. Late the following afternoon I crossed a very misty Porters Pass on my way back to Castle Hill. The dull light and fog stripped the colour from the world beyond the windscreen, mirroring how I felt inside.

Aunty Phyl and Uncle George had no children of their own, and Malcolm, Philippa and I, and Kenneth, her only brother's son, were her sole beneficiaries. I considered how her bequest to me might best be used to remind me of her. She didn't drive until she was forty five and her only car was a blue Vauxhall Viva with a monsoon shield on the driver's window to cut the wind and rain. She always wore proper driving gloves in leather and crochet, a hat and a scarf and she would change from court shoes to her driving brogues once in the car. This meant that goodbyes took a long time while she got herself ready and then she would have trouble with the clutch and bunny-hop up the road for the first fifty metres. The back of the car was always filled with Sunday School props and apples she was taking somewhere; rugs covered the seats to protect the upholstery. By the time John and I opened the Classic Car Museum she had stopped driving and the car was sitting in her garage covered in rugs. I pumped up the tyres, charged the battery, cleaned the spark plugs and parked it in the museum but John thought it incongruous among his British roadsters and so we auctioned it the night of the opening. Alan Gibbs paid $3000, which went to the Gifted Kids Programme. The car was given to a member of the Vauxhall enthusiasts club.

I thought of Aunty Phyl and the florescent blue Viva and decided what I needed was a decent car that would take me safely anywhere on the station accessible to vehicles. I could not keep using the manager's Land Cruiser. The Prado was an automatic and really dangerous on any but the most benign of farm roads. Old Blue, while an eccentrically delightful drive, would never make it to the blocks out the back either.

At the time, there was a very funny and irreverent television commercial that showed a couple of Black Angus bulls carjacking a new Toyota pickup to visit the cows on the next door farm. The tag line was 'the unbreakable new Hilux', which certainly recommended it to me. I thought I'd buy one for myself. I chose the double cab model in 'Champagne', for obvious reasons, with a tonneau cover for the back tray and the biggest bull bars. The latter have proved useful when separating the rams from the ewes. Black Face rams in particular become very toey and a nudge with the front of the Hilux encourages them to leave their play pen. The children from Benmore Station were the first to spot me driving it home and reported that I had a 'sheep shagger', which is what they're known as around here, after one of the ad's more memorable lines. It had its baptism crossing the Kowai River, and the Gunns and I christened it with champagne at Lake Rubicon and named it Phyllis. Then the very next week I stopped off at the Springfield pub for farmers' Friday night and put my first ding in the bumper reversing into someone else's car. Aunty Phyl would not have approved.

Cars and trucks are a recognisable extension of their owners on local roads; not just farmers and farm workers and inhabitants from the surrounding towns, but also the other regulars — the stock, mail and courier drivers, the rural contractors and road maintenance gangs. It did not take long before people recognised Phyllis. In the city, neighbours can drive by without even making eye contact. Country people wave when passing. I spent some time experimenting with waves. What would be the right kind for a high country farmer? An index finger casually raised from the steering wheel, right hand lifted briefly, a wiggle of the fingers, or the arm to the elbow extended up and out from the window? I tried them all and settled on a right-handed half wave to the right with index finger raised, like a windscreen wiper.

At some stage on these regular drives I found myself starting to look at the fields I passed as a farmer might. Previously I'd driven through what I saw as scenery; now I found myself thinking that the wind must blow from the south west because of the position of shelter belts, or noticing who had Herefords or Charolais or Angus. Even when I was flying into Auckland, I'd find myself thinking, 'God, that's lush. It's so green and there are so many sheep per hectare.' So often when you pass high country fields, you can't see any sheep at all. If I happened to be driving with someone rural, I would not risk gestimating about matters like breeds. I rather prided myself that I could recognise a Merino, a Black Face and a Perendale but I was much less sure about Romney, Coopworth and Corriedale. I'd be saying something safer, like 'they've put down a lot of silage' or commenting on the pasture. I noticed the state of fences and cattle yards and whether the sheep were fat or thin, well fed or under fed. I thought of my sheep, cattle and deer not just as animals but as a rack of lamb and an eye fillet, or a high quality garment; and not just as a farmer and breeder but as a mother. I was jealous of pastures or stock that looked much better than mine. I was always jealous of Brooksdale's flats and constantly needed to remind myself that they have so much more rain than Castle Hill and lie a thousand feet lower, a truth constantly reiterated by old codgers in the pub who'd tell me, 'Chrissie, you've just got altitude against you, not attitude.'

It was April the first, and I thought I'd play an April Fool's on Andy, so I went down to the shed where we were doing some drenching and said, 'Andy, there's stock on the road!' He started to pack up quickly before my gleeful 'Big April fool!' stopped him. Then about an hour later Jo came running in to say that our two pigs were on the road. Oh yes, we thought, we've already done that. But when we went outside, there they were running and squealing while a group of pupils from St Andrews College tried to shoo them up the drive. They looked hysterical on the asphalt, like women in tight stirrup pants and high heels. We didn't have any dogs there so we grabbed a pig bucket full of nothing and banged it to try and lure them off the highway. They were uncontrollable, but in the end the thought of food triumphed over freedom and we herded them back into their enclosure. They had escaped through the fence which was weak. They were normally kept in place by an additional electric wire but this day the fencers were working up the road and had turned it off.

The weekend after Aunty Phyl's funeral, Oxford was celebrating one hundred years of the town's A & P Show. I sometimes drove down to Oxford on Sunday mornings for the small farmer's market and in the short time I had been living on the station, I'd watched the town beginning to change. The supermarket had moved up the main road and in its place Jo and Ross Seagar were beginning the lengthy resource consent process to convert the buildings into a café, kitchen and tableware shop, and residential cookery school. The first day of the Oxford Show was all about livestock, while Sunday's feature was the most incredible display of old farm machinery and vehicles. There were Clydesdales and bullock trains, stationary and moveable engines driving threshers and chaff cutters, every age and variety of tractor plus ploughs, discs and cultivators, balers and spreaders. Tonnes of steel and smoke like huge, loud, smelly dinosaurs.

The most interesting models dated from the 1910s to the early 1950s. It was fascinating to see how so much changed after the Second World War when mechanical advances became very obvious. Their restoration was a tribute to those, mainly men, who spent countless hours bent over piston and axle. The moment I asked about one of their treasures their eyes would fill with the gleam of the committed enthusiast and they could talk for hours.

The other highlight was the South Island wood-chopping championships. Large singleted men with muscled shoulders, thighs and forearms, their whole body yelling power, brought their polished axes down within centimetres of their toes. It took all of thirty seconds to chop through a log a metre in diameter. They threw double-edged axes as if they were darts and hit the bull's eye dead centre. I drove home filled with smiles and happiness. There was snow along the tops of the ranges and at sunset they would turn the palest of gold and then pink above the skirts of ranges already black with shadow.

A party was planned for the end of April. The new cattle yards were finished and as it was school holidays Kate, Rob and the granny-kids would be visiting. Building the yards had been another learning experience. At the time of the incident with the cattle truck driver, when it became obvious we could no longer use the old yards, I was shopping around between Wrightson, Pynes and Goldpine for the best price for fencing materials. The Goldpine brochure had a number of cattle yard designs I liked the look of, thinking that if I wanted to increase cattle numbers I had best not choose anything too small. While we were deciding on designs, it was suggested that because the deer only had to be brought in twice a year, it would make sense to build combined cattle and deer yards. It certainly made economic sense, especially when the traffic in cheques was all going one way. Andy looked at the Goldpine brochure and agreed the designs looked good.

Next we needed to find the right site. The flats across the road from the main gate were ideal. They looked level but in fact had quite a run on them and I needed somewhere that drained well, preferably with trees to give protection from the southerly wind. Unfortunately, the first manager had dug a rubbish pit there and two of the precious windbreak trees had gone up in flames when he set fire to the rubbish; and it takes a long time for trees to grow here. Even the matagouri, which may be four hundred years old, stand only a metre or two tall.

In every other way it suited: there was good access for stock trucks and I would be able to put in a trough by running water from Spittle Hill. Pete Nichol and his dozer scraped out the yard area and we levelled it with forty-five centimetres of river stones from the pile we kept down by the Porter to maintain the river crossings. Only then could Geoff and the gang begin driving in the posts. Then Kelvin and Rog took over. Kelvin Kimber and Roger Mason came recommended as builders of sheds and farm buildings. Kelvin had also farmed deer and Rog spent a good deal of time as a shepherd and musterer and talked about working on Mt Algidus station for Mona Anderson.

One subtlety I had missed in picking a Goldpine design was that their business is founded on selling poles and roundwood products. I ended up with many more posts than a more experienced farmer would have used. But the finished yards were a lovely sight: a wonderful crush with a beautiful curved race leading to it and a raised platform where you can stand to much more easily inject and pour on drenches. The only improvement would be a roof and that remains on the 'to do' list. In the inventory of farm plant and machinery was an old loading race and, with an eye to reducing costs, I thought we could make do with that. We brought it across and positioned it. It was tattered and had to be tied with baling twine to one of the bays in the yards. The first time we used it it broke and we had to go back and build a proper race that the trucks could easily back up to. It was an example of sweating the small stuff, a false economy.

Snow doing farrier
work on Emma,
one of his
Clydesdales.

I had scrapped the idea of the combined cattle and deer yards after closer inspection of the deer. I failed to consider what it would be like to get them across the river and up the track onto the terraces above: I'd seen them run up hill and they are fast, very fast. The only way to try to keep some control would be to put a fenced corridor between the deer block and the yards, which would mean running high deer fencing through the Porter River, and I could imagine what the folk who fished it would say about that. Instead, when Rog and Kelvin had finished the cattle yards, I sent them across the Porter to start work on BigBucks, the purpose-built deer yards, so named because I hoped the deer would earn me some.

I invited everyone to the cattle yard opening, neighbours, contractors and tradespeople. On the morning of the party it began blowing and snowing, the flakes flying by on the horizontal — and it was late April, which is very early for snow even at Castle Hill. Bones, the publican at the Springfield pub, called to say he and Sharmaine would bring mulled wine. It was certainly welcome, another example of the generosity and consideration typical in the area. They arrived with urns, Aussie wine and spices and began brewing. Bones, as usual, asked how my work bench, his term for a bed, was going. 'No ram over the Torlesse yet, Bones,' was my standard reply.

Bones and Sharmaine were among the first people I met in Springfield, and they were warm in their welcome. She ran a very good pub kitchen and had a reputation as a great boss, good to work for. Bones is known far and wide. He has been a musterer, a great dog trialist, and owned and operated the local dipping contract before he bought the pub. When he bought Springas, one of his dog trialling mates claimed it was like leaving a rabbit in charge of the lettuces. His risqué doggerels have featured on *Country Calendar* and as well as pub quizzes he used to bring up girls from Manchester Street in Christchurch for entertainment. Grasmere, one of the oldest Canterbury stations and a high country luxury retreat, was horrified to discover he'd bought their old farm truck. It was still emblazoned with the station's name when he turned it into an outdoor snug after smoking was banned in pubs. He parked it in full view of the main road, built a ramp up to it with car, truck and tractor tires, planted the sides with tussock and placed an umbrella in the middle so people could smoke in comfort. He also has a reputation as an inventor. The first time I went to a party at his house, he gave me a demonstration of his most prestigious invention to date, the

Bona Fide Gudgeon Guide. He strapped the device to his leg, and balancing with straps here and there showed me how a gate would swing on an ideal axis. He sold the patent and it has since gone into production. I'm now keen for Bones to turn his attention to my idea for a ewepickerupper — like the sling Plunket nurses use to weigh babies that I can attach to Phyllis's bullbars and which would help me cart ewes around the farm.

On the day of the cattle yard opening everyone met up at the homestead first. There was no need to cool the beer. It lay in the snow. People congregated under the verandah around the barbecue turning slowly in its warmth while Pete Henderson on guitar sang country and western. Pete has a small farm in Annat and works as a rousie for a local shearing gang. He is much sought after to sing at A&P Shows and local parties. After lunch the wind suddenly dropped and it stopped snowing. The whole party togged up and decamped to the yards, the townies in cars and the others on foot carrying their glasses. I gave a short speech thanking everyone, and then my oldest grandson, Will, cut the wide green satin ribbon I'd tied on the double loading gates. I proclaimed Castel open. 'Castel' being the Old Norman French and Old English word for 'castle'. The farmers in the party wandered round as green as the ribbon while I told them that in a few years Castle Hill would be holding calf and lamb sales on the site.

Then it was back up to the house to continue the party. Old and young took turns on the 'Dohney ram' — the farm go-cart I'd seen one day when I was down at Terrace Motors to have the chainsaws sharpened. I spotted it and thought, 'God, that'd be fun', as I imagined roaring round the farm. It had roll bars and seatbelts, a steering wheel, lights and a horn, too many mod cons altogether for a vehicle without a generator, and the lightweight battery kept cutting out until we rigged an additional car battery to the tray at the back so it would recharge as we drove. It turned out to be far too low to manage the rough ground in the paddocks and tracks and it drowned you crossing streams and rivers; but it was great for playing like this. The granny-kids amused themselves somewhat dangerously by blasting people with water bombs from the doors-to-nowhere up in their dormitory as the adults zoomed round and round the house. Downstairs I tried not to notice eighty pairs of feet criss-crossing the pale grey carpet. True to form, day turned into evening and the drinkers moved from grain to grape to the high country tipple — whisky.

The yards were work-christened the following month. It was time to draft off the calves for the annual high country sale at Canterbury Agricultural Park in Christchurch and to scan the cows to find out how many were pregnant. Mustering cows with their calves is always a noisy and rumbustious business. Maternal instinct makes for feisty animals, intent on finding and protecting their calves. Quite often the calves are in nursery schools when the herd starts moving and there is much calling from calves and cows as they try to find each other. There are always a few cows that, having lost sight of their calves, are convinced they are back in some matagouri bush and keep turning on the dogs. When they have their calves alongside, and think that humans, horses or dogs are trying to separate them, they will charge with flared nostrils and wet mouths.

Dogs like moving cattle. It arouses the wild instinct of the hunt — they move in packs, barking and snapping at the cattle's heels. Cows are big animals — four to five hundred kilos — and quick on their feet, and it took a while before I felt confident enough to stand my ground against an obstreperous and protesting animal, arms outstretched, shepherd's stick clutched in my right hand. Calves, once separated out from their mothers, don't know where they are going. They don't understand what the dogs are doing, and they don't have a leader, so they charge in all directions, making them very difficult to organise.

That year the calves were weaned and sent to the sale the same day. We kept back about sixty replacement stock, but none of the steers. In the

beginning, I was absolutely paranoid each time stock left the farm that they would lose weight and condition before they reached their destination and we would earn less as a result. It became a real consideration when I turned on the six o'clock news that night to learn there was a foot and mouth scare on Waiheke. An anonymous letter claimed the virus had been released on the island. My first concern was that it would lead to discounting at the sale the following day. I called an Auckland friend, Mike Friedlander, for advice and true to form he said he was going out buying the next day! But at Inverary John Chapman didn't think the correction would be too great. I contacted the agent and decided to put a reserve of about $430 an animal in my top pens.

When calves arrived at Canterbury Park they were put in graded pens where buyers and sellers can view them from above on a network of narrow plank walkways. I climbed up to compare Castle Hill's calves with those in the highest grade pens, wobbling along feeling slightly dizzy as I looked down, the OSH stipulated handrails offering little comfort. The sale arena was like an amphitheatre, the seating stacked back from the floor where the auctioneers sat up on a stage. A big screen flashed up the farm, weight, price per kilo and how much was paid for each pen. When the auction started, we were up third after Mt White and Torlesse. The auctioneer announced there were reserves and then looked at me and asked, 'Will you sell?' I tried to work out the risk of not selling and trucking them back. They would go through the two weeks of losing weight that happens when calves are weaned and then the two weeks needed to build them back up before we could send them off again. We still wouldn't know what

Midge and me at our first ever dog trials, attempting the short pull, drive and yard — commonly called the cat and mouse. We have completed the short pull and Midge has the Romneys under control, their legs in unison, somewhat like army officers on parade, as they enter the drive. It was a dream run until we got to the yard, when the sheep decided captivity was not for them.

price they would fetch and it would be closer to winter with lower pasture growth; and we also didn't know when the snow was going to come.

I decided to sell and I reckon there was a five per cent drop in price that sale day, all the result of someone's idea of a prank.

My first calf sales were also meant to be the beginning of forging the Castle Hill brand. I drafted a certificate that would go with the calves declaring they were prime Castle Hill stock and composed a letter of thanks that we would send to every buyer of our calves together with a bottle of Johnny Walker Red Label and an invitation to visit the station. Not all the calves that year justified a certificate. Some were runty. On the day of the sale, I saw none of ours had made it to the top one or two pens. The following year I could see that people kept buying from the same stations. If Castle Hill was to break that purchasing habit, we would need to build a reputation for calves of real quality: hardy, strong, of good temperament and ready for fattening.

With the calves gone, the cows stood in paddocks over the highway from the yards crying well into the night. They paced and stared across the road. They seemed lost and stressed and took on almost human characteristics. The maternal in me can never get used to those sounds of bereft mothers mourning. I watched them, thinking that every year they do this: they give up their calves and they are also pregnant again by then, their lives a constant cycle of nurture and loss.

The cows were brought back into the yards to scan for dries — cows that fail to become pregnant after being out with the bulls. It was a howling cold day and I was with Andy and Simon Hewitt, the vet, trying to identify wet and dry cows using an ultra-scanner similar to those used in hospitals to check the development of human babies, except that here you use a probe. Every so often Simon paused, unsure what he was seeing on the monitor's screen. Then he would pull on a long glove and plunge his hand in to the cow all the way up to his armpit. If his probing confirmed it was a dry, it was usually a death sentence for the cow. I wanted to try too, fascinated to find out what he was feeling. I pulled on a glove and Vaselined it and then put it straight up the vagina, not at all the right place to be. There were great guffaws from Andy and Simon. I was meant to be feeling in the rectum for the uterus. Just then Tony Benny arrived to see me. He had been in contact about filming an episode of *Country Calendar*. They wanted to make a programme on how I was managing at Castle Hill, which was not

Opposite top: Snow and me during a visit to Grasmere Station.

Below: Duncan James of Benmore Station is presented with the Junior Musterer's prize at the Malvern District dog trials.

very well at that very moment. I extracted myself with reluctance; the cow's cavernous interior was the warmest place on the farm.

Over the afternoon Simon would take a scan where the result was obvious and then encourage me to interpret what I was seeing and feeling. I learned to find the outline of the calf, the backbone or the head or some other part, while watching the monitor, trying to match the information two different senses were giving me. Those pregnant in the first cycle were well formed but those conceived in the last cycle were difficult to tell. It was amazing, but it took time and I was holding up everyone else. While I probed in the warmth and the faeces, they couldn't wait to get back to their thermoses.

The results at the end of the scanning were a shock. We had bought the station on a promised ninety per cent cow in calf rate. This season only eighty two per cent of the cows were in calf. The big question was why. Did we not have enough bulls after all, or was the fault with the cows? Were they low in selenium or copper, essential minerals, which have naturally low levels in the soils throughout Canterbury? Simon recalled a fantastic farmer up the Rakaia who had fifteen per cent dries. They had tested his bulls and found all sorts of defects like screw cock or just a really low libido. We decided to bring our bulls in for testing before the bull sales later in the year. If they were not up to the job, then we would have to replace them.

Emily Crofoot emailed me to find out whether I was going to attend the annual Sheep and Beef Conference, saying it was an excellent programme. She and Anders were still recovering from a bad flood a month earlier at Castlepoint Station, fifteen centimetres of rain fell in three hours on

already saturated soil. Down at Castle Hill we needed a little rain. It was getting colder and we had already done some feeding out. Andy and I looked at the conference programme. He was interested in attending and I was happy to sponsor him. It was a continuation of my commitment to up-skilling staff that began with Books in Homes and the Gifted Kids Programme. I was eager, too, to talk through a couple of ideas for the farm with Emily and Anders. John Chapman was keen that we join a programme called Sheep for Profit developed by a Southland vet, Chris Mulvaney. I also wanted to get their thoughts on becoming organic. I was looking for ways to develop a niche that would give me added value, maximise my breeding and make up for not being able to fatten stock. I was thinking organic only for my cattle as the Merinos were constantly being drenched and injected and clipped. However, once I learned it took a minimum of seven years before you could be certified organic I did not pursue the idea any further. I needed solutions that would show a return long before that.

The conference was well worthwhile. It was useful to be able to learn about a range of new products and adaptations all in one place, as well as the history of some of the well-known agricultural companies like Gallagher's, manufacturers of electric fencing. It was also good for networking, even though neither of us knew many there. However, people started introducing themselves because by then we had been in the daily paper and the rural press and they realised I wasn't just a one-day wonder. My new life at Castle Hill had also featured in the first issue of *NZ Life & Leisure* and Mark Smith's photos had been seen by many. The focus at that year's conference was on dairying and converting to dairy, as many South Island farms were doing. The feature speakers were all stressing the same message about keeping to your strategic goals and the need to revisit and revise and write them down because when you get busy those goals become

Midge and I moving a mob of sheep along State Highway 73. One of the peculiarities of Castle Hill is its bisection by a very busy main road. I am always worried about losing a dog on the road. We tend to move the sheep very early in the morning. It is sometimes so cold that everything drips from the eaves of my rather long nose, which at such times is also rather red.

blurred and woolly. It was a good reminder.

I needed to ask where I was going. I'd had my airy fairy first mission statement which was all about having a profitable farm and recognising every inch of 'iconic' landscape and leaving it better than when I arrived. They were all fine aims, but to achieve profitability was proving much more difficult than I had ever imagined and I was a lot less sanguine about owning and surviving in a business with a steady cash outflow and no income-earning assets. Unlike so many of my earlier projects, where results and growth had come quickly, I was beginning to understand that farming needs a minimum of five years to start to effect any kind of change; to know whether what you have put in place works or not; and which way the markets are going. There was no use sitting saying the weather is terrible, the exchange rate's no good, and why aren't people buying superfine wool instead of polar fleece? Don't they know Merino is better? I was coming to realise that farming is about the twenty per cent you can affect, about making smart decisions and smart marketing.

More than my lack of farming knowledge, it was my lack of experience in doing the accounts that increasingly discomforted and depressed me. I had worked with organisations and bodies with big operating budgets and funds — the Lion Foundation, Salvation Army, Books in Homes and the Gifted Kids Programme — and had a fiduciary responsibility not just for raising money but also for ensuring it was spent in the right places and on the right people. But I had always had an accountant alongside. This was different. I was not used to this new world of depreciation, GST, payroll tax, and capital expenditure versus current expenditure. I also was more and more nervous about the rate at which my cash was disappearing. I was looking for income. People kept reminding me that I had plenty of assets, but the idea of selling required a shift in thinking; and there would have to be a buyer, as I had discovered when I tried to sell my Colin McCahon painting. The people buying art with the money to afford a McCahon had already completed their New Zealand collections and were starting to become more international in their buying. The next layer of buyers was purchasing works that rarely went above $50,000. In order to get the attention of that top tier, and the funds I needed, I had to go to the heart of my collection. Which was why, after a great struggle, I ended up selling my Gordon Walters. He was very desirable and very expensive because there are so few of his paintings.

Opposite: The two men in my life: Snow Cleaver, left, and John Bougen.

I knew I had some money, part of John's estate, coming to me from one of the companies he had invested in. I wondered if it could be paid to me in advance. It wasn't possible but the company's principals, Karim and Paul, became great sounding boards. Because John had been so good to them, they offered to help me and undertook an independent appraisal of the station. They looked at all the permutations and combinations of land, stock and staff and canvassed some independent advice while they devised a plan to provide me with a regular and dependable income without eating into my capital. It proved difficult to find a permanent solution, and it has continued to.

Perhaps the best thing they did was to bring a couple of people with years of experience in the farming sector to look over the station. Karim's father-in-law, Rod Preston, owned a meat works in Wellington that processed over a million sheep and cattle each year and had also farmed beef and sheep. He had a good feel for the market. Andrew McGovern was a very experienced sheep and beef farmer from the Wairarapa. What they had to say cheered me considerably. Rod and Andrew were impressed

with the work that had gone into the farm and Andrew was particularly impressed with the quality of the new fencing and stock handling facilities. There was also much more level and gently rolling country than they expected and they could see the potential for it to become significantly more productive with irrigation and more intensive fertilisation.

Their short-term suggestions to improve profitability were to sell any dry ewes to preserve grazing, to cull all but a high quality nucleus of deer and divide the enormous deer paddock so we could separate stock, to buy in calf heifers to replace the ones I'd sold earlier in the year, and to build up cattle numbers as they would bring me the best net returns. They reinforced my move into a dual-purpose wool and meat producing breed such as Dohney or Perendale, and they encouraged me to rigorously trim costs wherever I could.

Over the next few months I put the suggestions I felt comfortable with into action. The advice and interest from Andrew McGovern in particular was fantastic. He took copious notes during the visit and rang a year later to find out how things had progressed. He visited again in 2007, so interested was he to see what has been happening. He also proved to be correct in his appraisal of the two bulls we had just bought, as we would discover when we tested them in spring. The only person not happy with their visit was Andy. We had not replaced the farm advisor, whose last task had been to move on the first manager. Andy was very keen to prove he could manage Castle Hill alone. I realise now he found my constant stream of ideas and suggestions that followed discussions I had with some of the very experienced farmers in the area undermining.

At the end of June, we brought in the deer for the first time since I moved to Castle Hill. Rog and Kelvin had finished building BigBucks only a few days before and I was having another deer crisis. The yards had cost so much I was wondering whether the best way to pay for them would be to sell the deer. This did not make great sense but once again people were counselling me to get rid of them. They told me the deer market was dead: $4 a kilo was a long way below the high times of $10 per kilo. On good days I would tell myself that having made that capital investment in BigBucks

I needed to stick with the deer.

This would be the first time many of the deer had ever been mustered, let alone been brought into yards, and we had been trying to prepare them subtly over the preceding days by laying a trail of barley and hay to bring them down to the race. Because it was going to be such a major undertaking, we decided to have the guy from MAF who would test for TB and the PGG agent who would appraise the stock, come at the same time. There were five of us on the day: Rog and Kelvin, Andy (who didn't like deer), Richard Smith of Mt White Station (who is passionate about deer and knew Castle Hill as he had managed it in the past), and me. We headed over with a quad bike, four other vehicles and assorted dogs. The man from MAF and the agent were due at one o'clock.

For the next four hours we tried repeatedly to bring the deer to the race and into the yards. We would get them close and then they would peel off again and again. Sometimes they would turn and move in a single mass, like a school of fish; other times they would break from the mob in several directions, scattering deep into the vast deer block. Then we would have to go all the way back and start again. It was enormously exasperating. The dogs had to be firmly managed because they can agitate the deer, making the situation worse. With the five of us spread out across the terrain in two trucks, a quad bike and on foot, we looked like a World War II mission in the Desert Campaign, and it felt almost as challenging.

It became apparent we had made a mistake in the configuration of the yards. We only had one large gate leading from the vast deer block to the first holding paddock, which was also too big. What we needed, and have put in since, was a wing fence from the gate that funnels them through to the start of the race on the way up to the shed. (Now it only takes us two hours instead of four to bring them into the yards.) Once we finally had them through the holding paddock, they began to move up the wide open race and then into a number of holding yards that got progressively darker and darker, gradually calming them down, until they reached the shed which is totally enclosed and dark.

In deer yards, unlike sheep and cattle yards where everyone is shouting 'up-up-up' and the dogs are barking and leaping between pens, it is very quiet. The deer need to be moved slowly to be safe. Ron Schroeder, the PGG agent, was amazingly gentle with them. Despite their beautiful long-lashed eyes, I thought they were scary. I was working the solid gate they

Snow's Clydesdales pull a sled with posts, waratahs and wire for new fencing on the Emu Block.

passed through to the pen outside after TB testing. They'd come through dazed and then suddenly see the light and leap, often to head height. This was no place to daydream; I'd snap to and stand back. I thought of the earlier suggestion of calico 'wings' and tried to imagine how we would have managed the stags and wild does with something so flimsy.

The first animal through the shed's circular pens and then out into an outside yard with high solid sides had been one of the largest stags. Confused at being outside but not yet free of the yards he panicked and began to race round and round, ripping off the whole of one side of his antlers as he tried to get out. The big antler hung over his eyes and there was blood everywhere as the poor animal went berserk. Richard got his gun from his truck and shot him. I saw my investment going down in front of me.

The TB testing was a two-stage process. On this first day, David shaved a small patch on the neck of every deer, inserted a needle and injected a tiny amount of TB in solution. Three days later we had to bring all the deer in again so he could check the reaction, but this time we had to muster without Richard, Rog and Kelvin. There was Andy and Harry and their dogs; I counted the Hilux as my dog. To our dismay David thought one of the reactions was rough and so ten days later we got them all in once more. These were meant to be my trouble-free deer that only needed to be brought in twice a year; the good news was that MAF gave them the top clean bill of health, C10, which means a minimum of ten years free of TB. It is really important to maintain your C10 status — to lose it requires beginning the count to ten all over again — and it is one of the reasons we have possum, hare and wild boar hunts, all animals that carry and spread TB.

At the time of the yarding, prices were abysmal: velvet was very low and venison was poor. However, both France and Germany were trying to decide whether to start selling farmed venison out of their hunting season. Despite constant reminders that others were turning their backs on deer, my natural instinct kicked in: if everyone else was leaving, I would hang on. We sent three generations of deer to the works and kept just one hundred and ten breeding hinds and eight stags. There was no way the stock truck and trailer could cross the Porter or negotiate the tight turns up and down the tracks from the terraces. The truck uncoupled its trailer and left it back across the river, ferrying loads of deer across and transferring them to the trailer.

We had also removed the antlers from the spikers and stags while we had them in the yards, using Kelvin's portable crush which looked a little like a caravan you might see at an English country fair or circus. We'd elected not to build a crush at this stage because we did not have a sufficient volume of deer. It was also unusual to have all the stags with such big antlers, another result of not having been yarded for two years. We sent them one at a time up the covered loading race and into Kelvin's covered trailer with cloth sides until they were held by the crush. Once they were secure, Kelvin used a fretsaw to remove the antlers. Magnificent though they were, it was far too dangerous to work with stags with hard antlers and they can do serious damage to each other in the roaring season, when the hinds come into heat ready for mating. The carton of antlers went into my garage after I found out hard antler was only fetching about $4 a kilo. I had almost forgotten about it when a man turned up eighteen months later offering $40 a kilo. I kept a few pieces for nostalgia — maybe one day they will make knife handles or even the end of a hill stick — and sold him the rest.

One medium-term option for further development Keith and I had already discussed was irrigating the flats. With a good reliable source of water, we could greatly increase their productivity and that would provide more feed for Castle Hill stock, with the potential to fatten them ourselves rather than selling them on to someone else. As a breeder, and without the economies of scale, all I could expect was the best price on offer; the profit went to those who bought the stock to fatten. (2007 figures showed New Zealand sheep farmers get as little as ten to fifteen per cent of the total value of growing and slaughtering lambs, and transporting and selling them to overseas consumers, while the big supermarkets in England capture up to sixty-five per cent of the value.) More productive flats could also provide more baleage and hay to sell.

One of the sources of water we relied on was the spring that rose on Spittle Hill, which was then owned by John Reid, who had twice been the owner of Castle Hill Station and who was the developer of the alpine-style Castle Hill Village. We had been grazing the two paddocks on Spittle Hill as if they were ours when he rang to say he wanted to put his Highland cattle on them. I immediately recognised my vulnerability if I also lost

continuity of water. It had not taken me long to realise that a mild winter like the year I arrived, and the one now predicted to be coming, might be pleasant for farm workers and animals but there were drawbacks in a region with such dry summers and low annual rainfall, an average of 89cm at the homestead and 140cm on the hills. It made us very reliant on a good winter, meaning one with plenty of snow, to make up the difference. With limited snow melt you don't get enough water going back into the farm's springs and there is not enough water in the soil.

McMillan Wells came up to scout the ground. They cruised around, following the water race that has come from the limestone rocks for a hundred and fifty years, looking for a likely spot for a well. It needed to be close to a power source to run the pump that would take the water up to tanks at the top of the flats and then gravity would run the irrigation pipes to the troughs from there. They found a place about fifty metres from the Old Quarters. To make doubly sure, and because I've always wanted to see one in action, I invited a water diviner Keith knew. An old chap and

My huntaway dog Pearl (formerly Please, until teasing made me change her name) as a pup.

his wife turned up and walked a grid with instruments that looked a lot like wire coat hangers. When the diviner reached the same spot McMillan's had indicated, his dowsing rod began twisting round and round. He showed me how to hold one, and I am such a believer that I willed it to work. I marked the spot with a pile of irrigation pipes which have slowly disappeared over time.

The next question was how far down would we have to bore to access the water. The diviner didn't know, and McMillans said it could be anywhere from ten to forty metres, possibly more. Digging the well would cost $8000 for every metre so I put that idea on hold. I had a consent to put down a well to use for stock purposes but not for irrigation. Consents for irrigation are becoming increasingly difficult to get in Canterbury as the spread of industrial-size dairy farms leads to greater demands for water. That is not an issue at Castle Hill, where the station is the only one in the valley drawing off water. One option to irrigate the flats was to draw water from the Whitewater Stream, which has a heavy flow. This time I needed reports on potential effects. Irrigation expert Bill Allison completed a report on water flows, and Fish and Game and NIWA studied the impact on the Waimakariri River and its fish life.

In the meantime, I began looking for land on the flats around Sheffield and Russell's Flat to lease or purchase and explored the possibility of leasing a farm to the north of Oxford. Land on the flat would give me a fattening block, a balance that a number of high country farms have. But having bought something as big as Castle Hill and feeling I had spent all my money, I was frightened to buy somewhere else and wasn't as focused as I usually am. Every month the prices kept going up as land was bought for dairy and lifestyle blocks, until people were saying there'd be no more farms between Christchurch and Springfield except for dairy and lifestyle, especially if permission is granted to put in the Central Plains irrigation system. The system is a multi-million dollar project that would stretch from the Rakaia to the Waimakariri River and require a huge dam that would drown a lot of third- and fourth-generation-owned farms. I equivocated too long. Now buying or leasing land on the flats seems out of reach unless I borrow, and I have a phobia about borrowing money. It is like mortgaging future earnings. Instead, I followed one of the farm advisor's

last recommendations, one Andy concurred with, and sent hoggets and steers for grazing at Aylesbury. We still do that periodically to give them a boost when feed is low.

for almost a year we had been beating a path to the Pit paddock to dump rubbish and now you could see it from the road, a pile of debris and junk that was steadily growing, looming up like a funeral pyre. When a rubbish dump reaches that size you have to get written authorisation from the local council to burn it. Once I had permission, Harry and I waited for one of autumn's calm cold days, with blue in the sky and frost on the ground. We dressed the towering pile with diesel, threaded it with paper and lit it. Although we were on fire duty, we didn't think a bucket of water would be particularly useful. What Harry did have to protect against the fire spreading was a gun. He explained that possums often make a home in rubbish pits and have been known to flee with their fur on fire into the closest trees which they then set alight. I was expecting whole families to run out because it looked such a cool place for them to live, but in the end only one emerged, part of its tail on fire. It had barely reached the trees when Harry fired. He had to shoot it twice. The impact of the first bullet

Looking down from the Thomas Block towards the farm compound and the woolshed.

made it grip even tighter, the second brought it down.

The heat from the blaze was intense, hot enough to destroy everything in the pit, including scrap fencing wire and old wire-wove bed bases, and I had to keep moving Phyllis further and further away in case the pickup turned into an incendiary bomb. While we were keeping watch, Harry decided it was a good time to show me how to put on the new snow chains. I had tried unsuccessfully to fit them round the Prado's tyres the previous winter when I first arrived and failed dismally. I laid the chains out in front of and in line with the tyres and then drove carefully onto the steel web, trying to stop in a place where it would be easy for me to hook them up when I got out. If it was as hard as this on a fine day in front of a fire, what would it be like in the snow? I confess I still don't know because I haven't tried. We change the tyres from narrow to wide on the manager's Land Cruiser in winter, because that is the most important vehicle on the farm, and I have made snow chains unnecessary by picking when, where and what I drive.

The east facing slopes of the Pit paddock going to Middle Terrace were the best of all places to collect the great field mushrooms that were springing up in rings on parts of the farm. I have always loved mushrooms and almost every day I checked White Horse paddock, Chrissie's or the Quarry paddock. I collected bucket after bucket, mad for mushrooms prepared any way. I made mushroom soup, mushrooms on toast, mushrooms with pasta. I collected a fresh bucket for Harry and I while we watched the fire, and that evening I had my poached eggs on mushrooms on toast. I kept going out to look across to Pit paddock. In the dark I could see the fire. It glowed pink and orange. Could I feel the whisper of a rising wind? It made me so nervous I kept driving down to the rubbish pit to check it. You can never count on the nor'wester staying quiet for long. The fire burned for two days, and until it finally died I couldn't completely relax.

From the first couple of months after I moved to Castle Hill, I had been battling to stop a lime company which was quarrying on the station. The quarry was partly in the new conservation area and on pastoral lease land, both owned by the Crown, and partly on land the station owned freehold.

I had been surprised to find a quarry operating, in plain sight of the main highway, in an area designated by Nature Heritage and DOC to be of significant natural beauty. I was dismayed to learn they had a forty-year mining permit from the Ministry of Energy and a resource consent for mining from the Canterbury Regional Council which did not expire until 2033. The contract for access over my freehold land was for a shorter period. However, the company had signed an agreement with the previous owner not just to continue quarrying but also to greatly expand the area to be quarried, which admittedly we had signed up to when we purchased. But now I was in my pure, leave-the-land-better frame of mind. An ancient landslide surrounded and enclosed an active landslide on the quarry site. Geological reports showed it was still moving. The owner said it was the worst day of his life when the slip came down, but they wanted to continue to work the quarry as part of their business. I had Geoff's gang fence off the area the company was allowed to mine and Harry and I began taking photos every week or so. If there was any movement outside that area I would then have sufficient evidence to stop access.

My desire to close the quarry made me unpopular with some of the surrounding farmers and I really didn't want to fall out with the locals. The quarry had been operating since the 1960s and lime is an important fertiliser for all farmers in the region, even though we are in limestone country. The lime from the Castle Hill quarry is very fine and of very high quality and a proportion is used to colour concrete paving stones. Although there is another quarry on Porter Heights Road, and the lime works is not just reliant on the station's quarry, the high quality of our lime means it is easier to process. I thought after all the conservation talk by the Crown and concerns about maintaining this special landscape that I would have strong support in my efforts to stop the quarrying, or at least to prevent it doubling in size; the extension would turn it into an open cast mine that could be seen from everywhere. I had been led to believe DOC shared my concerns over the impact on the station and the area in general. It had taken a strong line in another case further south. However, despite finding that quarrying in an area like Castle Hill was inappropriate, and DOC's distress at the collapse of the back of the quarry, it failed to step up in the court case to stop it. Instead I received letters informing me that work would begin again.

I had been trying to arrange a meeting with Chris Carter, the Minister of Conservation, for several months. Twice I'd made appointments to

see him at his West Auckland electorate, and twice he had to cancel. I'd
received letters saying that the Crown would fast-track tenure review
but nothing had happened. It was almost a year since the Department of
Conservation, Nature Heritage Fund and I had entered into the partnership
to buy Castle Hill Station. I sent Carter a letter — a review of my first
year and what we had done on the farm, an indication of our commitment
to our side of the contract. I had invested approximately $1 million so
far, restored the historic Roadman's hut and was about to begin work on
the 1860s limestone cottage. We had repaired and painted all the farm
buildings, improved the on-farm roads, built new cattle and deer yards
and carried out an extensive fencing programme, particularly along the
main west highway. We had completed a weed control programme which
included the three greatest threats to the high country: gorse, broom and
wilding pines. We had also started planting native trees and tussocks, had
fenced off a section of red tussock, and had generally managed the grazing
of our stock in what I thought was a responsible
and sensitive manner. Furthermore we had given
many different groups and members of the public
access to the station. I asked again for a meeting
in the not too distant future.

I spent the actual anniversary of my move
south in Auckland. The *Country Calendar*
programme on Castle Hill was finally going to
air and I felt the need of family support while I
watched. The programme's crew had spent three
weeks coming and going from the farm as they
juggled filming a number of stories in the area.
They'd been good company, always ready for a
smoke and a drink and very complementary of
my roasted pork belly. They trailed me as I fed
out from the back of the Land Cruiser over at
the deer block, mustered cattle on foot across
the Porter River, moved sheep on the flats with
my Coke bottle filled with stones, picked up
bales with the tractor, worked with Keith and
Owen on the old buildings and walked among
the incredible limestone rocks. I need not have

worried. I thought we looked a great team and Castle Hill absolutely magnificent. There were complementary messages on my voice mail . . . and plenty of offers of tractor lessons.

I felt more and more part of the community. I was asked to an increasing number of parties and family celebrations and more people were dropping in. On my birthday Keith had given me a beautiful leather pouch for the knife he'd given me at Christmas. When I had first arrived no one gave me a chance, especially after my first manager left. But over time they were changing their minds. I was adapting too. I'd exchanged my Friday Zambesi pants for moleskins and check shirts. The high heels were gone and I was drinking Speight's, not chardonnay, although I was still on the twelve ounce glass, filled frequently, rather than a handle. There had certainly been really hard times, especially in the early days, but on balance I could say that my first year at Castle Hill had been a fascinating and glorious twelve months.

Castle Hill rams.

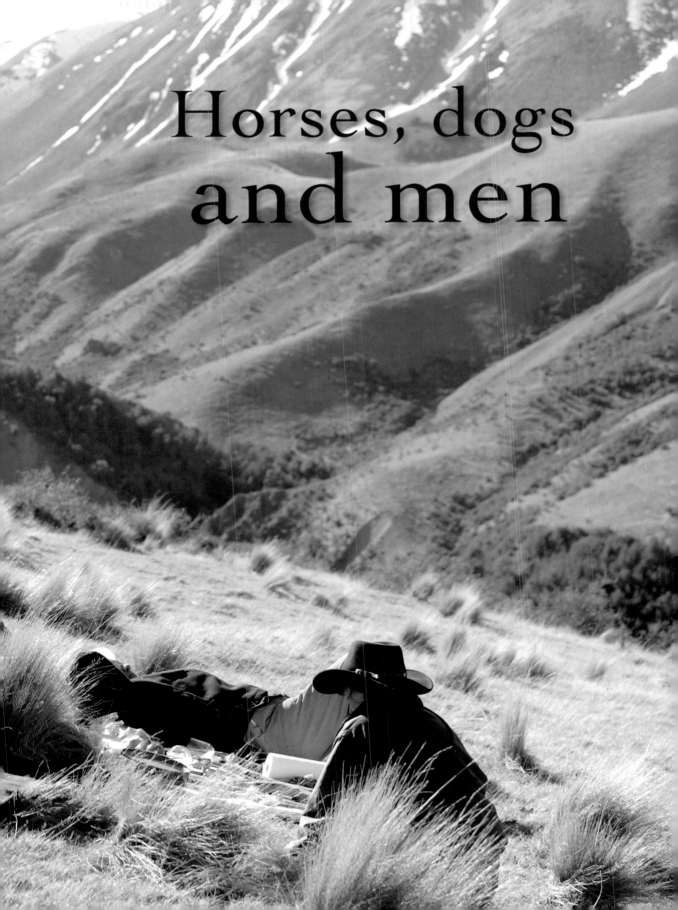

CHAPTER 8

Horses, dogs and men

Early one Wednesday morning I attached the Pratley sheep ramp to the back of the Land Cruiser and loaded the next porcine generation of Nelsons and Hamiltons into the dog crate. It was time for the kill again but on this occasion I was leaving it to professionals. They were going to 'pig corp' and hook No. 286, the Oxford Butchery hook. As I turned onto State Highway 73 I had a sudden image of Uncle George disappearing down the orchard drive on his way to market with his apples and plums. I rolled down the window and stuck out my elbow, my hand resting business-like on the wheel. In the rear-vision mirror I could see the mist withdrawing to hover over the braided waters rushing between the river terraces. Farmer Fernyhough, as Colin Giffney calls me, off to Christchurch. In the sheep yards the shearing gang would be at work shearing the ewes six weeks before lambing was due to start, the soft click of the hand blades drowned in the music from an old tape player. On their feet some still wore old style bag moccasins made by standing on a wool sack, tracing the outline of your foot and then sewing it up. Most, though, favoured the more comfortable and modern sheepskin version.

I studied the winter feed in the flats as I drove, the pigs' trotters a series of quick clicks as they jostled for position. We'd had a cold snap earlier — lots of snow, then sunshine, then strong winds and scudding snow again — and had brought the stock close in to make it easier to feed out: two to three bales of baleage for every nine hundred ewes supplemented with turnips in the winter feed paddocks where we had been break fencing since June, and barley once or twice a week, unless the pasture was under snow. Then it was barley every day. But the snow didn't stay for long and after shearing Andy would begin set-stocking the hills ready for lambing.

I thought back to my intention to enrol in an agricultural diploma at Lincoln University when I first bought the farm. I'd thought of driving to class as just a three-hour trip, but once I moved onto the station that changed. It would have been fun sitting with the eighteen-year-olds learning in the Speight's tradition, but the lecturer suggested I'd learn as much or more doing the work out in the fields. John Chapman had a friend, retired from Lincoln and living in Darfield, who could help. Only an hour, and I'd be able to distil the learning relevant to Castle Hill. But then the manager went and Dad's Army and I became all-day busy. Instead, I constantly consulted my Lincoln manual. It became my Bible.

Occasionally I even recalled some snippet of information I'd picked up in the mid-1990s when I'd done a few farming papers through the Correspondence School. I'd studied sheep, beef and grasslands, and when the questions became too difficult, particularly in the grasslands paper, I'd say 'I'm a townie' to excuse my inadequate answers. At the time I thought it would be great if John and I bought a farm close to Auckland. I even contacted an agent and found what I thought was the perfect place. But John did the numbers and said it didn't make economic sense. I wondered what he would make of Castle Hill. I don't believe he would have bought it because the figures wouldn't have stacked up but he would have loved the connection to Samuel Farr. Farr arrived in New Zealand on the *Monarch* in 1850 with his wife-to-be and her family, Mary Ann Pavitt, John's great grandmother. It was Farr, a builder and architect of note in Akaroa and Christchurch, who released the first salmon smolts in the streams around Castle Hill.

I had stopped doubting and questioning my decision to buy the farm.

I just wanted to do better and better. I was acquiring more knowledge, and beginning to understand how much I didn't know. I had discovered that I could collect information wherever I went but had to realise that what works in one location won't work in another: you have to farm your farm. I could see my grand plan for stock and pasture, drawn up just after I purchased Castle Hill, beginning to reveal itself in increased productivity of the pastures and the increased productivity and improving health of the stock.

It was two and a half years since John's death, and farming theory and practice weren't all I'd learnt. I'd had to master a number of new social skills. I'd learnt to dine alone in a restaurant. The waiter would look at me and say, 'All the tables are gone but would you like this stool?' and you would often end up facing a wall. Or people presumed you were waiting for someone, as if it was unusual for women to eat alone, and so tended to seat you next to magazines. When I was a teenager, being overlooked on a Saturday night was the kiss of social death. Now I was spending Saturday night with *Woman's Day*. I also had to learn to sit in the back seats of cars, regardless of car sickness. Learn to accept graciously the allocation of beds away from home, for instance kids' bunk rooms or, at best, single bedrooms. And learn to go to movies alone and not have the stimulation of being able to discuss the film afterwards.

Cloud engulfed the Land Cruiser and its squealing cargo as we neared the top of Porters Pass. On the other side it was raining. Sometimes the meteorological equivalent of a shower curtain falls over Lake Lyndon, on the station side of the pass, and drifts up to the turning to Porter Heights ski field. It stops moisture from the south; sometimes it stops the rain, sometimes the sun. When I sense a change in the weather I turn to the south from my castle eyrie to see if the curtain is drawn. By the time I reached the outskirts of Christchurch, the rain had cleared. The pig works was in Waterloo Road, home to Kia car sales, office furniture manufacturers and retailers, panel beaters, accountants and small business operators. In the midst of all this clean industry and suit-and-tie trade was an old sign reading 'Alliance Sockburn' beside a drive that led to the killing chain. I knew it was the right place because there was an awful lot of squealing going on. Big trucks were backed up to loading platforms, dwarfing the Land Cruiser and its small consignment. My pigs trotted down the gang plank; Nelson and Hamilton off to their Waterloo. Soon I had four more hams in the deep freeze, helping the growing consumption of pork in New

With Minnie. She has her ears back and a wild rolling eye. We never really became friends.

Zealand. The woman who had never owned a freezer before the farm now had three, and a walk-in as well.

I was splitting my time between working with Andy and Harry on the farm and with Keith, who was finishing the Old Quarters. Because it was mild we could continue the restoration work; once the temperature drops below ten degrees Celsius it is too cold to apply paint. Fencing could also continue because the snow wasn't settling, so there were always contractors around. Winter is supposed to be the season when you tidy out the sheds. Mustering slows down and most of your time is spent break-fencing the winter feed and feeding out. You live much more intensely in the feeding-out period and usually I was so tired I'd by-pass the sheds and go in, build up the fire and watch television. It was time for pea soup and my favourite, oxtail with mashed potatoes. There were moments of relief when someone had a birthday party or I risked going over the Pass to Friday night at

Springas. There we'd ask each other, 'How is it for you? My tractor's mucked up; can I borrow your plough?' 'Any stock losses?' And, 'What are you reading?', a question that always provoked a pang of guilt as I still wasn't.

Richard Smith's fortieth birthday party was a wonderful diversion in the midst of this. Richard manages Mt White for its owners, the Turnbulls. Mt White covers 126,000 acres, the third largest privately owned station in New Zealand. It is a four-day ride from the homestead to one end of the property. They still muster the traditional way, on horses and on foot. You enter the station across the rail line and a bridge over the Waimakariri, where the river's multiple braids narrow briefly to a single strand. There were seven gates and a forty five-minute drive on a gravel road that is slushy and potholed in winter and dust deep in summer just to get to the homestead and the party which spilled from the house to the big lawn with its spreading trees. There was singing and laughter and five hours of smiling.

Richard and Sheri have two young boys, who until recently were home-schooled, although it was difficult alongside all the work on the farm. Sheri also looks after about a hundred beehives and makes her own honey. But in 2006 the Correspondence School, once the educational mainstay of remote rural families, had only six hundred and forty full-time students classed as isolated, a tiny group among the twenty three and a half thousand other mainly urban students. As a result the Smiths lost their Correspondence School liaison teacher who used to visit regularly. The alternative modern communication technologies the school is now adopting do not apply in an area with no cellphone coverage and very poor internet connections. The closest school is in Springfield, an hour and a quarter away, and so with a partner they bought a place in town and Sheri and the boys live there during the school week while Richard stays at the cook shop with his musterers. It is a far from ideal situation. Many rural families feel the government is slowly stripping away all the supports and systems that have long been there to keep country communities alive and viable. They feel undervalued and forgotten.

It was coming time to say a reluctant farewell to Harry White. His three to four months at Castle Hill had stretched to nine, and it would soon be time for him to leave. While things were relatively quiet in the work calendar I arranged a special Saturday lunch for him with Andy, Keith, Chris and Geoff, the fencer, at Terrace Downs on the Rakaia. On the day, there was one more in the party. Earlier that week I had received a call from a man I had met at a restaurant in Auckland just after I purchased Castle Hill. I was dining with a friend who was pointing out rather forcefully the life-and-death toughness of farming. She thought me far too soft to deal out the summary justice required: all dries to the works. As we were leaving we stopped to talk with a friend of hers at an adjoining table. His dinner companion said he had heard about me. He told me he was a Timaru boy and that he envied me my new home. Now he, John Bougen, was on the phone. He was on a Books in Homes tour, visiting schools as a Duffy Hero, talking to the children about the importance of dreams and his adventures, which included a pell-mell trip with his cousin James Irving to visit one hundred and ninety one countries in one hundred and fifty seven days, enter the *Guinness Book of Records* and help promote Save the Children. John was in Picton and his options were to be lonely for the weekend or come to Castle Hill and take some photographs of the high country. I tried to dissuade him, warning that Picton was a four-hour drive from the farm, not two, but he came anyway. He said he had been fascinated by me and what I was doing after our conversation fifteen months before.

He arrived in what turned out to be characteristic fashion. I was down in the compound with Andy when a car went hurtling past, slowed suddenly, and did a U-turn. It returned, drove up the drive and screeched to a halt. Next morning was a photographer's dream, a day that cleared slowly, the mist rising and falling as it withdrew. I invited John to join us for Harry's farewell. At lunch I went round the table asking each person what they would choose if they were granted one wish. Andy wanted a farm of his own, Harry said he'd like to have a helicopter and licence to fly it, Keith wanted to conduct the Berlin Philharmonic and Geoff thought he'd love to be jumping out a bedroom window at eighty nine with the wronged husband chasing him. John said he'd like to knock off the remaining thirty five territories, dependencies and autonomous regions he had not been to, and I said, somewhat predictably, my wish was to make Castle Hill profitable. As we were walking out Keith said to me, 'I think this guy's interested in you.' I didn't believe him.

The restoration of the Roadman's hut was finished so John and I ended the afternoon there with the ubiquitous bottle of whisky, playing dominos and tiddlywinks to Eric Clapton and Bob Marley. We sat for a while on the little seat outside by the front door. It was nice to feel the warmth of someone so close beside me. Above us was a vast star-studded arc of southern sky, the Milky Way and constellations so much brighter and clearer than city lights and pollution allowed. It made the closeness and warmth more palpable. I wondered if maybe Keith was right. John wrote me a long thank-you letter. He continued on his tour of Books in Homes schools. They were schools and places I remembered visiting and we began to exchange letters and emails, sharing experiences of Hero and Book Assemblies and the children. He became a weekend visitor, staying in the 'west wing'. He made a point of meeting some of my children. Then he disappeared on another of his adventures, this time to circumnavigate the Mediterranean with a friend in a Kangoo delivery van.

In September we brought in the bulls for testing to assess their libido after our dismal calving percentages. There were the two Black Angus from Kakahu, my very first farm purchases, which had cost over $11,000 and so were expected to be very good. I had inherited Old Black and a Hereford and a couple of others with the farm. Andy, Harry and I went out early one cold and miserable morning and brought the bulls in close to Castel, where Simon Hewitt the vet joined us. I'd been told what to look for and what to expect. The first sign of interest from the bull was flehmening — nose

Work around the farm

Clockwise from top left: Snow clipping hooves as a protection against foot rot — when sheep get foot rot the horn keeps growing and curling up, hence the name farmers give them: Arabian slippers; dead sheep are dispatched into the offal pit; with Snow, starting our day on the phone to contractors. I haven't really worn him out!; dangerous work with deer in BigBucks: I hold a spiker's (a young stag) head with a beanie while Snow removes the antlers; every twenty days we bring in the sheep to stand in the foot rot bath, which is filled with zinc. I pour in sacks of zinc powder, wading into the crap in my muckboots and testing the consistency using a whisky hydrometer. We live, and could almost sleep, in our muckboots, they're so comfortable.

up, teeth bared, top lip pulled back, and dribbling. Next came smooching — rubbing on the side of the heifer, showing interest, and mounting without serving. Finally, serving, and I was instructed to watch for cork screw which was apparently best seen from the right hand side of the action. The bulls' libido was graded according to their behaviour: three serves in under five minutes — very high libido; three serves in under ten minutes — high libido; two serves in under ten minutes — moderate libido; and after that it all deteriorates. We had half a dozen heifers on hand and chose the biggest.

Before we began leading in the bulls, she was clamped in position within the yards and some Vaseline was rubbed around her vagina. I sat ready, stopwatch in hand, notebook on knee. The first bull entered, wandered round and did nothing. We were all freezing and wondered whether the cold was affecting the bull. Next in was Old Geoff, the Hereford, who began flehmening, but nothing more. We brought in one of the expensive bulls from Kakahu. Nothing. Then we milked the testes of the most likely candidate, No. 34 from Kakahu, called Gramps after my father, and smeared the semen round the heifer's rear end. This often makes the bulls more aroused as they compete against each other. Even this did not help, so at that point we elected to abandon the way we were going about things and try something else.

We injected about three of the heifers with prostaglandins to bring them into heat, and about four days later re-tested the bulls. We put the heifers together because they try to mount each other, supposedly a bit of a turn on for the bulls. On yet another misty morning, Simon came back and we started the process again. We picked a heifer, a very feisty young lady, which, like a Southern woman, was not going to be told what to do. In order to get her into the yards and secure her, I had to attach a rope to the Land Cruiser, tie the other end around her neck, and reverse to pull her into the crush. She was too contrary, and scary, to be attractive and we had to swap her for another. I set my stopwatch.

We brought in the first bull, one of the two from Kakahu. It mounted but forgot to get out its penis until it was too late; served at two minutes twenty, drooled heaps and served again at six minutes fifty seven seconds. Lots of licking and rubbing followed, but no further action. Grading: moderate. The second of the Kakahu bulls served in an impressive ten seconds with lots of flehmen followed by a few false mounts, plenty of licking and smooching and then another serve at nearly eight minutes. After that, no further action.

Grade: moderate. Old Black sniffed on arrival, mounted at forty seconds but didn't follow through, mounted and served after five minutes and mounted again but failed to serve at twelve and a half minutes. We decided he could stay as a backup bull. Old Geoff, the Hereford, was in next. Eleven minutes of flehmen, which does not get a cow pregnant, sealed his fate. He would be sold to the works. The two young bulls which we had just bought in a stud sale were below average. One looked the other way. I wrote in my notebook: 'Just spent $4500 on a Ferdinand lookalike.'

Simon signed a declaration saying they were not satisfactory and we were able to return them and get our money back. It had been another cold morning in the yards and I warmed myself with a glass of wine with lunch while musing on fertility. There had been no high libido machines and we would need to buy a couple more bulls. Once again John Chapman came to our aid. He lent us a pair of two-year-olds to put with the heifers on Father's Day. When the job was done, they went to the works.

In October I started paying particular attention to the rain gauge. It is supposed to be the wet month and we really needed the rain. Pasture growth traditionally starts again and the moisture readies the ground for new pasture and winter feed to be sown in November and December. I was also looking for someone to start work on the 1865 limestone cottage. It was one of the earliest buildings in the area still standing, and one of the oldest limestone houses. My brother Malcolm kept warning me not to over-capitalise and with this in mind I employed a valuer. On the strength of his report, which showed the property had increased in value, I felt confident about going ahead with The Limestone. I asked Suzanne Pickford, who had done the landscaping round the Old Quarters and had building contacts in Christchurch, if she knew anyone with the kinds of skills necessary to restore the cottage. All the floors were on a slope, the beds were on bricks, there was a gas heater with a flue up the chimney of the old fireplace and a rusted ball and claw bath standing on three legs. It was the most significant of the buildings and it looked the hardest to restore.

Ever since I'd moved to Castle Hill I had been looking for books about the station and the high country and their histories. There were classics like *Station Life in New Zealand* by Lady Barker, L.G.D. Acland's *The Early Canterbury Runs*, the much sought-after *Waimakariri: The story of Canterbury's Gold Rush* by Robert Logan, and the recently published *From Tussock to Tourism: The story of the Central Canterbury High Country* by David Relph. But the rarest and most treasured is a compilation of writings and diaries simply called *Castle Hill*. One of the diarists is John Enys, who with his brother Charles bought the sheep run in 1864 from its original owners, the three Porter brothers. In 1858, the Porters had bought two runs, a total of 25,000 acres and had added two more runs by 1861. When the Enyses bought Castle Hill it covered 35,000 acres. John followed a family tradition not just of keeping a diary but also of keeping the entries brief and to the point. In the diary of one of his ancestors at Enys Place near Falmouth in Cornwall is an entry written at the time of Queen Elizabeth I. It reads, 'Today we saw the Armada go up the Channel.'

The limestone cottage was one of several houses and homesteads built by successive owners of Castle Hill. John Enys, for instance, built a house of upright slabs of pit-sawn timber he called Trelissick which was later dismantled when an Irishman called John Millikin bought Castle Hill in 1908 and moved the house, along with the cookhouse, men's whare and sheds to Flock Hill, as he had renamed the eastern portion of the Craigieburn run. Enys had added a

Me and my fencer Geoff Rogers, at the Erewhon horse sale. Note my broken wrist.

sitting room to Trelissick built of ordinary weatherboards and Millikin carted that to the limestone cottage, also built for the Enyses, where it became the kitchen. All that is left now of Trelissick is a few foundation stones and a pear tree at one corner. Acland describes the Enys brothers as the 'good old-fashioned type of squatter'. Although they spent considerable periods of time away from the station, they were serious about their farming. There is a wonderful account of mustering Mt Torlesse in mid December 1868 from Enys's childhood friend, E.R. Chudleigh, who kept a much more evocative diary for his mother back in England. Some of what he describes would be familiar to generations of shepherds and musterers who have worked the Canterbury tops right to the present day.

'[December] 17 . . . We went five miles to the base of Mt Torlesse to be able to make an early start in the morning. We were all up at 3 a.m., had breakfast and off. Four of us went to the top in three hours and had a glorious view. It was too cold to stop long, so McLennan [the head shepherd] and I started along the top and reached the appointed rendezvous at 11 o'clock. Those at the foot collected the sheep with their dogs as we drove them from the top and sides. We all had a great feed and then a small sleep and about 2 p.m. we went off to muster another part of the country. We got back to camp about 6 p.m., had tea and turned in.

18. Had breakfast over before 5. The ground is alive with blowflies; the meat is full of maggots and the blankets not protected by a mackintosh covered with blows. We were off again and by 9 o'clock had the sheep at a river we wanted to cross, the yards being on the other side. We were two hours crossing. The sheep would not go in. We took them up and hurled them in, but no, back they came again and, breaking into small mobs, rushed past men and over dogs in a most determined way, but they gave in after a two hours fight and crossed. The sheep were fairly beaten and so were we for as soon as I had a bath and a good dinner, I slept for three hours.

19. At the woolshed yards all day drafting the strange sheep . . .

23. Eight shearers, one packer, one fleece roller, one picker-up and five outsiders. I took [charge of] the shed this morning and all the men appear good fellows.

24. Slept in a tent at the shed. Commenced soon after 5 a.m. and left off at 6½ p.m. I had the whole shed inside and out to look after this morning as all the station men and Enys were mustering. I started 15 bales of wool for

Christchurch by Markey and co.'

In the last four full days shearing, they shore just over two thousand seven hundred sheep.

John and Charles Enys were an interesting pair. Charles, the younger of the two, was known as the best shot in New Zealand and his prowess on the billiard tables at the Christchurch Club was reported to be 'staggering'. John's interests were more academic. Acland lists them in descending order as ferns, moths and butterflies, cats, people and sheep. Charles shared his love of cats and at one stage they had five felines. Charles let his cat lie round his shoulders during meals and help itself to titbits from his fork; John's sat quietly on his knee. John was the first to discover the fossil beds in the limestone of the river gorges and grid-ironed the cliffs above the Porter and Broken Rivers to preserve them. Today's fishers can thank him for introducing English brown trout and the Loch Leven and American trout to the surrounding streams. The two of them were hardly ever in New Zealand at the same time. When asked where the other was, the inevitable reply was that they were back home with a 'bucket in the well' to refresh their funds.

In 1888, Charles became seriously ill and returned to England where he died. The eldest brother died a short time later and John inherited Enys Place. He put Castle Hill in the hands of an agent and returned to look after the family estate. The property was leased for several years before being sold at the turn of the century. It was one of the leaseholders, Lewis Mathias, who discovered a great number of greenstone fragments behind the limestone homestead. It would appear that Castle Hill was on the network of old Maori tracks through the area to food sources and safe seasonal passages. According to Ngai Tahu, Kura Tawhiti (Castle Hill) and the nearby ranges were famed for kakapo and their ancestor Tane Tiki, son of the great chief Tuahuriri, sought the birds for their iridescent green feathers to make a cloak for his daughter Hine Tiki.

Work began on the limestone cottage in spring. For the first time, the tradesmen from Christchurch had nowhere to stay on the farm. I put them up at Springas pub, which Kate and Rob had bought when Bones and Sharmaine decided to sell. However, the builders' wives were not keen on the arrangement and the men ended up travelling every day from Christchurch. The best contractors were Paddy West, his son Ben and co-worker Daniel. Paddy came from one of the northern islands off the coast of Scotland and limestone was in his blood. He had done restoration work at Christ's College and also on Christchurch Cathedral (the limestone baptismal font at the Cathedral is made from stone from Castle Hill donated by the Enys brothers). As Paddy began restoring the cottage to its original configuration, I marvelled at how the early builders had dragged huge lumps of limestone down to the site, cut the blocks by hand and fashioned a snug, simple and beautifully proportioned house.

We put back the window that had been replaced in the 1950s by a door. The walls turned out to be less stable than we thought and took more work than expected. We exposed two of the interior limestone walls. The thick blocks showed hand adzing and when I stripped the wallpaper from the plaster it was seven layers deep. I kept pieces to date it. We exposed the lintels and found they were made of beams of black beech that still had bark on them. A surprise awaited us when we opened up the ceiling to put in Batts for insulation. It was already insulated with tussock. There is now a glass panel and light in the living room ceiling through which you can view the tussock and chimney. Paddy and his crew made good the original fireplace. Outside, they built the most beautiful curved limestone wall which protects and separates the cottage from the drive and compound. In the pretty garden bay to the north, there are old fashioned bulbs and grape hyacinths and I have now planted some tulips in memory of Jo Acland. When you sit in the cottage or on the front porch, you can feel the years. It has a lovely air about it. It is so cool inside in summer that I understand why the thick limestone blocks and the tussock lining to the tin roof were preferred materials.

My original plan for The Limestone, as it is now called, was to have Riki live there and we would have drinks and dinners for guests. She had left Books in Homes and was due to come south in November to manage all the accommodation. Tourism was back on the agenda and I was talking to a big inbound travel agent about the top-end market and starting the process of creating brochures and a website. Then, while we were working on the cottage, I thought it would be perfect as a café, something I had been considering as I watched the tourists and climbers toiling back and forth from the rocks. With that in mind, I added an extra lavatory. But that idea lasted about ten minutes; images of buses and campervans blocking my drive made me change my mind and I added a second bedroom instead. Big jobs like The Limestone excited me, and the more people said it would

The Limestone

Built for John and Charles Enys
in the late 1860s, The Limestone
has been completely restored
and furnished.

take too much to restore it and advised me to push it over, the more I'd say I could do it. But after all that restoration work, God, did I want a well somewhere that I could take my bucket to, like the Enyses.

j

John Bougen had been calling me regularly since he left on his Mediterranean road trip, sometimes daily, our deepening connections weaving through the ionosphere. Then one day he rang to say he was leaving the tour and returning early. He was missing me and Castle Hill too much and would be back by the end of November, in time for tailing. The interest he was showing and the questions he was asking made me feel I had found a real mate who would also be devil's advocate for me and my ideas. It was a long time since I'd been courted and now here was someone with a growing interest in me and the farm. I was pleased he was coming back.

It was hot and dry as we began direct drilling the paddocks with rye and fescue for new pasture. Andy was rolling the newly sown areas to keep in the moisture. The rain forecast to fall later in the week didn't arrive, and on Saturday I watched the nor'west wind raising layers of topsoil in thick ochreish clouds from the freshly drilled fields. It is considered risky to plough at Castle Hill because the wind can come up without warning and blow hard. There is a famous story about the contractor ploughing at the Enys block when the wind began blowing and all the topsoil ended up on the other side of the road. That was why we changed to cross slotting to plant seed because as the seed is deposited into one hole and the fertiliser into another alongside, it disturbs the ground less. We would never go back to direct drilling. At the Grasslands Conference I'd heard that seventeen per cent of New Zealand's GDP is in the first fifteen centimetres of its soil. I felt I was watching the potential for my contribution disappear.

Suddenly everything was happening at once. In amongst the builders and plumbers and stonemasons, fencers and general help, Riki arrived, then John, and the day after our first guests, Kate and her team for the Pumpkin Patch catalogue shoot. The models were a mix of Riki's granny-kids, local children I knew and children from Christchurch chosen by Pumpkin Patch. I went to watch one of the photography sessions out on location. The country kids sat on rugs by trucks during the long waits; the city kids sat in cars.

John moved into the homestead and shifted from the west to the east wing. The master bedroom is tiny and to this day it looks like a student flat. There is no space and clothes don't get put away. There are always suitcases out and they just get re-filled from the floor. The bathroom is even smaller and there is plenty of jostling to get to the basin or shower or mirror. The best thing about the room is the bed; I insisted on the most comfortable when I was buying for the station.

We started to meet my mates as a couple, and when people rang to see how I was I would introduce John into the conversation. Friends would nudge and ask, 'Is this the ram, Chrissie?' For a while they were very protective, hesitant to fully embrace this new person until they knew him better and saw the genuineness of his commitment to me. They were constantly saying to John, 'You're not going to hurt her, are you?' When you are living on your own in the valley, there is not a lot of courting in the conventional sense. Instead our relationship blossomed over boning out the dog tuckers and other farming tasks. We had interests in common; we both collected art and although I have not done anywhere near the travelling he has, I am a good traveller. We are both athletic and in the increasingly light evenings we had competitions hitting golf balls from the house down to the cattle trough in the next-door paddock. His shots were longer but mine were more accurate.

There were adjustments to be made. As people grow older they become more set in their personalities; what has happened in their lives reinforces who they are. I always maintain that every person is like a job lot at an auction: there are gems you want but with them comes some dross. Everyone is a mixture, only the balance is different. With John the negatives were smoking and snoring but they are far outweighed by the positives, the gems — sex, the emotional high when you have someone who is showing real love and caring for you. My stomach turns each time he holds my hand or arm, or when he is in the driving seat and we are going somewhere as a couple. I get cups of tea in the morning at half past six and he is a sensational cook. I used to say to myself, 'I've got plenty of good friends. I don't need someone alongside me daily', but I had forgotten how natural and wonderful and warm it is to have someone who cares for you above all others.

I had adjustments too. Living twenty-four hours above the shop, or in

Local events

The Cass Bash is an annual event that attracts a great crowd. The 2006 Bash marked the first time that the Valley team (lower right) had beaten their annual opponents, Railways, for years. Ross Urquhart and I had an unbeaten sixty-run partnership and I was named Man of the Match.

this case the wool shed, is a new experience for me. I had a real reluctance to let someone share my dream. For the first time I was on my own and almost growing up. Until then I had gone from living with my parents to living with Allan Tattersfield and then John Fernyhough, until I lost him. Then came Castle Hill. Every so often I'd find myself thinking that this was going to ruin my new hard-won reputation for doing all on my own. But then I'd see John working so passionately and so hard and know I had to change. I had to stop being so terribly possessive of my farm and start using 'we' rather than 'I'; and I had to listen more. And the reassuring thing about John is that he doesn't have to be here. He has successful businesses in property and retail and to begin with he kept going north for work. But over time the balance changed as he fell in love not only with me and Castle Hill but also the whole essence of high country farming. This was where he stayed now, except for occasional forays on business.

With our tailing done and knowing Ross Urquhart at Grasmere was about to start, I volunteered John and my services, a very high country thing to do. I felt more confident after my second year on the tailing line. I was given the clippers to mark their ears, worked out a system and began carefully: Mt Misery and males one side and Grasmere and girls the other. Heather Harrington was there and I started chatting, horse talk, she being a horse whisperer. We'd been talking for a while when I suddenly realised I was clipping the underside of the ears instead of the top edge. You mark them along the top so you can identify them more easily when drafting. I was appalled and confessed to Heather that I thought I had marked about fifty the wrong way. She told me, very nicely, not to worry; but after our picnic lunch, when Ross was so grateful, he was walking back through the mob that were about to be released when he suddenly began swearing and shouting. He grabbed the clippers and waded in amongst them, clipping them in the right place while the sheep ran in circles, little beads of blood flying from their ears. It was hideous and I felt dreadful. However my sense of dismay was ameliorated with an end of day Speight's on the lawn.

After watching and waiting for rain, we approached harvest time for the hay and baleage in drizzle and damp, the opposite of what we needed. At least there was fine weather for my annual Christmas carols party back in Auckland, where I danced the tango in a splendid Christmas Fairy costume and very high red shoes. My partner was Norm Hewitt, an old friend from Books in Homes days. Driving away from a catch-up breakfast in town I caught sight of myself in the rear vision mirror. I looked exhausted. At a cocktail party, holding my glass of bubbles, I dropped a piece of smoked salmon on the carpet and as I bent to pick it up I was assailed by the sight of my hands, nicked, scarred and very obviously working hands in contrast to my refined urban surroundings. Although I always looked forward to my visits back to Auckland, I was feeling slightly alienated. While people were interested in what I was doing, my conversation was becoming more farm focused, and after a short time talk would return to their shared Auckland lives. I found I was even more uninformed on general topics. My children had always joked about the way what I was doing took over my conversation: Oh no, they'd cry, she's talking about Books in Homes, about gifted kids. Now it was farming.

Back at the station, the weather was still playing games and the season was late. Keith, my saviour and the mainstay of Dad's Army, was leaving. He was going back to work for DOC and his first job was to restore the Avoca Hut on Broken River at the boundary of the original Castle Hill run. On his last day the two of us went down to the terrace above the Porter River for a picnic. He had his sandwiches which Chris always made for him and I pinched one for old time's sake. They were consistently delicious and I would often steal one at morning tea. It was like swapping school lunches, except I didn't always have something to offer in return. We talked about the past eighteen months, remembering all we'd experienced, what we

A handsome Castle Hill ram with wonderful turned horns. His fine wool fleece weighs over four kilograms.

With John, Pearl
and Midge.

had learned and the things that had made us laugh. Keith had been doing a university paper in Classics when he started working at the station, and getting A+ for his essays, and one of the things I appreciated most was that he added tales of the ancient Greeks to the farming conversation. Among his favourites was Xenophon, mercenary and writer, whose book *Anabasis*, an account of a campaign against the Persian King, was used as a field guide by Alexander the Great when he first reached Persia.

Then, barely before she had settled in, Riki had to leave too. She became ill and needed to be close to hospital services. The farm, more than an hour from the nearest hospital, was much too far away. Her daughter, Fleur, and husband and family had recently shifted to Christchurch and so

Riki moved in to town to live with them; and then they moved back to Auckland. I was sad to see them go. Riki and I have done so much and been through so much together and I had been really looking forward to her becoming part of my new life at Castle Hill.

Christmas Eve was spent making hay. The contractors have such a short season and everyone wants them at the same time. They run constantly between lowlanders and high country farmers like us with our differing climates and states of readiness; and sometimes the two clash. The weather was still far from ideal and we stacked the bales like outcrops of high walls, facing the northwest wind to protect the ones behind from rain and to help finish drying out. They stood in the fields like huge randomly placed sculptures. Andy and his family went away for Christmas and left John and me in charge. With the season so late, the baleage, which we generally try to have done before Christmas, had not been started. There was a ten-day burst of sunshine forecast to start about 27 December. We spent the last days of 2005 and beginning of January working desperately to get the just cut lucerne and meadow grass ready to be baled and wrapped. It was a dismal and costly exercise that year. We were raking eighteen hours a day. In some paddocks it was hardly worth it; they only produced about six bales and the lucerne had seeded too much which meant some of the nutrient value had been lost.

The baleage contractors worked on under lights as we brought down the bales from the fields for them to wrap: three on the tines of the tractor and ten stacked on the Penrose feeder. The baleage paddock at night is like a stage on which tractors and trucks move in a ballet, emerging into pools of light, circling in the darker corners, their work lights flashing. The young guys get very little sleep between jobs because of the huge pressure to get everyone's baleage done in good time. On New Year's Eve we worked until midnight. Kate and Rob and the family were staying, and during the evening I joined them briefly for a glass of bubbles and then went back to the paddock where I was working. While I raked slowly, the

Overlooking the glacial terraces of Deer and Ghost Flats across to the Castle Peak.

baling machines moved quickly around me. I failed to see a bale and raked over it, jamming the prongs together. I thought it would be all right to keep going but they came after me like the highway patrol, lights flashing. I was removed from the tractor and spent the rest of the evening with John in the John Deere to try and put as many bales as possible under shelter as the forecast was for more rain. We took a break the next day for our New Year's Day party.

Andy came back with his family at the end of the first week of January to say that he was leaving. He had given six weeks' notice before coming to Castle Hill but now he was telling me that as he was still owed some holidays he only had four days left to work. I said it wasn't worth it and that he may as well go straight away. It was totally unexpected and came just as we were entering a really busy period. In the midst of what felt like disaster, we had one positive — John Tavendale, 'Tav', the new farm advisor. We

had been without one since Andy arrived as he was keen to run the station on his own and did not want the oversight of an advisor. John Chapman and Emily Crofoot had both continued to stress the importance and usefulness of having a third voice, especially someone like Tav, who had spent a lifetime in the area and had many prominent and successful high country farmers amongst his clientele. They had both recommended him. I called Tav and explained what had happened. He was shocked. However, in the paper that morning he had seen an advertisement from a farmer returning to the area wanting a job as a farm locum. Tav knew him and said he would sort something out.

I was hurt and surprised by Andy's actions. We'd had a meeting a couple of days before Christmas and he had given no indication he was considering leaving or that he was unhappy. I knew he was not pleased to have a farm advisor on the scene again and he was uncertain what John's arrival would mean to him as farm manager. We assured him that John's presence and role on the farm would not affect him. But John has this huge energy and would work all daylight hours, not stopping for lunch, because that is his way. His practical strengths are a wonderful contrast to the sensitivity of his photographs. His father was a builder and he had done some farming as a young man in the north of the North Island, so he had multiple skills that were enormously useful on a farm, especially one remote from towns and services. When you cannot call for help, you have to 'chop your own wood'; to solve problems and work out how to do things yourself, wherever you are on the station. It is especially hard if you are a woman, and a woman who does not like asking for help. You learn to make good use of the simple machines — the lever, pulley, screw, wheel and axle, inclined plane and wedge.

Even with those aids, I had known I was of limited use to Andy. Unlike a man, I couldn't throw a hay bale or bang in a post, and after my disaster with Moss, I still didn't have any dogs. I realised, too, that I had remained rather insensitive to the impact of my constant suggestions that we try the latest thing I had been talking about with one of the neighbouring farmers I admired. We were both beginners in different ways, and when I failed to get him to change his perspective, the prospect of having someone as experienced and avuncular as John Tavendale to talk to him became very

The Station flats and the Porter River from the air.

attractive. I also wondered whether Castle Hill's isolation was too hard on a couple with a very young family. A number of farmers had talked about that and how hard it often was on the wives. I would need to take all this into account before we began interviewing for a replacement.

In the meantime we had the temporary manager Tav had found for us. Lindsay McGrath was crossing Cook Strait as Andy left. He'd been working up north after selling his farm at Oxford and wanted to get back to the south. He stayed with us in the homestead initially and then moved into the manager's house. Lindsay came with three dogs — Brandy, Whisky and Patch — and the most distinctive voice. He was a master at yelling 'That'll do, that'll do!' He was weather-beaten, reliable and kindly, and told me everything he had learned in his many years of farming.

John had ridden horses in the past and now he was on the farm full time he realised he could have a horse of his own. It is an unavoidable truth that to manage Castle Hill effectively you need horses. Even without the tops it is very hilly, and when mustering stock from one paddock to another it is necessary to go to the furthest ends of the field they are leaving to ensure a clean sweep. Most people would rather use the bellows of a horse than their own lungs, and that's particularly true for an asthmatic like me. There was also a temptation when you have enormous blocks, as we still did, and no horses and could not reach most of the farm by vehicle, to set stock and come back in two or three weeks. What we were trying to do with the newly configured farm was to manage the pastures, our food, by doing another of the 'Fs', fencing, dividing them into smaller blocks. One of the first decisions that came out of an early meeting with John Tavendale was to look at increasing pasture and winter feed. By then we had put in one great strip from the highway to the edge of the terraces above the Porter River. Now we would try breaking in two large paddocks, Ghost Flat and Deer Flat, over the river. They were 50 metres lower than the Porter terraces, and so not as cold, and they faced west so had some protection from nor'west winds. They had a good stream running through them, no matagouri bushes and only scattered tussock. And lastly they were flat and fenced.

We were over getting a quote from one of the local spraying companies when some people from DOC passed on their way to check on the fencers. They wanted to know if we had approval to spray and re-pasture on what they reminded me was Crown lease land. It had never crossed my mind. I was farming it and improving it. But according to the pastoral lease, I had to have permission from LINZ and they in turn check with DOC. Eventually they both gave their okay and we cross slotted it but the process made it a month late.

Ray Ward-Smith had been the person sent out by DTZ on behalf of LINZ to find out what we were doing. He had worked for the old Lands and Survey and had been up and down the high country all his life. After he had looked over the paddocks he came back to the house for a cup of tea. The conversation turned to family and he mentioned that his son had horses. Andrew had represented New Zealand in eventing but now wanted to go to Massey University to do a veterinary degree and so was selling them. John was immediately interested and said he would like a horse or two. Ray said they would bring a couple for us to look at.

I've never been a horsewoman. My experience of horses was limited to the odd ride on elderly horses one step from the knackers' yard. What I had learned in these brief encounters was that I was allergic to them. (I didn't suffer from allergies and asthma as a child. They developed suddenly in my thirties, after I left my first husband. I've always believed it was the stress and the guilt of that decision, of discovering that I was not a person who breaks a contract easily, that triggered them. My friend Lindsay Baragwanath still remembers the time we took our kids to Ohakune to ski and went

Two of my early Castle Hill staff, Harry White, at left, who came to the farm just after graduating from Lincoln, and my previous manager Andy Bitmead.

out riding one day. By the time I got back to the small chalet where we were staying — five in a bed and some on the floor — my eyes were red and swollen. We'd been asked to drinks that evening and I had an idea teabags would help reduce the swelling, so I soaked a couple and put them on my eyes. Tracksuits were coming into vogue as casual wear and I had just bought one at Vance Vivian, a menswear store. I thought it would be perfect for alpine drinks; one of Lindsay's daughters asked if I was going for a run. I removed the tea bags from my eyes. They had left big brown stains. At the party I mingled, panda eyed, with women in silky ensembles and high-heeled boots.

The horses arrived with Ray, his wife Kath, and Andrew, plus a pile of saddlery. I climbed on Jimmy, John got on Jerry Maguire, and Ray and his son mounted their thoroughbreds. Kath decided, wisely as it transpired, that she'd read books up at the house. We started off, one small circle around the huge horse truck and then down the drive and over the highway to the farm road to the river. What followed could be called a series of unfortunate events. First, Jerry Maguire kept going sideways, turning this way and that until John became frustrated. Ray took Jerry to try and sort him out but as we reached the track down by the river Jerry McGuire reared up and Ray ended up underneath. Andrew raced back to his father to see whether he had been hurt or worse, and my horse Jimmy took off after him. Luckily Ray was all right.

We continued down to the river and I was feeling fine, rather pleased I'd survived the unexpected dash, when suddenly Jimmy did a little jump, dropping me off. I was wearing boots with heavily corrugated soles and my foot stuck in the stirrup. He began dragging me, bang, bang, bang, along the rocks. As the others tried to stop him I managed to wrench my boot out and Jimmy took off. I made myself get up and checked see if everything worked, insisting fiercely that I was okay. They took me at my word and rode on while I walked home. By the time I got back I was in agony. Kath made me cups of tea and I had a bath. It turned out I had four broken ribs and a badly scratched back and I thought I would never get on a horse again. John went ahead and bought Jimmy and Jerry McGuire. We agreed it was just a freak accident. A short time later, at the annual picnic at High Peak, I wobbled around in the paddock in Clergerie high wedge boots with my broken ribs as the men all regaled me with stories of mates who'd died or been badly hurt when the same thing had happened to them.

We put Jimmy and Jerry Maguire in Frizzells, the paddock behind the house, and I flew with John to Auckland, very sore and shaky and with my confidence nearly as battered as my body. Lindsay McGrath was installed and we had two weeks in which to drive John's car down from Auckland via Haumoana, where the Frizzells were still living in my bach, and Castlepoint. After all our conversations and emails, it was wonderful to finally visit Emily and Anders and their station and to see what they had achieved. They carried twenty eight thousand stock on their 7000 acres, very different from us. It was well run and intensely monitored. Emily gave me some of their operational and management protocols. The day before we arrived, we heard prices for lamb had plummeted, a drop of twenty per cent on the year before, and at a time when the New Zealand dollar was strong.

The day after we got back to the station, Castle Hill and I featured on the six o'clock news. A few days earlier I had taken a phone call from a reporter on *The Press* asking me about one of our farm roads. The day we got back I was also contacted by TVOne for comment. The stories were the result of protests by a group of residents from Castle Hill Village about work we had been doing to improve an existing farm track that led down from the Thomas block out to State Highway 73. The original track had been put in about 1920 and then during the World War II it had been used as a running track for training Home Guard soldiers. It was reopened to reach stock during the great snows of 1992. The protestors complained the work had been carried out without resource consent and that a new road had been cut, disfiguring an area designated 'outstanding landscape'. This scar was clearly visible to them from across the river. The story in *The Press* quoted one of the residents, identified as a Maori expert, claiming the work had 'desecrated sacred land'. In little more than twenty-four hours I'd gone, as my son David said, from hero to zero. However, previous owners were very supportive. Jill Blackley knew it had been refined by her father and how treacherous the track could be in the wet and snow.

Work on the stock track had begun in mid December and Pete finished it while John and I were away. It gave us access to a 2000-acre section up the back of the Thomas that we were dividing and fencing and we needed safe access to it. The old track had some serious deficiencies and the spectre of OSH, and the ongoing saga of the Berrymans*, made me very aware of my responsibilities for the safety of those working on the farm. We had deviated for a short section, where the steepness of the old track made it unsafe, and installed culverts to stop scouring of the existing track. In the past, it had caused farm vehicles to have to drive onto the surrounding tussock land, causing damage. Once again I had no idea I had to apply for resource consent to maintain and upgrade an existing track.

My timing could not have been worse. There had been a number of high-profile incidences where local body luminaries and others had carried out major projects without getting permission and then had resource consent awarded retrospectively. The most obvious local example had been the big tar sealed road and parking lot and the grassing of an entire hillside carried out at neighbouring Flock Hill in preparation for filming a few scenes for *The Lion, the Witch and the Wardrobe*. The station's owners were paid handsomely for the use of their land and the consent given after the fact. People were becoming tired of those who were getting away with such blatant flouting of the RMA. I felt I had been chosen to make an example of. A procession of representatives from the various bodies involved came to look at what we had done. The Selwyn District Council, DOC, ECan and Mark Solomon for Ngai Tahu did not consider it a problem. Mark completely understood the necessity for the work, saying that you cannot farm without tracks.

LINZ had to respond to the neighbours' concerns and protests. They found there was no evidence a consent had ever been granted for a track in the Thomas River area and wanted me to apply for one. The issue dragged on. In June, I was served with a summons from the Selwyn District Council to appear in the Christchurch District Court the following month. I was accused of committing a criminal offence against the Resource Management Act, and having had only the odd speeding and parking ticket, I was horrified. Arguing my case was expensive. I employed a lawyer in Christchurch, a QC in Auckland and commissioned a report from a firm of surveyors to show how minor the impact was of the work we had done. After all this expense — in excess of $25,000 — the council

* The Berrymans were prosecuted for failing to maintain a bridge built on their property by the army, which subsequently collapsed causing a death.

withdrew the charge. Instead I was instructed to apply for retrospective consent. It was granted on the condition that the hard edge of the new cut be re-contoured to blend in with the existing slope and the new slopes planted with pasture grass and local tussock to match the surrounding vegetation. What resulted was a much greater scar than the scratch we originally made.

Things were not going well on the horse front either. Jimmy had taken a dislike to Jerry Maguire and spent his time kicking him. One afternoon I was walking back from tending the hens when I noticed that Jerry was lame. John was in Auckland; he suggested leaving it until morning and checking again. Next day Jerry Maguire was even lamer and I called the vet. Jimmy had kicked so much and so hard he had broken a bone in one of Jerry Maguire's legs, usually fatal for a horse. It was bad, but we could send him to an equine hospital, where for vast sums they might or might not be able to fix it. The alternative was to put him down. I suggested a cup of coffee up at the house before checking once more to make sure his diagnosis was right. Unfortunately it was. I called John again as Jerry was his horse. He did the sums and didn't want to send him to hospital. I held Jerry Maguire's head while the vet inserted a huge needle in his neck and gave him a lethal injection, assuring me the horse would go down peacefully. But he didn't die easily. As the blood oozed up the injection needle he lurched, jumped, went down and got up again and all the while I tried to hold his head. Eventually he lay still. The whole time Jimmy and another horse stared from the next paddock.

The vet washed his hands and left. I didn't want Jerry Maguire lying there upsetting the other horses, so Lindsay put a length of chain around the rear legs, attached it to the tines of the John Deere and hoisted him up. The only problem was that even with the tines fully raised Jerry Maguire's nose was still nudging the ground. We had to take him like that, head down, trailing blood, along the highway with traffic slowing and drivers staring, then in through the gate to the offal pit paddock where the tines and body became entangled in the pine trees before Lindsay manoeuvred around. At the pit, after a great effort to get the distorted

More work around the farm

From top left: Tallying the sheep as they leave the drenching tank, where they have been soaked with organic phosphates and zinc sulphate to guard against flystrike, lice and dermatitis; working on the conveyor belt at the annual pre-tup good health day, smiling as ewe No. 2000 gets her shot of five in one with selenium; feeding out from the John Deere during the 2006 big snow; Midge helps me catch an orphaned lamb.

and bleeding body as close as possible, we dropped him in and he landed perfectly on his side. Looking down on him I thought of the great white horses etched into the Wiltshire hillsides in England. By this stage Lindsay was crying. Although he had done this sort of thing many times, he said it never got any easier. He suggested he make us a cup of coffee and as we left Jerry and the pit he quietly confided, 'Only the good die young.' I didn't want to get on Jimmy again. I was off thoroughbreds and looking for a station hack.

John was not only buying animate items for the farm. He bought tools, a farm bike, a post driver, a slasher to top the paddocks and cut the grass along the side of the road, and his pride and joy, a 90hp Massey Ferguson tractor. It may well be one of the few in the high country. A tractor with no cab is not a popular choice in minus fourteen temperatures — but it has turned out to be invaluable. I like driving the 'Mighty Massey' because, unlike the John Deere, you have all-round visibility. You can see what the forks are doing and it makes it much easier when picking up hay bales. The negatives are that the wheels have been set so that it has a narrow wheel base (and so it can feel like it is about to roll on a hill) and there is no sound system. It felt good to have someone else who wanted to become a partner in more than just the physical work.

With February came mustering, weaning, drenching and culling of the sheep. My ribs were still very sore, especially during tasks that required turning and bending, such as tapping a spring for a water trough. After that particular job I took a break, went home, ate one of the Darfield bakery's outstanding pies and lay down for a while. We had help for the last great muster that season. There was John and Lindsay and me, Stew Gunn's shepherd, Louise Buick, and Geoff Rowlands from Springfield. Ever since Louise had been a small child she had dreamed of having her own team of dogs and her own off-road truck with a crate to hold them. Now she had them all and the job with Stew on Brooksdale. It was the first time I'd seen a woman working her own dogs; the first time I'd mustered alongside a woman shepherd. She took me with her on the top beat, walking the scree slopes to the south of Prebble Hill. It was scary. You work your way around the side of the hills, not down them. She taught me to put my hill stick on the up side of the slope we were traversing to help maintain our footing, which is totally against one's natural instincts. I was also doing a fair bit of sliding around on my bottom. About eight old ewes, behaving more like goats, took themselves up the rock face onto a ledge way above the river. They sat up there, refusing to move, and in the end Louise had to scramble up to get them. The lower hillsides and flats beyond were Sahara-like and the sheep came down in dust clouds. By the end of the day we had them all in the tailing-yard holding paddock. Early next morning we got back to find half of them had disappeared. One of us had forgotten to close the lower gate.

The dipping contractors arrived and set up in the sheep yards. Around them the pens filled with sheep and lambs standing patiently under the sun, pushing head first into the shade from an old tree. Across the toast-coloured paddocks the rails of the cattle yards appeared to ripple in the heat distorted air. The dip is a large raised corrugated tank, open at the top and surmounted by a turning arm that showers the sheep packed inside with a thick spray of dirty yellow coloured liquid. The sheep entered reluctantly, pushed and chivvied up the ramp by the dipper's beardy dog, the old style huntaway, with occasional help from Lindsay's 'That'll do' dogs. But on release the sheep needed no encouragement, skittering and slipping down the ramp on the opposite side, leaping to freedom. Their wool was darkened by the dip, the curl separated and accentuated. The dipper and his wife are two of the few people I've met who say they like Perendales: 'sheep with brains'. Leave one of the tank's doors open while you get water, says the wife, and if it's Corriedales they'd still be standing there when you get back. But Perendales, they're smart. They'd be out of there in a flash.

This last big muster was also what ended my time without dogs. All I had to bring the sheep from the paddocks on the flats over to the yards was the Hilux and the hill stick Mary Lou had given me. I would drive a bit, toot, get out with the stick and push the sheep a little and then get back in, drive and toot. It was very slow and inefficient, and I began to feel as if I was almost expected to bring the scones. Just as with the horses, it was plain I couldn't take full part in the running of the farm without dogs either, and I did not want to be relegated to the maker of morning teas and lunches. There could not be more than one Moss.

I called a very well known dog trainer, Dick Carmichael, who holds annual dog auctions. It took ages and I kept phoning him, and then Ed arrived. He was a huntaway and the size of a small horse. He looked more like a chap's dog, and John rather liked him so he took Ed and I kept looking. I wanted a heading dog rather than a huntaway because they are

The rewards
of labour

Now Selling
Pen 1328
Tally 15
Tot Wt 2540
Avg Wt 153.3
TB Status C12

Last Sold
Pen 109
Tally 25
$/KG 2.353
$/Head 475

CANTERBURY LIVESTOCK AUCTION CENTRE

PGG Wrightson

Since I've had Castle Hill the
managers and I have worked steadily
to improve the infrastructure and
raise productivity. Once run-down,
the station now has new fencing and
cattle yards, among other things.
Clockwise from top left: Baleage in
tight, neat rows; mown lucerne
waiting for the balers to arrive; at the
cattle sales with PGG Wrightson
stock agent Craig Miller; Castle Hill's
sales figures up on the auction
board; BigBucks, the new deer yards.

more intelligent. Then I heard about Guy Redfern, and that is how I got Midge, short for midget, a small black and white heading dog. Guy ran her up White Horse paddock and showed me how she worked. Then he recorded her command whistles onto the voicemail recorder on my phone. The only problem was the Witch of Springfield, a demon tidier, wiped them and when I went back to check they were gone. Guy had arrived with Midge just as I was completing my third sponge for the chocolate log competition at the Malvern A&P Show in which Jess Gunn had entered me in as a joke. There were strict rules: no cream, only jam in the filling, and it had to be with the judges by 10am. I got to the show just in time, paid my $2 entry fee, and came third, winning $1. The Gunns ate the log in a tasting session on the way back to Brooksdale and pronounced it excellent.

Midge became my constant companion. I took her everywhere with me and was shocked I was not allowed to have her inside and let her lie on the carpet like all the family dogs we'd owned when first I and then my children were growing up. At the same time, I began to understand that I had never had the same depth of feeling for any of them as I have for Midge, and I guess that is because she works alongside me. Once I had Midge I could move stock a long distance through all sorts of terrain, through tussock and matagouri and rivers. I became much more observant of pasture, and its

Looking west across the Porter River to the homestead flats. Castle Hill Village is in the distance at left and the Craigieburn Range is behind. From left: Mt Enys, Mt Cloudsley, Mt Izard and Mt Cheeseman.

condition. I noticed that where hill land faced north-west it was burnt off and in the lee more protected. I had the time to study my stock, to speak to them. Midge found ways to overcome her size disadvantage. Sheep and lambs may be hidden under the kale in the winter feed paddock, or under the snow tussocks, but she is always leaping up, fixing their position. She will sit and look until she spots them. I might see two Perendales and send her out and begin to wonder where she is and the next minute she comes over the hill with twenty. Cattle must seem huge, with their legs and hooves flying at head level, but she runs in and out of them like the tide, and bares her teeth.

There are times when she has her off days and I wonder whether she is coming on heat. We might be flushing out sheep from the manuka and she will become so frustrated she gives up and wanders off out of sight, which is so against her normal modus operandi and really annoying. Sometimes she doesn't respond to her 'sit and look' command. I yell at her and others tell me she may need a tickle-up — the stick. But that is not for me. I prefer the Sue Bradford style of behaviour modification. She is also a fussy eater. Tux isn't to her taste. She likes neat little Eukanuba, and when she gets a leg for dog tucker, she picks at it in her kennel and it joins a growing pile of bones right at the back. When you are cleaning out the kennels, hers is the only one where you have to take off the lid to remove the skeletons from the cupboard.

Getting Midge proved to be the key to my love of farming. She is an extraordinarily loyal dog. If I am there she will not move on or go with anyone else, even a group of dogs she likes to be with. While I am away in Auckland I miss her. She has made real to me what Peter Newton means when he talks about his 'one and only'; and I now understand why Snow Cleaver, when his favourite dog died, drove all the way to Whitewater to bury Jim where they did their last muster.

CHAPTER 9

Breaking and remaking traditions

The arrival at Castle Hill of our new manager
Snow Cleaver marked another turning point.
John Tavendale had advertised for a replacement
for Andy immediately, but this time we looked for
a stock manager because we didn't want to be in
a situation where control was vested in the farm
manager. I was looking for someone who was skilled
with stock and could demonstrate it; who would ask
the right questions about the farm; who could look
at the pasture and know what was needed to make
it flourish. I wanted someone who had experience of
farming in the Craigieburn-Torlesse area and who
was pleasant to work alongside.

Snow Cleaver was Northland-born, from a remote
farm where they made extensive use of horses, and
yet he was a typical high country man. When he was
still young he had seen an article in a magazine about
the South Island high country and made a pact with
a mate to find a way to get down there. His mate
died but Snow came anyway and has never left. He
started on southern farms as a musterer when he was
eigtheen and has worked his way up to manage farms

for a wide range of people, including LandCorp. His previous job had
been as manager of Mt Hyde in Otago, another station with a fearsome
reputation, where he had worked wonders and turned it around.

You know just from the way Snow talks that he brings with him years
of experience. He is one of the last generation to muster the tops of the Alps
and Canterbury ranges. He knew Castle Hill and its previous managers
and thought it a place with unrealised potential, a place that even given its
altitude could do much better. He arrived with his dogs and some of his
horses, moving into the manager's house with Lindsay just in time to help
him do the annual draft with Tav, a good introduction to the station's stock.
We had delayed preparing for tupping until we had a new manager, simply
moving the ewes from paddock to paddock and not giving them barley, the
great hot carbs that ewes and rams need at tupping time. We had almost left
it too late in terms of their health and fertility, and now began feeding out
generous quantities of barley in readiness for Father's Day on 1 May.

Feeding out barley required another new skill for me, backing with a
trailer. I found long draw-bars were slightly easier to manoeuvre but the
barley feeder's short and to get it into filling position under the silo was a
nightmare. The paw marks and dog licks and mud and dust on Phyllis's
back window didn't help. After what seemed like hours of repeated backing,

accompanied by screaming and swearing, I would be forced to ask for help, which a high country woman hates to do. (One of my best achievements this year has been to finally manage on my own.)

Because the mob was a long way up the paddock, for the first few days I sent Midge out to bring them down. It only takes a day or two, even with a change of vehicle, before stock recognise the barley buggy and come running. I would put Phyllis into low gear and set a straight course. The grain is released by a string. You either sit in the cab while you pull the string or walk alongside. As the barley pours out the sheep line up, head to head, feeding. At the end of a line, the buggy drops a little mountain underneath as it stops, and it is not long before the greediest sheep become aware of this and push their way under to reach it. In each of the paddocks I also dropped big pinky-coloured blocks of salt licks (used to combat copper and selenium deficiencies).

Shortly before Snow arrived Lindsay went to Palmerston North for a weekend of golden oldies rugby. He came back feeling sick and we all thought he had food poisoning or a stomach bug. But weeks passed and he didn't get any better. He was irritable and clearly unwell. He kept assuring us he was fine, but he became so sick he eventually put himself to bed for a couple of days, something Lindsay had never done before. Snow thought there was something badly wrong. Crutching began and Lindsay insisted on getting up and going down to the sheep yards. I was in Darfield to collect Toxovax injections from the vet when John came racing in to tell me he had just delivered Lindsay to the health centre. He had been standing at the back of the shearing shed leaning on his mustering stick, looking like Moses, when he suddenly collapsed. John went back to the farm, and I stayed with Lindsay until the ambulance came for him and I then followed them to Christchurch Hospital. They found he had gall stones and an infected gall bladder and he was there for weeks. He didn't return. His wife came down and picked up his dogs, and once he was well enough they went back north. They have a place at Waipawa now and every so often he'll call, and when in the south come visiting, always interested to know how things are.

I had not attempted to get on a horse since my fall. I told John to take Jimmy but I knew I would have to try again before too long. Snow Cleaver is a great horseman. The first time I saw him drafting calves from a group of heifers, separating those feisty, neurotically protective first-time mothers from their babies, it was like watching a rodeo. The ground was sloping and very uneven and there were big old matagouri bushes, some over two metres tall. Snow was on Emma, a Clydie-cross, chasing, changing speed and direction, pivoting almost on the spot, mirroring the movements of heifer and calf until he eased them apart. Now that he was here, I felt it was a good time to pick up the reins again. He has heavy walking horses, very different from highly strung thoroughbreds, but on my first time back in the saddle, I became terrified when we reached Whitewater and began crossing, remembering the day I had crossed the Porter River and Jimmy had dislodged me. I dismounted, annoyed with myself but too scared to continue. I could still feel occasional twinges from my ribs.

Dave and Wendy from Hororata Nurseries were up planting round The Limestone and knew my horse story. They thought they might have just the kind that would suit me, an eighteen-year-old pacer called Timmy who had a strange gait and was not a big mover. He had hung around the back of hunts carrying elderly, frightened and failed hunt riders. If he hasn't already been killed, they said, we'll track him down for you. And so Timmy arrived. On my first ride, Snow led Timmy and me round North Face and then left me to ride home without the lead. Because of his age, Timmy stumbled frequently and tended to fall further and further behind, suddenly lurching forward in order to catch up. As I was to discover, he also didn't like heading off alone; he was used to years of following.

He arrived unshod and one of the first tasks was for Snow and his son Jack, who act at the station's blacksmiths, to shoe him. I'd never seen a horse being booted up before. The brazier heats up, the blast of hot air reminding me of a high summer nor'westerly, and the long tongs hold the shoe until it is white hot. Adjustments in shape are beaten in. When it is a perfect fit, it is plunged briefly into cold water before being applied to the smoking hoof and hammered in place with square nails. Then the hoof is filed — a full pedicure. I didn't know hooves grow like toenails.

There are times when Castle Hill basin can feel very remote from the rest of the country, let alone the world. Anzac Day always reminds me of how international politics have reached into the heart of even the smallest of New Zealand communities. I've attended the Anzac service at Springfield since I arrived. In 2005 Anzac fell the day after the big party for the opening of Castel, and only Kate and her kids and I made it over Porters Pass to the morning parade and a beer in the pub afterwards. The service is held in the Springfield Community Hall. Everyone is there, young and old, in their Sunday/wedding/funeral clothes. Some of the farmers seem uncomfortable in such townie gear retrieved from the back of the wardrobe. Trousers finish above the ankle and the ties are thick and striped. The chaplain is from Burnham Military Camp and there are half a dozen soldiers in khaki, representing the armed services. The organist plays the upright piano and we all sing the National Anthem and 'Abide With Me' or 'Oh God Our Help' slightly out of tune but with a feeling of being one, of being free, and of remembering the personal and the universal. We sit in rows facing the Roll of Honour boards that hang on the north wall. That is when you see how small communities are affected: two or three sons taken from one generation or succeeding generations in just a single family.

Each year I knew more people to talk to, needed fewer introductions. And each year I recognised more names up on the honour board. There were Millikins, descendants of a previous owner of Castle Hill, John

Millikin, who began his New Zealand life carting supplies to the stations and railway works along the West Coast Road; one boy was lost in World War I and other in World War II. Two Evans boys and two Gold boys, all lost in World War I. In all, the twelve sons of Springfield who did not return from the two World Wars, big numbers in such a small community. At the end of the service we followed the few remaining veterans outside, where the flag was raised and lowered while *The Last Post* sounded mournfully in the freezing morning air. Wreaths were laid and then all of us quietly placed our poppies at the base of the flagpole. Everyone trooped inside for cups of tea before heading up the road to the pub in the hope of a shot of something stronger.

There were now only a couple of weeks to the annual calf fair at Canterbury Park and I was hoping for better pen positions than in 2005. After the low eighty five per cent calving rate the first year and the subsequent testing of our bulls, I took more notice than I might have when the bulls had gone out at the end of December. Andy put cows, heifers and bulls together in one huge mob in the Whitewater block. I wasn't sure the bulls would even find the cows in its 2500 hectares, and cows have such a short period in heat in their twenty one-day cycle. Near the end of their

On Tarndale during a cattle muster. Note Tarndale's grimace and my anxious smile.

second cycle, when you hope
that they are all in calf, I
insisted we move them from
Whitewater to the Thomas
block where we were
fencing. At least for the last
cycle bulls and cows could
see each other. I was pleased
we did. On scanning we
found ten to twelve per cent
of the cows had conceived
in that last cycle, which was
unusually high. Even so, we
still only had an eighty two
per cent calving rate. It was
well worth a less uniform
mob just for that gain.

With Hamilton and
Nelson, from whom
I get the most
aromatic bacon.

Once the bulls were
back in, the cows were put
right out beyond Emu block
for calving where there was
standing hay, according to
Andy. We had not subdivided the paddocks by then and the cows stayed
up in the hills and only came down to the Montana flats to have their
calves. Then they stayed down, moving back and forth from Broken River.
I thought the standing hay was well gone by then and brought over bales
of hay and salt licks, plain and multi-mineral. It must have done them
good because Castle Hill calves were in the top pen at the sales and earned
favourable comment for their quality in the newspaper. I watched with
pride as they entered the auction ring and milled around looking lost and
slightly stunned. Our calves have such lovely natures that I was almost
tempted to put my hand up, as I did when I red-spotted my collections in
the Anderson Fernyhough Gallery. I felt we earned our 'High Country
Vigour' stamp that year.

Once again the calves had left behind crying mothers that clustered at
the fence across the road from the cattle yards. At midnight there was a call
from a cartage company. They said one of their drivers had contacted them;

Snow walking out of the traces with his Clydesdales Jock, Emma and Banjo.

there is no cellphone coverage between Lake Lyndon and Arthur's Pass. He was down on the highway near the cattle yards and there were cows everywhere. John and I found a huge rig outlined in lights like a circus truck, its headlights blazing. We had just completed installing a new gate in the road paddock and the cows had broken through hoping to find their calves in the last paddock they'd been. We pushed them back through the gaping gate, wired it closed, and hooked up a double electric fence along the whole length, gate and fence, imprisoning them until morning. Despite all our fencing work, determined stock find ways through. A month earlier we discovered a hastily scribbled note stuffed in the doorjamb at the homestead. 'Bull on side of road 500m down Castle Hill straight from your turnoff. Don't want to see it be steak!!!'

There was no doubt winter was on its way. In the mornings the Hilux's windscreen was white with frost and mist hid the stock until the sun was in its stride, taking the moisture skywards bit by bit to leave a blue-sky day. The matagouri that sat by the river bed of the Porter carried perfect spider webs on every

branch, glittering like Christmas decorations. But in the changing seasons
you can be caught by a sudden reversal, a freezing cold sleet and wind
that feel as if they come straight from the South Pole. The field mice had
started their annual search for warmer accommodation and the mouse traps
in the garage were working overtime. They snapped and tapped around
the concrete floor. In the Roadman's and Old Quarters you needed to be
vigilant: they've been known to hop into the beds. It was the time of year
again to think about 'tidying the sheds' — the stables, the workshop, the
walk-in freezer, and the woolshed. John had become our weather man.
Every morning he turned to the back of the first section of *The Press* to
check the forecast for high country Canterbury. He watched the orange
wind sock by the cattle trough in Chrissie's paddock, my very best present
from him, and checked his fancy watch that gives barometric pressure. He
became extremely accurate in his predictions, and terminology; while Snow
and I talk of thick rain John insists, correctly, that it is snowing.

On the morning of 11 June, we had sixty millimetres of rain. John
was taking hay across the Porter River to the deer, driving the John Deere
with six bales on the back of the Penrose debaler. The force of the water
jack-knifed the trailer despite its three-tonne weight. He boosted his way
out but then had to get back with an empty trailer. Being John, he thought
he'd give it a go. He tends to drive with the left hand door open to let out
his cigarette smoke. As he reached the centre of the river the water poured
into the cab until it was 30 centimetres above the floor. Behind the tractor,
the trailer floated about like confetti. The John Deere pulled through but
others haven't been so fortunate. One of the fencers almost lost his new
truck when he picked the wrong crossing early one morning and had to be
towed out. I was luckier. I took Phyllis, weighed down with bags of seed, to
the crossing I had just seen the cross-slotter use only to have the Hilux die
in the middle. There was green water over the windscreen and I was almost
submerged. I barely made it, throwing great plumes of water to either side
as I ploughed on and up the bank.

On the morning of 11 June I left for a week in Auckland, stopping for
lunch at the Gunns' on the way to the airport. As usual weather was part
of the conversation. The heavy rain that fell later had been forecast and
we all thought the barometer was too high and the temperature too warm
for snow. John thought differently but even he did not predict what was
coming. Next morning he called at seven, as we always do when one of

*Opposite: Feeding
out in the big snow
of 2006. Two feet of
snow lay on the
ground for two
months. The feeding
channel was cleared
by snow plough.*

us is away from the farm. There had been a huge snow storm overnight, the heaviest fall in forty years, and this was particularly wet snow, much heavier than the last big fall in 1992. It was the beginning of what we call the two-by-two winter — two feet of snow for two long months. John had to manage the first forty eight hours. Snow had taken a day off to collect his horse truck and Clydesdales from down country and ended up having to stay two nights at Springas because the Pass was closed. Ever the consummate farmer, he had brought all the sheep down from the hills onto the flats before he left. The cows, bulls and deer were left on the hills in an area where there was good shelter.

For the first couple of days no one ventured down Highway 73 except John on the big John Deere with the snow plough I had bought somewhat reluctantly in 2005. During those mild winters I'd thought Keith and Andy slightly odd with their constant talk of the need to replace the old plough. Since then it had lain forlorn in the shed; in the winter of 2006 it was the equivalent of the Westpac Rescue helicopter. John snow-ploughed the main highway and made feeding-out channels for the baleage. He fed out

State Highway 73 alongside the Roadman's, cleared to create a narrow passageway by our snow-plough.

a hundred bales in the first four days and we continued to feed out up to twenty five bales a day. In the paddock beside Old Quarters the sheep supplemented their diet by eating the bark off the pines along the northern fence line. A year later the trees were still trying to patch their wounds. After the snows, we settled in to a succession of days of incredible beauty, especially when viewed from the warmth of the homestead's underfloor heating. We lived and worked in a white world where the tops of the ranges sat crisp against vast blue skies and you had two sunrises and sunsets each day, the pink and gold that stained the snow morning and evening reflected on the pristine slopes opposite.

The mildness of the previous winters meant there had not been much need to feed out baleage. I found doing it difficult now; it was like a complex acrobatic act done in an ice box. The snow settled and a series of frosts sealed it. The feeding-out tracks were like glacial terraces that wove their way through the flats. The Penrose only takes four bales at a time and if we were feeding out twenty five a day that meant a lot of driving back and forth. When I reached the paddocks the animals would be running up and down the feeding channels begging for food. The bales sat two at a time on the conveyor belt on the open trailer with another two carefully balanced on a side rack. Once in the field I'd cut the twine round the bales on the belt and tie back the ends; then, with the stock following eagerly, drive slowly along the feeding channel between two-metre-high banks of snow. The bales crept along the belt, through the rotating blades at the end and out to the ravenous stock. I drove constantly looking back over my shoulder to ensure I stopped the belt before the metal plate at the back of the bales hit the blades. Because I found the bales so heavy, I tried to park at an angle so I had gravity to help me tip the second pair into place, but I still found it difficult. And by the time I finished I'd be desperately cold. Snow jokingly accused me of misrepresentation as we clunked through the icy channels: 'Chrissie, you told me this was much warmer than Dunedin — look at it!'

It was definitely a time for comfort food, and unlike Mary Anne Broome (Lady Barker's name during her time on Steventon Station in the Malvern Hills) we were well provisioned. In the great snow of August 1867 Steventon lost four thousand of its seven thousand sheep and almost all its lambs. Their stores were virtually exhausted when the storm struck, the winter order of supplies, groceries and coal still in Christchurch. Trapped in the homestead by deep snow, with her husband in town on business, Lady

Barker ran out of food for cooking and fuel for heating. Her two young maids retired weeping to their beds, saying they might as well die warm. In contrast, Castle Hill's pantry is like a small grocery store — tins, jars, bottles and packets lining the shelves, and the multiple freezers well packed. I am prepared for unexpected guests, weather bombs and pandemics.

If I'd been in the city and it had been snowing or raining I'd have stayed inside, turned up the heat, poured a drink and put on a rack of lamb. On the farm, whatever the weather, you are out attending to something. I thought about the stock, whether the sheep were in the right place, how the cattle were managing. We suffer from a lack of good shelter belts and we wanted the stock to be in the lee of what shelter we had. I dug out the pigs and ensured they could get to their trough and that the hens had enough grain and their water was not frozen. They had virtually stopped laying in the short winter days.

The dogs almost go into hibernation in winter because there is little work for them. We had moved their quarters in the autumn after I'd seen them shivering in a southerly underneath the pine trees at the back of the stables. It was a bleak sunless position. Although my cheque book was meant to be on holiday I couldn't bear to see them like that. Their new enclosure, The Dogs, is beside the northern wall of the old tractor shed, a series of kennels suspended in a row. Faeces can be high-pressure hosed off down a drain and into a sump, all very hygienic. Even though it is more protected, we still have to chip off the ice when we go down to feed them. I put Midge closest to the shed because I thought she'd get reflective heat but instead the snow roared down the corrugated iron wall and settled on her. I've since moved her further along the row, hoping it will be a warmer position. In the old days the musterers' dogs had a really tough life. No dog motel for them. They were tied up at night under a matagouri bush or in half a forty four-gallon drum, summer and winter, in torrential rains and hoar frost and snow, and fed on wether muttons with no fat. Many died of distemper.

A storm like the one in June pulls small communities together. The neighbouring stations called each other once phone lines were repaired. Not everyone got their power back as quickly as Castle Hill; it's one of the advantages of being on a main highway. At High Peak Station they were without power for six days and it was five days before a grader cleared the road. The families on LandCo farms in the isolated Lees Valley gathered together each evening in a conference centre that had a generator. In the warmth they prepared and ate their evening meal, watched television and compared notes on how each of the farms and families were coping. The Chapmans at Inverary in the Ashburton Gorge had less snow than us, but they were seventeen days without power or phone. When I could finally contact them, John said he had quite enjoyed the candle-lit dinners, but Anne said she had become depressed at having to manage without power for so long. When our neighbours from Grasmere and Mt White were finally able to go south to Christchurch, they were shocked to see how much snow there still was at Castle Hill. Our fall was much heavier and longer lasting than theirs. They called to apologise for being such neglectful neighbours.

The storm was the most costly in the country's history. The Canterbury region was paralysed and some ten thousand houses lost power. In Darfield, the snow caused the roof of the relatively new swimming pool to collapse. Insurance claims topped $42 million. The greatest damage was to the electricity and phone infrastructures and to the paddocks of winter feed that were crushed under the weight of the soggy snow. The other damage of course was to farmers' pockets. That perennial 'D' of farming, debt, got a little bit deeper.

Once the snow started to disappear we began break-fencing the battered winter feed paddocks. The turnips survived but the rape and kale broke and fell apart as they thawed, like salad greens that are mistakenly frozen in the back of the fridge. Once more I wished for someone to invent a better electric break-fencing system. The single wires blew around and became caught on the most miserable of grass stalks and the new, supposedly improved, netting was incredibly difficult to get snug to the ground. I stomped into the house at the end of one particularly trying day and suggested that perhaps we needed to leave unplanted paths through the feed, like fire breaks in a forest, so we could set the break-fencing more easily. The poor weather continued with the coldest and wettest spring for years. It stunted pasture growth. John Chapman said it was the slowest spring growth he could remember. I felt sorry for the lambs, starting life born in a puddle, but I was extremely pleased with their numbers. When we had pregnancy-scanned the ewes in August we'd found an incredibly high in-lamb rate for the station, and the annual drafts for which the meat works had only offered us $12.50 and that we had put to the ram instead, were now full of twins.

All through the winter and early spring we had maintained a high level of supplementary feed. It was costly but it paid off in the lambing rate and the good condition of the lambs. I soon learned I was not the only one who farmed passing fields; farmers are constantly looking at each others' stock. When Snow arrived he couldn't wait to get what he called the 'dog tuckers' away from the road and out of the front paddock by the hay barn and pig pen. I'd placed them close to the killing yards thinking only of convenience. He made sure the paddocks along the highway became the display windows for Castle Hill. He and I moved the mixed-age ewes with their lambs into a roadside paddock, and as we drove away I thought, 'They look fantastic. People will be saying we've had a good lambing.' And they did. They rang spontaneously to tell me they had never seen the stock looking so good. I could feel my chest fill with pride as I said that it was not just me, it was the team.

Every year on the last weekend in November Barry Drummond hosts the Cass Bash, when the railway workers play the valley in a one-day cricket match. It's another of our local institutions and everyone is there. Barry is the unofficial mayor of Cass. He came for three years to manage the railway, with its little station that painter Rita Angus made famous, and is still there twenty years later. Canterbury University's Cass Field Station, also painted by Rita Angus, is just across the double rail lines, and further along by the siding is a series of little huts in various stages of decomposition. At Cass Bash time the whole area is alight with lupins. We go for the day but some make a weekend of it and camp for a nominal fee. Barry has a marquee and when he's having a party the Cass Club is open. There is karaoke on Friday and he has bands for Saturday night; the first year I went the Waratahs played. A Maori group come over from the West Coast and put down a hangi in the morning and take it up at five. Not only is there chicken, pork, lamb, potatoes and kumara, but also Christmas pudding which is served with great jugs of custard. In 2004, when I knew hardly anybody, I was taken under the wing of Victoria and Olly Newbegin, past owners of Cora Lynn and Grasmere Station. When I moved

to Castle Hill, Victoria thoughtfully gave me the postal addresses for all my neighbours, a list of alpine plants that do well at our altitude, and told me about getting fresh fruit and vegetables delivered direct from growers. That was when I was thinking about paying guests.

The Cass Bash playing field is in a paddock opposite Grasmere Station, just past the entrance to Craigieburn, where Johnny Westenra farms, on a flat area that Barry somehow manicures into a cricket pitch. The outfields are another matter: one part is over the entrance road, another by the Mt White mailbox and yet another on a really rough paddock covered in stones. There is always some kind of excitement during the game. Last year I went out early to umpire and gave LBW to a chef from Grasmere. He flew into a rage and had me removed. Then everyone jumped to my defence. It came time for our side to bat. One of the rules of Cass Bash cricket is that you can't go out until you have scored a run. I kept missing the ball and needed a quick lesson in how to hold the bat. Ross and I then had a wonderful sixty-run partnership and at the end of the day I was awarded 'Man of the Match' and a bottle of wine. I couldn't wait to tell my kids.

The autumn equivalent of Cass Bash is Paddy Freaney's Easter tournament of what is best described as coarse golf. Paddy and Rochelle Rafferty are the ex-owners of the popular Bealey Hotel. They made international news in 1993 when Paddy claimed to have seen and

My mother, Gladys Don, surrounded by her fourteen great-grandchildren on her ninetieth birthday last year.

photographed a moa while out tramping. They are also mountaineers and have climbed some of the highest peaks in the world. They take the summits around Arthur's Pass, which most of us find a difficult and asthma-inducing climb, at a canter. This year I was invited to a barbecue and pre-tournament practice with Ross and Daniel Urquhart, Heather Harrington, Richard Smith and some of the musterers from Mt White Station. The golf course runs up and down slopes through drainpipes laid across Paddy's garden, which is no bigger than the average city plot. You navigate through the hebes, flax and tussock to the water hole — a killer — where one can double one's score. The putters date back to the 1960s and the balls have bounced off countless trees and rocks. You take your beer with you when you play and everybody is within 20 metres of each other. It is hilariously chaotic. Silver cups of all sizes and shapes, once awarded to past winners of wood chopping or netball or croquet or dog trials, are handed out for all manner of prowess and then gathered up at the end of the day ready for the following year.

We stopped practising when it became too dark and began the barbecue. I'd taken a bottle of whisky as koha and while we were eating our meat and salad it was decided it should be opened. One of the boys from Mt White said that when you come in at the end of a muster you have to drink whisky out of the lid. The lid started circulating and I noticed our voices growing progressively louder as we extolled the quality and skill of our golf shots. The thought of having to drive home brought my evening to a sudden end. Next afternoon Paddy and Rochelle turned up with our formal invitation to the tournament. They were in a bad way. Paddy had mentioned the spa to the Mt White boys who'd insisted they turn it on and they had finally left at four in the morning. Paddy told me I'd 'missed a great one'. 'Thank God,' I thought.

Winter returned to give us a farewell slap early in December. Snow and I had been going to move the hoggets into Plenty and I was up at half past five for our six o'clock start, but the night's rain had turned to snow and so I thankfully went back to bed. John and I began the seasonal negotiations of the newly coupled about whose family we saw when for Christmas and the holidays. Then just before we went up to Auckland I fell in the cattle yards and broke another rib . . . and one of the rules of farming. In the cattle yards these include no running — the rule I had broken — no jumping down from the railings, and no dogs. I thought it was an unnecessarily harsh way to acquire that information. But my troubles were not over: while with my granny-kids up at my bach at Mangawhai I slipped down a bank in the wet and shattered my right wrist.

We arrived back at Castle Hill before New Year. I'd had a couple of days in hospital and was in no shape to do my share of farm work, or much else initially. At least the new pain made me forget my ribs but I had no idea this kind of break and my right arm in a cast would incapacitate me quite so much. John not only had to take over all the cooking, he also helped me dress, put in my contact lenses, cut up my food, and fetched and carried all manner of things. It was a lot to ask someone but he did it tenderly and without complaint. I didn't like to imagine what it would have been like if I'd been alone.

When I think of John I am constantly amazed at just how skilful he is in such a wide range of things. Both Colin Giffney and I have welcomed the business knowledge and advice he has brought to the farm and his sense of humour leavens many a day. He's fantastic at plumbing and irrigation and an excellent post driver. He placed a hundred posts in the new outside sheep yards with the greatest of precision. Since he bought a four-tonne digger whole paddocks have been contoured and irrigation lines buried so we don't have a repeat of last winter's frozen pipes. Snow and I have a bet that within six months John will be looking at a twenty-tonne digger. Geoff is fencing the ridge between Whitewater and the Rocks and has a small bulldozer, and John is already waxing eloquent about how useful such a machine would be. There is no end to a high country man's toys.

My family. From left: Julie, James, Emma, Grace and David Tattersfield; me; Will, Kate, George, Jack, Alice and Rob Hellriegel; Joe, Chloe, Symmone and Leo Tattersfield.

If you were writing a profile of someone you would want to be part of your life on a farm, John would be that someone. An old friend rang when he heard about John and me and said, 'I wondered why I was walking around smiling and then I realised if I was writing a job description for you, it would be John. He's mad, but not as mad as you.'

There was no way I was going to sit up in the homestead and nurse my broken arm. I could at least continue mustering although the gates I already had difficulty in opening were now almost impossible. I had no grip at all. First there were the many permutations of latch. A few are perfect, some are made of twisted wire, others have been put on by fencers with superhuman strength who set the gate latches so far apart a woman, especially one with a ruined right wrist, has no chance of opening or closing them. There are the catches made of horse shoes and, trickiest of all, the chain that locks with two cut links. The gates themselves have their own challenges. Some drag and catch on the ground, some have to be lifted or swung down on in order to release tension on the latch, some have abandoned their hinges and are propped with baleage twine. And then there are the old Taranaki gates; opening and closing them always seems to involve a tussle. One of the many farming inventions needed is an easy way to open gates, perhaps by running over a pressure pad that sets a spring; nothing electric or hydraulic that would freeze or short. Or maybe someone could develop a catch that a dog could open. I would love a million dollars to spend just on gates and fences.

Every February, the thirty-pupil Springfield School has its major fund-raising event of the year when they provide breakfast for supporters of Coast to Coast. 2007 was the race's twenty fifth anniversary and there was no way I was going to miss that, even if it did mean being at the Mt White Bridge at four in the morning to be ready when the sun rose around six and the famished supporters descended. The men — John, Rick Hill from Flock Hill, Richard Smith from Mt White, Waka James from Benmore, Stew Gunn from Brooksdale and Stu Stokes from Russells Flat — set up in a row, their barbecues fired up to cook fifty kilos of bacon, thirty dozen eggs and hundreds of hash browns, all served on white or brown bread, while they talked farming. I lined up with the girls with paper towels and tomato sauce, and tried to keep abreast of the farm talk. In front of the Taege Tent, affectionately called the party tent, was a school desk where people paid their money: $6 for The Works, very different from Parnell prices. Coffee and tea were served from the back of a ute; no latte or flat white here, just black or white. The all too emaciated contestants forgo breakfast, focused on the next stage of the race, the kayaking section. They set off down the Waimakariri to the bridge near Oxford with good luck notes and bananas and other snacks taped to the front of their kayaks.

The weekends of the Coast to Coast and the Wildfoods Festival at Hokitika in March are the closest State Highway 73 comes to resembling a city rush hour, except that all the traffic moves in one direction. The cars go past the gate like lice over a dirty sheep's back. John says we may as well have Castle Hill Towage signs for the farm trucks. We are constantly rescuing vehicles. There are cars in the drains, cars that hit bridges, cars splayed on fences and cars down river banks. We also have drivers who have run out of fuel. Over the Christmas period we buy in containers of petrol because there is a constant stream of motorists who have miscalculated the

Local volunteers join us to muster the 2500-acre Whitewater Block.

distances between petrol pumps and need a few litres to get them through. Because the farm compound is so close to the road we have had to padlock the diesel pump to stop people helping themselves. The last time that happened they not only stole fuel but also left the tap on and we returned to find the contents of the tank on the ground. It is not easy to get a tanker up immediately to refill it, and all the farm vehicles run on diesel.

The one activity my ribs and wrist put a complete stop to was riding, and if I am honest there were times when I didn't mind. There had been a couple of incidents with Timmy. I had finally prised him away from following, although he didn't like it. Out one day mustering with Snow on the Lower Thomas, Timmy was so intent on turning round to follow Snow while I was intent on pulling his head back in the direction I wanted us to go, that the bridle broke, the bit came out of his mouth and next thing I was over his head and onto the tussock. I scrambled up, not wanting Snow to see I had fallen, and made myself get on again. Timmy's erratic pacing and stumbling and the difficulty I was having in breaking his propensity to follow were beginning to bother me and I thought it would be good to find an easier ride. John said he would buy me a horse for Christmas, and early in December we went to see Rex and Denise Mitchell who manage one of the LandCo Farms in the Lees Valley.

We followed a narrow, precipitous, unsealed road that wound through the Ashley Gorge and over the Puketeraki Range while the Ashley River snaked back and forth beneath us. Then suddenly we were through, looking out on the fertile valley flats stretched below. Rex had a four-year-old mare called Minnie for sale who Rex said was too slow for the Lees Valley musterers. She was a smallish horse and liked women. All that sounded good to me. She was delivered to Castle Hill but I didn't have the chance to ride her because of my ribs and then my wrist. Once I was ready to ride again, I found I didn't like her all that much. She had an attitude that showed in the whites of her eyes and the way she laid back her ears.

I was still looking for a safe, sturdy, reliable, big-lunged beast but they were not easy to find even though I rang people like Richard Smith, who still musters Mt White the old-fashioned way; no helicopters to the tops for

him. What I wanted was a station hack of the old variety, something Snow
and I began to talk about while we were out mustering. Snow breeds horses
and he knew exactly the kind I needed and gradually he, John and I came
to the decision that we would start breeding a line of station hacks. John
and I felt lucky to have Snow's expertise and name behind this new venture.
We bought nine brood mares, five in foal, from Slade Farm, a thoroughbred
stud north of Amberly, and planned to put Snow's Clydesdales over the
thoroughbreds to get good station, trekking and eventing hacks. We also
bought a colt and are getting about five brood mares from Birchwood,
which is being de-stocked now it belongs to DOC. The first Castle Hill
foals are due in spring 2007. We believe they will fit a niche in the market,
and with luck there will be one that is just right for me.

I'd also started looking for a huntaway because I found that even with
a heading dog as good as Midge you still need noise to move sheep. Up
until now I had been using some not very effective huntaway stand-ins:
a jerry-made percussive device fashioned from a piece of alkathene pipe
about forty five centimetres long, split at one end with a supermarket bag
attached by its handles, and an old octagonal tea tin with stones inside tied
up with baling twine. There was also the inconvenience of having just the
one female working dog because when she goes on heat you lose your work
mate for three weeks while she stays in the bitches' boxes. I heard that
Snips Prentice had a huntaway that had just given birth to a litter of pups.
The dog's aunt had been a New Zealand huntaway champion and so the
breeding was there. Stew Gunn was getting a pup from the same litter and
said he would choose one for me. His method was very scientific. He told
me he put a bottle of bubbly on the lawn and the first one that ran to it was
mine. Even though she arrived covered in puke from the drive over Porters
Pass, she was a beautiful looking pup. I called her Please partly as a joke
but it came to rebound on me.

Please turned out to have a natural instinct to run up behind mobs but
I needed to train her. I received plenty of advice from Snow and others on
how to go about it and would start and then get too busy to put in the time.
I treated her much as I do myself when starting something I know nothing
about, which is to begin and presume I'll pick it up in the process. I would
head off with Please and expect her to know almost by osmosis what to do.
I could get her to bark behind a mob and, with the odd throw of a stick,
to come back to 'Wayleggo', and if I said 'Stand' she would bark without

moving but I could not put reliable sides on her. In the sheep yards she'd sit and bark but then I couldn't get her to be quiet, and she would walk the wrong way, scattering and dividing the mob. She was also exhibiting an unwelcome predilection for the hocks of the last sheep. The shearing gang doing our crutching was heard discussing how polite I was to the dog at the bar at Springas. They didn't realise Please was her name. I was no longer so amused by my choice. I felt I was pleading and getting nowhere. The constant shouting had wrecked my voice. Snow said it was not too late to change her name. I sent her away to Graham Fechney, one of Snow's dog trialling mates, to learn her sides — left and right — and even some obedience. Four weeks later the re-named Pearl returned. She was now nine months old, slightly more obedient and not quite as crazy. My voice was no longer hoarse by eleven.

Summer is the time for sheep dog trials and Snow's arrival in the area with his reputation for excellence with dogs had spurred the local dog trialists to amass as many points as possible to get a team to the national trials. The season had already started by the time Snow, John and I went down to the Malvern Collie Club's Springfield trials. Snow was using his huntaway Tom for the straight hunt and the zigzag and they completed both with ease. I had Midge with me and Snow entered us in the short head drive and yard. I had no hesitation about entering even though I knew nothing, had never been to a dog trial, and only watched *Tux Wonder Dogs* occasionally. I must admit I was quite taken with the idea of being a 'maiden' and not just a maiden but a 'district maiden'. My first attempt was built on a number of sketches Snow did as he explained how you entered the drive from the front, followed your dog and sheep through the hurdles two thirds of the way up and then, when you reached the pen, did not let go once you put your hand on the opening handle until the penning was complete. I'd been told not to go early in the day but to wait until the sheep started to tire.

I watched a few of the pros and noticed there was a dress code: moss green moleskin pants, caps carrying the brands of drench products, John Bulls (boots), a dog stick (which is shorter than a hill stick), and whistles made from tin, plastic or pounamu. The two judges were sitting in their cars, feet on the dashboard. There were lots of mustering stories while people waited. Everyone talked about how difficult it is to muster with dogs now because they are so used to mustering with the toot of the quad bike or Hilux and the sheep are much more attuned to those sounds than the quiet of a dog.

When my turn came, the person releasing the three Romney sheep was way up the hill to the left almost behind some trees. With a lot of 'Over!' and 'Where!' from me, Midge brought them down and into the drive and started moving them through the hurdles. In my excitement I went round the outside of the drive until a yell from the judge reminded me I also had to go through the hurdles. We reached the pen and I unlatched it. Time was running out — you only have fourteen minutes. I stood like a mannequin with my arm out. I didn't think I could move an inch. I had no idea you could stretch your body and leg as far as you were able in any direction as long as it was not in front of the gate. Before I could finish the judge yelled, 'Time!' I closed the pen and returned the three sheep to the holding paddock. Waka James was there and was so complimentary about my first attempt that I felt great. John told me he was extremely proud of me.

Now I was eager to get to the Glenroy Collie Club's two-day trials at Fighting Hill on the Rakaia. It takes a sizeable community effort to organise dog trials: there are the lunches, the bar, the judges and people to hold and release the sheep. The cook shop was opened and a little hut set up for the bar where the trialists reminisced about their run and their dog. Women from the surrounding farms provided lunch. There were cold cuts and delicious old-fashioned salads: potato, sliced iceberg with half eggs,

Icicles hanging from the spouting outside my bedroom.

beetroot in vinegar, and mayonnaise made from sweetened condensed milk. Then there were biscuits, slices, fruit cake, and tea and coffee to follow. The food was set out on tables covered with clothes and adorned with vases of flowers; all this for $6 a plate. Annette Millar, who has a South Suffolk stud at Peak Hills, was there making lunches as she has for years, and it meant a great deal when she told me how wonderful it was to see someone holding up the women's side. I was the only one competing this year.

I was so keen for my second attempt at the short head drive and yard that I went early in the day. The sheep were Snowdon Perendales, and perhaps if I had waited until the afternoon fatigue might have blunted some of their characteristic high-spiritedness. Once again Midge brought them down faultlessly and after some to-ing and fro-ing we got them into the drive. But there we stuck. We could not get them through. Time! The judge, knowing I was a maiden, came over to talk to me. He said I was doing fine, I just needed to support my dog more, and I had a *great* little dog. I had the feeling the subtext was, 'Pity about you'. Next was my first attempt at the long pull. I could see Annette and the other women in the cook shop looking out the window. This was quite different. The Rakaia is infamous for the nor'west winds and it was blowing like hell. I was yelling against the wind, further handicapped by using my voice instead of a whistle. I sent Midge up the right side but three-quarters of the way up she decided to cross over, a cardinal sin, and lost us points. Nevertheless she

A smiling Lady Hamilton with a second-generation Lord Nelson.

pulled them down and into the circle of white painted river stones. I had to line them up with the sheep and me inside the circle and Midge outside, but by then I was hyped with adrenaline. I was trying to get her inside as well when the judges yelled and gave me the thumbs up. I was so excited at my first completion that I impaled my Zambesi pants on the barbed wire fence putting the Perendales back in the holding pen. The cook shop women were full of congratulations.

We had been talking about re-instating the Castle Hill dog trials since

Snow arrived. They were not part of the official trial season, more a day
out for friends from town and country. Bones, who is well known in dog
trialling, said he would lay out the course once I had a pen. I tried in vain to
locate the original Castle Hill cups, following a trail through several of the
neighbouring stations before giving up and ordering new winners' trophies.
After a week of vile weather the day of the trial dawned calm with blue skies
and sun. I confined myself to releasing the trial mobs for the short head
drive and yard from the limestone rocks at the top of Chrissie's paddock. I
could not have competed anyway. I'd caught a cold which had developed
into pneumonia and I had no voice, especially not for shouting commands
at dogs. There was no way I could stay inside either, when this was the
inaugural Castle Hill sheep dog trial, the first in the valley since the 1970s.

We put up the Taege party tent. Kathy made a scrumptious feast of our
hams and venison patties, and people brought their own tables and chairs
and drinks. It looked like a line-up for Bunnings. The trials started at ten
o'clock, town and country mingling, kids everywhere, Pete Henderson and
mates on their guitars, everyone relaxed and roaming between dog watching
and admiring the restored buildings. The competitors adopted the wait-
until-they're-tired approach and so they were still competing as the townies
packed up and the sun went down. We had to have a two-stage prize giving.
Mark Smith from Mt White had won the Junior Musterers' Race; as they
had arrived by plane they needed to be away before sunset. The second
prize-giving took place by candlelight, chief judge Bones officiating. There
were cups for all events and the overall winner, Roy Veronese of Snowdon,
won the Castle Hill Cup, an old trekking billy donated by Snow which was
as close as I could get to a replica of the original billy which I daresay was
made of sterling silver. Oh for those annual Merino's wool cheques of the
fifties and sixties!

I had been wondering for some time whether I'd made a mistake buying my
Dohney rams. They had seemed like a good idea when I was looking for a
way to stay with fine wool and get a bigger meat carcass but I'd learnt that
I wasn't really in a position as a new and relatively small farmer to pick
up a niche breed like Dohney that no one knew about. Farmers weren't

used to buying them to fatten. They have no history with Dohneys and would rather buy Black Face because they knew in six weeks on the land they could make a predictable amount on each sheep. I rang Paul Jarman, who had bought Dohneys before me and been enthusiastic about the way they were performing. I'd been watching mine leaping over the sheep yards, crazy as Perendales. I asked Paul how his were doing. 'Oh no,' he said. 'We got out of those mad things!' Now we've got them as hoggets and they'll be going to the terminal sire this season and the lambs will be off to the works.

The Perendales had been much more successful in giving us a great balance between fine wool and a big meaty body and we decided to increase numbers. However, my experience with the mixed-age capital stock Merinos from Berwen Station made us careful about where we sourced them. The Merinos had been the best of Berwen's breeding unit and I'd thought Omarama and Twizel would mean a good transfer but I didn't know the Omarama weather, drier and kinder than Castle Hill, and the terrain not as high. They never prospered. They did a massive Merino sulk, got sick and generally looked more like dog tuckers. Two years later, most of them are still not bouncing around in the top mobs. There were Perendales for sale at Millers Flat which Snow thought would be much more compatible with Castle Hill conditions, and the sellers, the Barclays, were very well respected. We bought some beautiful two-tooths at $100 a piece and three of his rams, which had come from the renowned Ruddenklau Perendale stud. We also bought some top quality Perendale rams from Annabel Tripp at Snowdon and half a dozen excellent South Suffolk and Poll Dorset rams from Annette Millar at Peak Hills. Now that we have built up our Perendale numbers, we shouldn't have to buy in any more as we will be breeding our own replacements.

Despite our success with the Perendales, I was still attracted to Merinos, partly because of the role they have played in the romance and history of the high country, and also because I truly believe that the

fortunes of fine wool will rise again. I had not considered buying a stud
until I knew Ross Urquhart was definitely leaving the valley and moving
up north. He'd been a man of a thousand farewell parties as the decision
to leave Grasmere waxed and waned. The Urquhart name first appears on
high country runs in the 1870s and has long been associated with Merino
sheep. Ross's Merino stud came from the Tripps of Snowdon, one of the
oldest in the New Zealand stud book, number 118. Annabel Tripp says they
were reluctant to let it go but keeping it was no longer economic. She told
me to look for sheep with the prefix 'A' because they were one of their best
blood lines, with excellent fleece quality and good frame weight.

Ross knew that I needed new Merino blood if I was serious about
staying with the breed. Snow and John agreed, and Ross said he would
give us first pick of his stud before his stock was sold. Snow and I went
down to Grasmere to spend a day going through the various mobs, working

*With Snow and Ross
Urquhart, examining
Ross's stud Merinos
just before he
retired from
Grasmere Station.
These original sheep
will form the nucleus
of the new Castle
Hill Merino stud.*

in the one-hundred-year-old shed. Daniel, Ross's son, drove the sheep in and as they ran through towards the light we grabbed them and turned them on their backs to check their hooves. Soon there was horn and blood and clippings everywhere while conversation between Snow, Ross, Daniel and I ranged over mustering, the old days, old friends and old dogs, and parties. At one of Ross's many farewells he decided to have a competition to see who could hit a golf ball the furthest. I suggested covering the balls with silver paper so they could be seen more easily in the fading light, which didn't work. In the end, because I can do no wrong in Ross's eyes, he declared me winner and arrived at Castle Hill two days later with my winnings — $2 — and wine. If Ross borrows a cigarette he returns a packet, typical of him and high country generosity. If there is one sin in the high country, it is meanness.

Every so often the three of them would stop, step back and roll a cigarette for smoko. We talked about Iraq and they got stuck into the reforms of the 1980s and 1990s and how it had affected them; about how the promised trickle-down effect had not happened, and about their fear of ending up having to live in the city where their lot would be no better because it is so expensive. Lunch was a loaf of bread with butter, tomatoes and bacon made from wild pig. When we had finished working on the sheep, Snow and I ran the ones we had chosen through the race in mobs of thirty, looked at them more closely and weeded out a few more. There was a sense of timelessness to the day but also the realisation that it would soon be the last time for Ross. He was doing the opposite to me in moving to join his wife Louise in Orewa, almost the city. Meanwhile Daniel had gone to bring in the hoggets to put them through the shed and footrot bath. But they have minds of their own and decided to visit the grounds of the up-market Grasmere Lodge before he was able to turn them around. They came bursting in the doors of the shearing shed. Snow and I couldn't stop laughing. In the end we chose a range of mixed-age ewes, hoggets, ewe and ram lambs, and eight rams of varying quality. They became the nucleus of my new Merino enterprise. Ross had deregistered the Snowdon stud in 2004 after introducing Saxon and other blood lines, and I will have to work hard to get the registration back.

Once the decision was made to begin a Merino stud we looked for other good blood lines. The Tripps had told me that in their time they'd had really great success with the stud rams which had come from Moutere

and Matangi stations. Everyone talks in hushed tones when mention is
made of Moutere and the Jopp brothers, and so Snow and I went down to
Alexandra to Moutere Station and bought two fine stud rams from Tony
Jopp. Setting up a stud meant another review of our paddocks. A stud
needs many much smaller paddocks close to the homestead because there
are a lot more lambing beats. Lambing is due around 15 October and I will
be out with my shepherd's crook and handbag — not, this time, with its
usual ammo of lippy, foundation and blusher but with my stud notebook,
felt pen and ear tags. You need to mark the lambs as they are born, pairing
them with their mothers, to keep an accurate record of blood lines from
the ewe and ram. I feel we have already made a good beginning. After only
three months at Castle Hill the condition of the one hundred and thirty
eight stud Merinos has improved enormously and there is amazing variation
in wool. There is the sought-after black tips that protect the wool from the
rain, heavy crimping and light crimping, some oily, some dry, bright white
fibre and not so white, and the very best of all — fine white oily wool with a
good crimp and purple skin.

Since I moved to Castle Hill I have become more aware of the vast gulf that
now exists between urban and rural New Zealand. Whereas once, only a
generation or two ago, the majority of New Zealanders had some contact
with the country and farming, , that is not the case now. Twenty years ago
one in four hundred children had direct access to a farm; ten years ago it
was one in twelve hundred; and in 2006 it was estimated to be around one
in three thousand. Ten years out, one in fifteen thousand is the prediction.
It is troubling to see this pattern: such separation constitutes a real threat to
farmers in losing urban sympathy, understanding and support.

I've become aware of it in the behaviour and attitudes of the 'weekend
warriors' and the growing number of residents in closely housed country
enclaves like Castle Hill Village. Gone is the old understanding about
seeking permission before going onto a farmer's land, about the need to
shut gates and keep dogs on a leash especially at lambing time, about the
fragility of so much of the high country and the damage that can be done
by four-wheel drives and mountain bikes. In the gathering up of the high

country estate to form great conservation reserves and parks, people have also been led to believe they have the right to walk or drive or ride not just in those areas, but also on the privately held freehold and leasehold land that adjoins the conservation areas. There is a story well known in the back country — possibly true, possibly apocryphal — of an exasperated farmer who found a couple of trespassers mushrooming in his paddocks. He followed them back to their house in town and began picking flowers from their garden. When they demanded to know what he was doing, he explained he was simply taking their flowers in exchange for the mushrooms they had taken from him.

I've had my own perception shift. When I lived in the city DOC were heroes. I had such a positive attitude to them. I still feel positively about much of what they do and for the quality of their workers on the ground. In our case we have been particularly lucky with the person assigned to

Castle Hill, Chris Stewart, whose father was a trustee of Books in Homes
with me. But since moving south, where I have DOC as neighbour and
partner, my goodwill has in some part been replaced by frustration and
disappointment. There has been the continuing dissatisfaction with the
stalled tenure review process, despite NHF's and DOC's commitment to
help speed the review. The department has been responsible for fencing off
the conservation land and for the first stage of the review process — the
survey and survey plan. Three years after purchase, not only has the
survey plan not been lodged but the survey itself has not been completed,
and the review process cannot begin without that. It is no wonder farmers
refer to 'ten-year review'.

But there are more pressing matters on the ground, literally. In mid 2007
DOC owned more than forty per cent of the South Island, and while I totally
endorse the purchase for posterity of iconic and environmentally important

parts of New Zealand, the random purchases and avaricious behaviour
remind me of a land grab. However, of greatest concern is the apparent
lack of intention or even motivation to maintain the DOC estate. There
is a marked proliferation of gorse, broom and wilding pines on land
now held by the Crown through DOC and the NHF, making it ironic
that DOC's corporate colours are green and gold. Castle Hill's former
owner John Reid had an almost humorous interchange with DOC over
some DOC land adjoining an area he is developing near Queenstown.
He wanted DOC to clear the gorse and broom on its property as
he was trying to keep his land clear. They said they couldn't, it was
companion planting — protecting desirable species they wanted to
grow. John asked to see the protected plants and under every gorse
plant was broom and nothing but broom. I am not sure the department
has the money or resources to manage and care for the land it already
holds and which it bought in order to preserve. Keeping farmers as
lessees with protective covenants and access arrangements seems a far
more sensible course.

So much of the conservation land now abuts working farms that
the spread from those areas of weeds and of hares, rabbits, possums,
deer, wild pigs and goats, which spread diseases like TB and do
enormous damage to pasture, adds to the already substantial costs of
farming. The money that could be spent on fencing is spent instead
trying to control the weeds that spring from seeds blown from DOC

*A mob of Perendales
on the Enys Block.*

land. In late summer 2007 one of Dad's Army, Simon Henderson, returned to remove the wilding pines on John's Point. They come from seeds carried on the prevailing northwest wind from the Craigieburn Reserves and from the Canterbury University-owned Flock Hill. It is only three years since NHF purchased the Cheeseman area in the sale of Castle Hill, and already broom, gorse, briar and wilding pines are on the increase. There is no accountability for what spreads from DOC land to neighbouring farms but, as farmers have found, they are quick to demand action if traffic is the other way.

There has also been a delay in the Crown Pastoral Lease renewal, which was due in 2007. We received notification of the proposed increase in the annual rent, from $6000 to $84,000 plus GST, six months late. The eleven-year rental is based on the original station area, two-thirds of which is now held by the NHF. The government has estimated the rent based on what the pastoral lease would sell for if it was freehold, a smart way to get around the amenity values that the Labour government is keen to see represented in pastoral lease rentals. I bought Castle Hill Station in good faith based on the Land Act of 1948, which fixed its rental on land exclusive of improvement and for pastoral purposes only. Farm land has increased in value over three hundred per cent in the past eleven years. The market value the government attaches to pastoral leases is being driven by the DOC/NHF purchases of high country stations, and our rental increase (now fourteen times the level I paid when I arrived) is simply a reflection of the high prices that the government and a few foreign owners have paid in recent times. The value the government sees in amenity values is arguably just a way of validating the premium they are prepared to pay; our sheep seem to care little whether their daily view is iconic or prosaic. The report of the government-commissioned High Country Pastoral Leases Review disagreed with the arguments for including amenity values in pastoral leases but the government, in cavalier fashion, chose to disregard its findings. It appears now that the issue of rental valuation will have to be resolved through the Land Valuation Tribunal and the High Court. Although the government says it does not wish to make farming uneconomic, for properties such as Castle Hill, in what is acknowledged as extremely difficult country, adding amenity values to the existing rental terms will make it exactly that. There is a growing suspicion among high country farmers in Canterbury and Otago that the unstated aim is to make farming in these areas untenable and so rid the high country of agricultural enterprise entirely.

The hard winter and wet spring of 2006 presented us with a gift for 2007. A wet start to summer, the substantial fertilisation programme, cross-slotting new pasture and winter feed on the flats, and Snow's decision to test-plant swedes which he thought would do well, provided us not just with record amounts of baleage and lucerne hay but also with good in-ground feed. Altogether it gave us the opportunity to turn Castle Hill tradition on its head. Seasonal lamb prices were appalling — less than $2 per kilo when it is impossible to farm a lamb for less than $4 a kilo. The meat works were holding farmers to ransom. What started life as farmers' co-operatives have ended as companies where the farmers' interests receive little consideration. John, Snow and I looked at our options. The peak selling prices for ewe lambs are in November–December and then again in August–September on the shoulder season. Castle Hill has traditionally sold in January–February to fattening or cropping farmers to finish off. It is hugely costly to feed lambs over winter. This year it was different. We decided to carry our lambs, born in October, through to August–September, and to sell before they cut their first teeth and become hoggets, at which time their price plummets.

In an even greater reversal of past practice, PPCS offered us a mob of four hundred and eighty lambs under its 'Lamb Plan' to fatten and finish for the meat works. The company was short of feed options because cropping farmers were very late getting their crops in and they offered to pay us for every kilo the lambs put on, to a top weight limit of forty-two kilos. We had reservations about the lamb plan's worth. We had to crutch and drench them and they required a lot of mustering until we settled them in the big tussock blocks at the back of the farm. There turned out to be very little return, especially as some of the lambs were already well above thirty-one kilos when they arrived. I'm not sure we would do it again, even if we were able. And I am ambivalent about aiding and abetting the big meat companies' agenda. Nevertheless, that we had been able to take on stock to finish, and hold ours instead of sending them away, was an incredible change on past practice.

There were other successes to feel good about. After buying the farm on a sixty eight to seventy per cent lambing rate, we had achieved over one hundred per cent with our Merinos in 2006, which was unprecedented. I could not wait to get down to Springas and skite. Snow had said he could lift the percentages at his job interview, to a certain amount of scepticism I'll admit, and he had more than proved it. The calving story was just as good. We were in the top pens at the calf sale, but prices were down on the previous year and certainly down on predictions. My letter to the buyers with their bottle of whisky told them they had a bargain. And when we scanned the cows in May 2007, there was a ninety eight per cent pregnancy rate in the mixed-age cows and three-year rising heifers, and seventy per cent in the two-year rising heifers in their first year with the bulls, and they had only been out for one cycle. The others were out for two. When Kate and her friends stopped for a drink at Springas on their way to stay in Old Quarters for Queen's Birthday weekend, they were told how incredibly successful the team and I had been in turning the place around. The locals said it was the best it has been in one hundred and fifty years. I wasn't convinced they could accurately judge that far back, but it was really nice to hear.

The good times spilled into autumn. Fathers' Day for the rams was more like Fathers' Week. The speed of the operation and the multiplicity of mounts would make all chaps jealous. The ewes hounded the rams, eleven and twelve at a time, all flushed and ready for tupping. The poor rams didn't have time to turn round, eat a square meal, or watch the rugger. This has been the first year I've noticed such overt copulation. It must be the fitness of the rams and the ripeness of the ewes. Now we look forward with anticipation to 2007's lambing rates.

When I am driving up to Castle Hill now I sometime reflect on that first twelve months and how tears would fill my eyes. These days I smile, eager to be back there, and if there are tears they are tears of joy. I am proud and very glad that I took that blind leap of faith three years ago and went out and bought a slice of paradise.

> While I stand on the roadway, or on the pavements grey,
> I hear it in the deep heart's core.
>> W. B. Yeats, *The Lake Isle of Innisfree*

CHAPTER 10

Postscript

Shortly after I began living at Castle Hill my sister Philippa sent me a magnetised photo of her daughter Steph, my brother and sister and our mother on Steph's wedding day. She said it was so I wouldn't forget them. It is still on the fridge today and she need not have been concerned. Who I am and much of what I do is inextricably linked to the family I was born into.

I think I've been lucky in my life. I was lucky in my parents and the philosophy of hard work that they inculcated in me. To say hard work brings results may sound simple but so much in life is about that. My parents were perfect examples. At ninety my mother still starts her day with the seven o'clock news and is up at half past seven, except on Saturdays and Sundays, when she gives herself an extra half hour in bed. I am lucky that my brother Malcolm also has a farm he is passionate about. It is totally different to Castle Hill, smaller and with ten times the stocking rate and income, but in the early days especially he was someone I could talk to and whose advice I could trust. I've been lucky that I could share my dream with my sister and her family, who didn't forget me and came south to visit and experience my new world. And there are my three children, David, Kate and Joe, and my son-in-law Rob and daughters-in-law Julie and Symmone and the wonderful granny-kids they have given me. The greatest costs of my love affair with Castle Hill has been separation from that family, seeing less of my mother in her last years although I know from our phone calls that she celebrates what I am doing because she knows it makes me happy, and missing my granny-kids growing up, seeing them at sports days or in the choir or talking over what's happening in their lives and watching them develop.

I am incredibly lucky with the team I have around me now at Castle Hill, and the two people at its centre, John and Snow. Snow with his honourable sense of hard work, his love of and sixth sense about stock, his generosity in imparting all he has learned of farming to me, and his dry sense of humour, helps me and gives me confidence in what I am doing, and complements me when I do well. John is truly a partner in this adventure. His strength supports me and stops me from tripping, from falling over. We've begun to build a history together. Of course there are apprehensions when you start to share your life and invest in love, more so than when you were young; so if he is the ram then I hope I'm not the annual draft, just the mixed-age ewe. We're best friends, mostly, and we love doing the same things. If you succeed in making your partner happy, it makes you happy, and I am all about happiness. One can wake in a bad mood — John calls it my foetal position — and the day seems lost, hopeless. But even those days have bright and beautiful moments. Ours is a very simple balanced life.

I look back at the changes of the past three years and am amazed, even though I think I am a truly positive person whose optimism sometimes verges on barely acceptable risk. I love taking on new challenges; I just go for broke. With Castle Hill I bought a farm that many who knew better would not have touched. There have been a lot of people on Castle Hill since the Enys brothers first farmed it, and all of them made a return when they sold on, but it was rarely profitable as a farm. I, too, could have settled for just the capital gain but that is not enough for me. I want to make it profitable. However, in the process farming has had some lessons for me. I am constantly surprised when things don't go well after I've put so much effort into them. I was having a grouch about bad venison and lamb prices recently when Richard Smith said, 'God, Chrissie, you're sounding like one of us.' I took that as a huge compliment. When I bought the farm people would tell me they admired my pluck but that I'd never make ago of it because the country was just too hard. Well, I have made a go of it. In 2004 the lamb weaning percentage was seventy, now it's one hundred and five per cent. In 2005 only eight five percent of our cows were scanned in calf, now it's ninety eight per cent. In 2005 only seventy two per cent of our deer were scanned in fawn, now that's one hundred per cent. The kill-out weight of the lambs fattened on Castle Hill is now 18.9 kg and when we took the last lot to the works the manager said they were the best presented he'd seen that season.

I've been used to expecting quick results, and earlier projects like Books in Homes and the Gifted Kids Programme fulfilled my expectations. Farming has forced me to become more accepting of the things I cannot change or control. That acceptance, so foreign to my natural character, is born out of the fact that you cannot influence eighty per cent of what happens on a farm. The remaining twenty per cent needs you to farm very smart, very well, and to be flexible at all times, and about time. There is no point fretting if you or an agent or contractor is not there on time. Things change, agendas are set by the willingness or otherwise of the sheep and cattle and deer, by how your dogs feel, and most important of all, by what the weather is doing.

Sometimes I try to imagine the future for stations like Castle Hill. I wonder what a fragile place like the high country will be like under the new conservation regime. I wonder whether we will still have people working on the land when it is so difficult now for them on so many fronts. The spread of lifestyle and the seduction of dairying, driven by corporate-run dairy farms, are changing the Canterbury Plains and contorting the land. Once you could have argued with justification that rural interests were over-represented in government policy and decision-making, but now they are dangerously isolated, ignored and misunderstood. Yet I notice that one of the personality traits among my farmer mates is a healthy fill of tolerance and compassion, and a general sympathy for the plight of others. One of the very best things about coming to Castle Hill has been the wonderful people, now my friends, who have been and continue to be so helpful, supportive and encouraging, perhaps because I give everything a go. Before I came here I'd been given a stereotypical picture of Cantabrians as very conservative and I wondered how I would make my way with them.

In the beginning, and sometimes even now, I was almost frightened to show the level of my ignorance. The older you get, the less gutsy you are about admitting you don't know something. For the first time in my life I have had to listen, and people who know me would say that is not my strong point because I keep butting in. They are used to me out there talking about anything and everything, whether I knew much or not. What I really needed was an ignorance log like the ones we gave our Gifted Kids. If I had set out then to ask all the questions I had about farming, it would have taken five volumes and I would still be adding to them. For many people the 'why' question can be very uncomfortable. They read it as a challenge and veiled judgement of what they are doing, rather than a genuine request for information. That has not been my experience with the farmers I've met in the last three years. I have found them open and quick to share their knowledge and experience.

Life is about learning, and for learning, and I know that each day I learn more, and every day I am more certain of my life on Castle Hill and my love for it. When I left Auckland and my house above Judge's Bay I wondered whether I could live away from the sea. I remembered the few times I had been to the South Island in the past and how I longed to get back to the familiar green of the North. The high pastures of Canterbury and Otago seemed harsh and parched. They only became beautiful after I began living amongst them.

Now I am happy in the mountains, with my hopes of a winter kind enough to allow us to keep our lambs on to when the schedule rises in the shoulder season.

Will we have the top pen at the next high country calf sale? I think so.

Will Snow achieve his ambition, and a first for Castle Hill, with a one hundred and twenty per cent lambing rate? I trust him to do so.

Will fine Merino wool become fashionable again? I believe so.

Will John and I continue to grow in our love for each other? I hope so.

And as I reflect on my very personal high country love story, I see in my mind's eye the quote from the *Psalms*, painted in gold leaf in an old fashioned script, that sits above the sitting room windows at Inverary Station: "I lift mine eyes up to the hills from whence cometh my strength."

High
country
recipes

Gerry's Famous Braised Sausages

8 sausages
2 tbsp oil
1 large onion chopped
2 to 3 garlic cloves chopped
4 tamarillos or tomatoes
1 cup of red wine (or more, and a
  glass for the cook!)

¼ cup of brown sugar
½ tsp salt
1 tbsp tomato paste
Tabasco to taste

Use a heavy pan; add the oil and brown the sausages over a moderate heat. Put in the onions and garlic and brown lightly. Peel the tamarillos, chop roughly and add to the pan with the rest of the ingredients.

Cover and simmer all day on the wood burner, stirring every so often. (Or cook for twenty minutes over a moderate heat if you are not doing it the High Country way.)

Serve with lots of mashed potato and peas, and more red wine.

Le Gigot de Sept Heures (Seven Hour Lamb)

1 leg of lamb
2 tbsp unsalted butter
1 tbsp olive oil
3 tbsp brandy
2 heads of garlic, separated into
  cloves (about 40 cloves)

160ml dry red wine
160ml chicken stock
4 large sprigs of fresh thyme
Salt & pepper to taste

Fill a large stock pot three-quarter full of water and bring to boil. Plunge the lamb or hogget into the boiling water and allow the water to return to the boil. Then reduce the heat to medium and simmer for fifteen minutes. Drain and pat dry.

Preheat an oven to 120°C (250°F).

In a heavy Dutch oven or casserole over a high heat melt the butter with the olive oil. Add the lamb and brown on all sides, about fifteen minutes. Add the brandy and ignite it with a long match. When the flames subside, add the garlic cloves, wine, stock and thyme. Season lightly with salt and pepper. Cover tightly, place in the oven and cook, turning twice, until the lamb is tender — about seven hours.

Remove the pan from the oven and transfer the lamb to a warmed platter and keep warm. Pass the other contents of the pan through a sieve, pressing firmly on the garlic to extract the cooked flesh. Return the liquid to the pan, place it over a high heat and bring to the boil, scraping up the browned bits from the bottom and sides of the pan. Reduce the liquid to a sauce consistency. Taste and adjust the seasoning. Strain into a small warmed bowl. Carve the lamb and then pass the sauce at the table.

Meatloaf

900g veal, pork and lamb mince
1 onion, chopped
4 cloves of garlic, crushed
350g mushrooms, chopped
120g egg plant, diced
1 tsp cumin seeds, toasted and
    then ground

1tsp black pepper, ground
Salt to taste
1tsp fresh thyme, chopped
75ml olive oil
120ml cream
2 eggs, lightly beaten
Bacon rashers to line loaf tin

Preheat oven to 200°C. Heat olive oil in a frying pan over a medium heat. Add onion and garlic and cook until golden brown. Add mushrooms, eggplant and cream, season and simmer three to four minutes. Remove from heat and cool to room temperature.

In a large bowl combine minced meats with cream and vegetables. Add cumin, thyme and eggs. Adjust seasoning to taste.

Line a meatloaf tin with bacon rashers, extending the ends over the sides of the tin.

Tightly pack meat mixture into the tin, fold bacon ends over the top and cover with foil. Place loaf in a roasting pan and put in the middle of the oven. Pour warm water into the roasting pan until it is half way up the sides of the loaf tin.

Bake thirty minutes. Remove foil and bake another forty-five minutes or until juices run clear when tested with a skewer.

Serve with potato mash and chutney. Serves six.

Venison Fillet

Marinade
2 tbsp soy sauce — I use Tamari
1 tbsp toasted sesame oil
2 tbsp white wine
1 tbsp palm sugar, grated or
    chopped

Sesame Salt
1 cup sesame seeds, dry roasted
    until brown
1 tsp sea salt

Mix together the marinade. Slice the venison into steaks and marinate no more than half an hour. Grind together the salt and sesame seeds in a food processor or mortar and pestle.

Cook the venison steaks on a hot barbecue using a little sesame oil on the plate.

Serve with sesame salt as a sprinkle.

Raspberry Jam

Fresh raspberries   *White sugar — for every 500g of*
Butter   *raspberries allow 500g of sugar*

Put the raspberries into a preserving pan or large thick-bottomed saucepan and bring slowly to the boil. Add the sugar gradually and boil quickly for five minutes.

Remove from the heat. Add a knob of butter and stir for twenty minutes or until all the sediment has been stirred in.

Pour into warm sterilised jars and seal with jam covers.

Quince Jelly

1.5 kg quince   *Sugar*
3–3.5 l water

Chop or slice fruit, including cores and skin as they are rich in pectin. Add water to just cover the fruit and cook in a covered pan until completely pulped.

Strain in a jelly bag or muslin. (The first time I made this I had neither so I improvised with pantyhose — Southern Woman's No 8 wire.) Measure the juice and allow one cup of sugar to one cup of juice. Heat the juice to boiling point. Remove from the heat and stir in sugar until dissolved. Return to heat and boil briskly until setting point is reached, about fifteen minutes. Skim to remove scum.

Pour into sterilised jars and cover.
If fruit is low acid, add two tablespoons of lemon juice.

Apple Crumble

1kg Granny Smith apples, peeled,
 cored and roughly chopped
100g caster sugar
1 cup plain flour
½ cup firmly packed brown sugar

1 tsp baking powder
3 tbsp rolled oats
100g unsalted butter cut into
 small pieces

Preheat the oven to 190°C.

Place the apples and caster sugar in a saucepan with a little water.
Cover and cook over a medium-low heat until the apple has softened.
Place apples and any liquid in a baking dish about a litre in capacity.

Place flour, brown sugar, baking powder and rolled oats in a bowl and
mix well. Add butter and rub in with your finger tips until the mixture
resembles coarse breadcrumbs.

Spread over the apple and bake for twenty to twenty-five minutes until
golden brown.

Serves six.

Glossary

A totally arbitrary and far from comprehensive Glossary of Farm Speak, some specific to Canterbury

AD — annual draft; a line of ewes mated to terminal sires; not the top mob, the next mob down often drafted for sale to the works

All hat and no horse — a talker, not a doer

Baleage — equivalent of silage in a bale; green or wilted forage (pasture, lucerne, etc) that has been baled and then wrapped individually or in a tube in plastic to create the anaerobic conditions that allow the ensiling process to occur

Banjo — long-handled shovel

Big red smile — to kill an animal by cutting its throat

Binder — a meal

Booted-up — a newly shod horse

Break fencing — dividing a paddock of feed with temporary electric fencing to limit the area of feed available to animals by doling it out in strips

Cleanskins — cattle that have not been ear marked or tagged

Coin — money, income

Crutching — removing the wool from the hind quarters of a sheep

Cryptorchid — a ram neutered by pushing his balls up into the body cavity where the body's temperature makes them infertile

Cull — to cut out, to remove from mob, an animal no longer suitable for breeding.

Dog tuckers — second-rate sheep and lambs separated from the general flock and generally held in one of the home paddocks to feed the farm dogs

Down the road — fired

(Just) down the road — a country measurement that could mean anywhere from a couple of kilometres to 50km; interchangeable with 'a couple of miles'

Duff — steamed pudding

Dung beetle — any worker, not a shepherd or tractor driver, who does the shit work; bottom of the heap

Dusters — bull's balls

Eye-chrometre — traditional old farming instrument for measuring distance, size, weight, length, temperature, wind strength and direction, etc, etc.; aka the eye

Eye dog — trained to control sheep by its gaze; also known as a heading dog.

Father's Day — the day rams or bulls are put out to mate

Four tooth — a sheep, 20 to 24 months old

Front foot — when a horse rears up pawing the air with its front hooves

Full mouth — a fully mature ewe with its fourth pair of teeth, more than 34 to 40 months old

Go to market — a horse bucking

Hay — pasture, lucerne, oats, etc., that has been mown, dried and baled to be used as supplementary feed

Heading dog — a dog that, without barking, heads off an individual or group of animals, controls the front of a moving mob or herd; also called an eye dog

Hill stick — see mustering stick

Hogget — a young sheep between a lamb and a two-tooth, approximately 10 to 16 months old

Huntaway — a driving barking sheep dog that barks on command (or should) to help move stock from behind

It smells so bad it would knock a buzzard off a shit cart — can apply to any smell

Long acre — grass strip along the road

Masting — when trees produce massive numbers of nuts or seeds; in Canterbury the high country Black Beech masts every two to seven years, most likely in response to favourable climatic conditions the previous year

Mixed age — term used to describe livestock of mixed ages, usually older than two years or after they have reproduced for the first time

Mocker — clothes

Moonlight grazing — grazing land that is not yours

Mountain oysters — sheep's balls

Mustering stick — prized possession, usually made of manuka and about 1.5 metres long; also known as a hill stick or nibby. I am going to take my hill stick to heaven so I can fight off the angels trying to fence me in

On the board — the area in a shearing shed where the actual shearing is done

OSH — Occupational Safety and Health Service, a government body attached to the Department of Labour tasked with ensuring work places and practices are healthy and safe, resulting in fewer work related injuries and deaths

Out the back end — to fall off the back of a horse

Peaked — exhausted

Pipe opener — a steep walk or climb before a muster; opens the windpipes

Rousie — rouseabout, odd job worker in the shearing shed

Set stock — move stock into a large paddock or block and leave them there for two or three weeks or more

Shed up — filling the 'night pen' of a wool shed or covered yards with sheep in preparation for the next day's shearing or crutching

Silage — pasture, lucerne, barley, oats, etc., conserved for supplementary feed by mowing, compacting and anaerobic preservation (ensiling) in sack or pit covered with plastic held down by old tyres

Six tooth — a 26 to 30-month-old sheep, basically a three-year-old

Snow-raking — to rescue a sheep from heavy snow. To walk up to the sheep, to create a chnnel for them to come down, Rakes are not used!

Spiker — yearling male deer that has grown its first "antlers" normally in the form of two single point spikes

Standing hay — tall grass

Stragglers — sheep missed on a previous muster (bad news for the shepherdess)

String — habit of sheep on a hill to travel single file

Sunday dog — one that refuses to work if the going gets tough, or if it is extremely hot

Swag — musterer's bedding roll. Snow Cleaver talks of farmers planting a flax bush at the gate so when they tell their workers they are off down the road they can tie their swag with flax

Tally — in the counting of sheep, 'tally' equals

With Lindsay McGrath

100. In the yards keeping tally can be done by cutting a notch in a stick, transferring a stone to one hand each time 'tally' is shouted, or, if you are working alone, standing by a gate post putting stones on the top

Taranaki gate — a makeshift wire and batten gate

Tarn — a small mountain lake

Terminal sire — a sire whose progeny are all destined for slaughter

Tilted flats — hillsides

Toe digger — really steep hill

Tupping — the act of mating or the period of mating for sheep

Two tooth — a sheep with its first pair of adult incisor teeth, anywhere from 12 to 18 months until approximately a year later when it becomes a four tooth

Wayleggo — the shouted command of the NZ High Country musterer and shepherd to his or her dog to call it off the sheep or cattle

Wether — castrated male sheep

Wilding pines — pine trees that are self sown, the seeds scattered by the wind; a large and fast growing problem in many parts of high country Canterbury

Valley Speak

Bitumen man — a townie

Blinking like a mouse in a flour bin — (self explanatory)

Brain fart — affliction of dogs and horses where they suddenly don't know what they're thinking, with unpredictable results

Ferals — city dwellers

Honeymoon morning — farm workers and partners can stay in bed instead of their usual early start

Lolly-pop licker — a useless dog that doesn't work; also known as 'a turner' — turns dog food into shit

Mud flats — a high country man's name for down-country flats

Nodder — a sheep with footrot, usually found in the dog tuckers paddock

Pakihis — clearings or bays in the bush; patches of open flat land

Piss/shit in your own time — a hurry-up shouted at a dog out working

Shingle scrapers — dogs, low and white, that get the sheep from high up on the scree; also known as gully rakers

(Someone's) like a mushroom — could pop up anywhere

Tail-waggers' town — where working dogs go after they die

Toe digger — really steep hill

Trim their feet up to their neck (and they never give me any more trouble) — used of Merinos, see 'big red smile'

Weekend warriors — town folk who head for the country armed with 4X4s, mountain bikes, hiking boots, snowboards and skis

Workbench — bed

You can smell the shit through his ribs — of a mustering horse at the end of a hard season